Contrib--

Danny Abelson
Paola Antonelli
Marisa Bartolucci
Aaron Betsky
Sarah Bodine
Sybille Brantl
Akiko Busch
Thomas J. Campanella
David Carson
Noah Carter
Megan Doyle
Sarah Duncan
James Marston Fitch
Barbara Flanagan
Peter Freiberg
Richard Gehr
Victoria Geibel
Carin Goldberg
Paul Goldberger
Roberta Brandes Gratz
Joseph Griffith
Steven Heller
Sean Hemmerle
Richard Horn
Jane Jacobs
Karrie Jacobs
Ben Katchor
Alyssa Katz
Barry Katz
John Kelly
Geof Kern
Conrad Kiffin
Verlyn Klinkenborg
Tim Kucynda
James Howard Kunstler
Peter Kupfer
Philip Langdon
Alexandra Lange
Criswell Lappin
Sandy Lappin
Kristine Larsen
Peter Lemos

Daniel S. Levy
Hugo Lindgren
Phillip Lopate
Alex Marshall
Jane Maybank
Nory Miller
William Mitchell
Andrea Moed
Amma Ogan
Mary Pepchinski
Sylvia Plachy
Nina Rappaport
Penelope Rowlands
Tatiana Samoilova
Luc Sante
Fern Schumer
Kirk Semple
Suzette Sherman
Julius Shulman
Ken Shulman
Michael Sorkin
Philippe Starck
Doug Stewart
Susan S. Szenasy
Wolfgang Tillmans
Antoinette le Vaillant
Veronique Vienne
John Voelcker
Christopher Wahl
Shawn Wolfe
Jeremy Wolff
Jim Zook

Photographs by David Carson

DESIGN IS

Metropolis Books
Published by Princeton Architectural Press
37 East 7th Street
New York, NY 10003
(212) 995-9620
www.papress.com

Editing: AKIKO BUSCH
Design Direction: CRISWELL LAPPIN
Photo Essays: DAVID CARSON
Production: CAROLINE GREEN
Art Research: SUZANNE CORT

Special thanks to Cathryn Drake, Nancy Eklund Later,
Julien Devereux, Kimberly Taylor, Danielle Masar Rose,
Marty Jezer, and Jon Raymond.

Heading and text font:
Dispatch by CYRUS HIGHSMITH/FONT BUREAU
Photo Essays Headings Font:
Union Square by PABLO MEDINA

Printed and Bound in China
06 05 04 03 02 5 4 3 2 1 First edition

Library of Congress Cataloging-in-Publication Data
ISBN 1-931648-00-X (hardcover)
ISBN 1-56898-314-X (softcover)

DESIGN IS

NEW YORK FASHION:

WORDS, THINGS, PEOPLE, BUILDINGS, AND PLACES AT **METROPOLIS**

MEN & LADIES

Edited by **AKIKO BUSCH**
Designed by **CRISWELL LAPPIN**
Photo Essays by **DAVID CARSON**

Metropolis Books
Princeton Architectural Press, New York

DESIGN IS WORDS, THINGS, PEOPLE, BUILDINGS, PLACES

A trip through 20 years of design and a voyage into the next 20 years.

Context has always been important to METROPOLIS. When the magazine was first published in 1981, publisher Horace Havemeyer III and then-editor Sharon Lee Ryder wanted to put design at the center of the cultural dialogue. They foresaw a time, as it has come to pass in 2001, when the design dialogue would grow wider and deeper than simply being the concern of the professions. They understood that architects needed to collaborate with the designers of interiors, objects, and graphics, as well as their clients, to create environments and products that serve their users—and serve them beautifully.

From the beginning, METROPOLIS has sought to be a good companion, one that is eternally searching for new ideas, finding them, and sharing them with equal measures of intelligence, urgency, and humor. Through the years the magazine has become a voice for those who believe that design matters. It has depicted the creative life of the designer as an inspiring and worthwhile activity. It has debated what our world looks and feels like, and has challenged our form-givers to do better. It has kept an eye on the past, assessed the present, and looked into the future when that was called for. It has shown an equal fascination with high design as with the vernacular—and at its best, it related one to the other.

In this compilation of articles and excerpts, as well as entirely new material written, illustrated, and photographed especially for this book, we present all that design is, was, and will be. We are especially grateful to Akiko Busch, METROPOLIS's first managing editor and a longtime contributor, for bringing together the many voices of design in these pages. We'd also like to recognize METROPOLIS art director Criswell Lappin for taking on the daunting task of designing this book—his first, as well as ours. We are thankful as well to Barbara Flanagan for the letter she has written to her son, an evocative perspective into the future and an eloquent springboard for all the pieces that follow. And we thank David Carson, whose photo essays open and close the book as well as punctuate every chapter, for making these pages come to life and for accompanying some of the best writings in design with his depictions of the metropolis—our rich, visual, always fascinating subject.

Susan S. Szenasy, Editor in Chief

Landscape of the third-floor retreat.
Illustrations by **Tim Kucynda**

DESIGN IS

A LETTER TO MY SON, AUGUST 21, 2000
BARBARA FLANAGAN

Dear Nat,

Even though I've known you for 15 years, I know much less about you now than ever.

What I know is this: it's your first year of high school; your voice is deeper, your head higher, and your patience much shorter than last year or the year before. If you would stand straight up you could pass for a grown man. In fact, you'll actually be a grown man in a couple years, and in a couple decades you and your friends will be running the show—ruling the world.

What I know very well, however, is your room. It's a complex space, layered with meaning—and stuff. Like the floor of an Amazon rain forest, it's covered with a dangerous tangle of vines that trips up all intruders: wires, cables, conduits connecting your machines—PC, printer, scanner, synthesizer, keyboard, modem, drum machine, and turntables—plugged into two inadequate outlets. Covering the jungle floor is another layer of organic disorder. Most of your wardrobe lies on the floor, flattened into waves of many plaids, as if a tsunami had beached a whole shipwreck of clothing there along with your sheets. Embedded in that shifting layer is the flotsam of your recent past: vinyl records, CDs, golf balls, shoes. Next to your lava lamp, dishes and snack wrappers also pile up.

I know you love your faraway third-floor retreat and the way it frightens the few grown-ups who dare to make the climb. If you'd let me clean it, for God's sake, I might learn even more about your inner life, along with the electronic realms you visit all over the world—while simultaneously composing electronic computer music, phoning pals, and buying more equipment on E-bay—long after your bedtime. But you decline ("No, Mom, I'll clean it myself").

You'd like your life to be private. And you'd prefer, frankly, that I take all my urgent concern, curiosity, and imagination and use it on someone else. But I'm your mother—and I cannot help but wonder about you, your immediate future, your distant future, and the fire hazard that is your room.

So here's the deal I will make. If you promise to uphold a reasonable level of health and safety up there, I'll agree to try to change my focus. Rather than worry about your current domain, I'll obsess about the place you'll inhabit later—when you grow up and leave the house. Will you be okay out there? Furthermore, I'd like to know: will the world be okay? Instead of redoing your room, I'll invest my meddlesome energy in designing your future. This is what I think life will be like, my son, in the year 2020.

You're 35, which is pretty old in this new country. A lot of it looks pretty much the same as it did when you were 15, but there are a lot of important changes that would be too big, or too small, to notice if you were a tourist. Age is one example.

Twenty years ago plenty of bored young billionaires entered politics after retiring (at 25). They didn't actually run for office themselves, but ran the people they wanted in office. So now, even though the boomer generation, mine, is still alive and kicking, a young and powerful minority has made new rules. The laws favor those under 40.

15

Another thing you can't notice is the way things don't move so quickly anymore. You'll recall how people used to race around harassing each other by cell phone and Palm Pilot? No more. Good things take a long time. Many time-consuming things are considered prestigious: long vacations preceded by long relaxation periods, foods and drugs absorbed into the skin through permanent body patches; night college (a four-year degree earned in ten years of REM course-editing while you sleep); long careers in long-perspective fields (those with 50-year time frames), including the enviro-warfare professions (the ones that manipulate climate over enemy territories).

The invisible changes are big. The USA is now the NAR (the North American Republic). The melting of the polar cap became something of a national security problem, with the flooding and all, so Canada agreed to merge with us supposedly to figure out how to keep their glaciers cold (1). The real reason, of course, was the massive industrialization of Mexico and the insecurity it engendered.

The good news is that energy is free and clean—it's solar at last. The photovoltaic (PV) industry finally figured out how to make cheap, thin PV film that can roof, laminate, or surround almost anything, then convert sunshine into electricity (2). Unfortunately all the equipment that uses that energy is expensive and underperfected. It's taken a long time to trash internal combustion engines and make the switch, especially since the NAR leveled most of its factories long ago. People still own cars—electric ones. But getting travel permission is not all that easy (3). Each citizen is assigned an annual mileage allotment according to what they do for a living and which Village they belong to. The average is 2,000 miles. (Can you believe 12,000 was the pre-allotment average? That's one change you must regret.)

About those PVs: the funny thing is that China makes nearly all the PV material used in this country but fuels its plants with only gas and oil. That's because the inevitable happened. You remember back in the 2000s, when we all squandered gasoline like there was no tomorrow, as if we actually owned the oil fields and called the shots? (Electing a Texas oilman in 2000 helped the illusion.) Talk about arrogance.

OPEC had the last laugh by making a defense pact with China. The cartel sells all its oil to China, and China protects the cartel. Who protects us? We're not really the global power we used to be; China could cut us off in a flash and supply Mexico instead. That's where all our diplomacy goes now—sucking up to China. To think we used to scold them like children. Most of the defense budget is spent on NDI (Natural Disaster Inducement, or enviro-warfare, the by-product of climatic research on the greenhouse effect). (Although Congress did halt the project to induce cloud cover over Mexico, our climate-control operations along the border are still maintaining, at phenomenal expense, the 3,000-mile air curtain keeping Mexico's polluted air from mixing with ours.) (4)

In short, we were forced to go solar. And as soon as we switched over everyone moved west, motivated by a mass misunderstanding. The federal government had been cranking out a lot of publicity about someday selling our photovoltaic energy surplus to other countries, especially China. And although every agency has been working on ways to ship electricity overseas, no one has been able to make that cost effective. Nevertheless

16

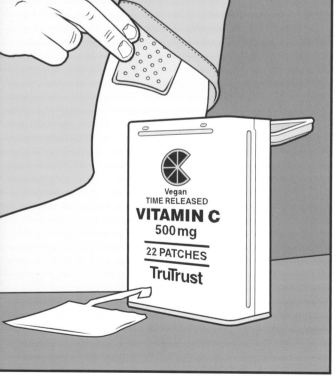

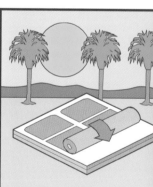

Clockwise from top left: individual solar-powered
transportation modules; new national boundaries of the
NAR; panels of solar film; solar-powered transportation
on land and in air; nutritional skin patches.

millions of people moved—a bit prematurely—to stake out acreage in the nation's sunniest microclimates and then wait for the arrival of technologies that could harvest and store shippable PV power, making them trillionaires. The phenomenon is like the California Gold Rush in many ways. But North Americans are learning that finding a mother lode is not the problem—extraction is. Now the Southwest is like New Jersey used to be, whereas New Jersey is full of ghost towns, like those Western former mining towns.

And that brings us to your house, deep in the New Jersey wilderness. It's not exactly a house, but rather a migratory way of life. After the Great Western Migration of 2011 and the Northeastern Real Estate Crash of 2015, you and five Yale class-mates bought Lambertville, New Jersey, for $2 million ($150,000 in pre-crash dollars). The town is a few miles north of the emptied Trenton, whose motto was, "What Trenton Makes the World Takes." Technically there is no Lambertville, of course. Your location is SE Quadrant, 200 degrees, Village 2306, mid-Atlantic climate zone, NAR. Your local downtown, as we used to say, is the Village farm. That's Lancaster, Pennsylvania. (They removed all the Amish tourist joints and rehabbed the fertile farmland.)

In "Lambertville" you live in "Smart Skin cocoons" (more about those later) of different sizes. Parked temporarily, they include a horizontal suite of connected row houses (exploded up in interesting ways) and a Victorian mansion overlooking the raging Delaware River, which occasionally floods the town, then recedes, sculpting new landscape patterns each time. You work in another series of spaces, also outfitted with Smart Skin enclosures: a former farmhouse, tavern, and warehouse. (The notion of living and working in the same unit—lofts or home offices—as your parents did, is now considered uncivilized.)

Most of your equipment is in a former lawn mower factory. (You'll be happy to know that there are no more lawns; only Village farmland gets irrigated.) When you enter your warehouse you feel like you're walking into a snowstorm. Everything is white: the floors, ceiling, even windows have been Smart-Skinned over to make a seamless square tube of space. And if you want a real snowstorm, the Skin system can simulate it by emanating cold air, the sound of wind, and dizzying visuals of blowing snow.

What's really cool is that you can also simulate the original factory, complete with brick walls, wooden ceiling, and the din of machinery. That's the modern version of historic preservation, as we once called it: keep the outside shell intact and reproduce the inside theatrically. (It's much easier than restoring that old Victorian house of ours; you hated all that smelly repainting.)

Anyway, you and your friends own a hotel—actually a series of cocoons parked in weird places—but hoteling isn't your vocation. Because Lambertville is well located in the abandoned East Coast, where the picturesque Rust Belt meets nature, the town attracts plenty of tourists. Most are erudite, wealthy Far Easterners searching for industrial American WABI artifacts to photograph and ship home. Originally the Japanese name for rustic refinement, WABI is an aesthetic that's hard to explain: it's neglect, followed by arrested decay that represents a moment in time. Think of the urns dropped by ancient Pompeiians as they tried to escape, later unearthed and left to age among the foundations. **Mainly foreign tourists like to see the American ruins (5).**

19

New York City is really the place you want to be, however. You're just waiting for your sublet permit, the visa that allows artists and craftsmen to stay in Manhattan for a couple of months each year—if their applications are accepted and processed (usually after five years), and if there is space available. **Most of the vacancies occur in the high-density servant towers—like dorm buildings for domestic labor (6)—** when servants accompany their employers out of the city on long vacations. You've also applied for a San Francisco permit just in case the New York one doesn't come through. But that's even harder to get because those WABI-loving foreign tourists (seeking out the picturesque earthquake ruins of 2005) bribe the entry officials and hog all the permits.

Living in one of those cities will help you advance your real career as a composer. What you compose is SYKE—short for psychological—music: electronic

music designed to influence behavior neurologically. The first intimation of SYKE music was Muzak, soothing renditions of popular music piped into public places. Later the French invented "son et lumière" shows that blasted classical music at tourists, as well as corny night lighting on chateaus. Mozart for babies and other fads followed, but the principle— using sensory input to mess with the brain—took a couple of decades to engineer.

Eventually biological research proved that the brain's synaptic responses to aural stimuli could be precisely predicted and programmed. At first SYKE music was controversial, especially when it was used with SYKE lighting design, an earlier form of so-called "manipulative environmental design." Critics said it was a diabolical form of subliminal advertising. But now it's ubiquitous. Most people have digital ear appliances embedded in their cartilage anyway, so they can shut off aural reception whenever they walk into a particularly hostile SYKE-filled setting **(for example, when police clear city streets at night using music, especially the irritating Curfew Theme, as if it were tear gas.) (7)**

The ear appliances explain why disciplinary SYKE no longer works, at least not in wealthier nations (everyone just tunes it out). Most SYKE is harmless; some is even therapeutic. Unfortunately, some people tune out too much. They get addicted to silence because it's so absorbing—like watching TV with the sound muted—so they have to be committed to silence-rehab clinics to get resocialized.

Famous SYKE composers work like painters did 50 years ago. No royalties—intellectual property laws, like copyrighting, were overturned in 2002—just the promise of big commissions. (8) Patrons order up SYKE compositions just as kings used to commission symphonies. The same sort of patron buys hundreds of highly customized compositions each year—sort of like sound tracks for living—designed to enhance family life, enliven a party, or boost a child's math ability. However, it's the institutional and commercial applications for mass auditing that most composers are after—things like worker productivity, crowd control in national parks, and elimination of jet lag on airplanes.

Remember when sound used to come from speakers? Now of course it comes from nowhere—or rather, everywhere: furniture, walls, ceilings, floors, and even sidewalks. Architectural Smart Skin made all of this possible. In the beginning the membrane was like flimsy bubble wrap filled with gases that you'd tack around the inside of a structure as if you were upholstering it. Current running through the gases would make the room glow. **(In 2003 its elderly inventor called the product "tents" made out of material that "merged the principles of "neon lights and electric blankets." No one cared.) (9)**

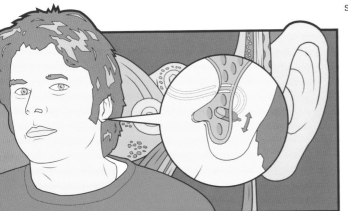

The breakthrough was wiring the membrane for sound. At that point the substance glowed while it vibrated: marketable at last, but not indispensable. Later, biotech scientists figured out how to make the wrapping material more like living skin—breathing, exuding, and receiving stimuli. First they produced a membrane with a more intricate and responsive cellular structure. Next they replaced the gases with advanced fiberoptics. Some years later they developed a way to make the Skin change temperature to heat or cool a space while emanating humidity, ventilation, and chemical mood atomizing (a mind-altering mist like ionized ocean breezes, only more potent). Different cellular layers perform different tasks. The whole system uses an astounding amount of electricity. And without PV tech, it wouldn't have flown.

Anyway, demand skyrocketed and prices lowered, until Skin was not much costlier than historic Sheetrock in pre-migration days. To keep one step ahead of China (since Skin is just about the last NAR product manufactured in-continent), the company kept developing Skin until it became much smarter than the original.

The real coup was rendering the cells self-sufficient so that each did its own "thinking," and could receive and transmit information individually. At that point it wasn't difficult to get the Skin to receive pixilated images from broadcast

21

sources or in-house transmissions. Think of DVD screens as quarter-inch-thick wallpaper; now imagine that the wallpaper is structural, like the foam-core, cardboard-sandwiched plastic architects once used for models—except this material is as flexible as an old neoprene wetsuit.

Only recently have the Smart Skin people perfected Spray Skin as an alternative to floppy membranes. You power-spray it on any surface, run a current through it—and the stuff crystallizes into an integrated cellular network. Using this method, you can erect a reusable inflatable structure, spray on the skin, deflate the structure, and get an instant architectonic shell. This system is great for taking over abandoned buildings, because you don't have to renovate them. Just apply Smart Skin and hook up to a portable PV-generation array pack to power any machinery you need. Most squatters like to keep a few rooms in their natural state of decay (otherwise what's the point of ruin-living?) rather than Skin a whole interior.

In the Southwest and West most of the postquake construction has been made of Smart Skin shells, formed into all sorts of bulbous shapes, sequined with thousands of shiny PV scales. Of course walls as electronic screens is nothing new; it was one of those old-fangled "futuristic" notions of the twentieth century. But the cool thing about Smart Skin is the way people started using it to design sensory sets—both abstract and realist.

Most people prefer the kitsch approach: prepackaged sensory settings. Sit in a vertical cocoon, eye contact the Amazon button, and all the surfaces come to life and convince you that you're in the middle of a rain forest. You get real-time image broadcasting with trees, birds, and slightly perfumed sticky air and herbal anesthesia (ancient tribal style), if your domestic intoxicant use taxes are paid up.

It's really only the city people inside the Metro-Gates (the ones who've inherited permanent residency permits) who commission abstract sets—the kind using experimental SYKE music and lighting effects. Some of them actually own the most advanced listening aids ever invented, which were banned when you were a kid. They infuse your bones with sound by stimulating the musculoskeletal system with from within. You have to get the implants, of course. **(Call me old-fashioned, but I still don't approve of embedding electronic devices into the skin—including those telephone wrist gadgets.) (10)**

But that's why you want to get to New York: to find implanted clients and refine your craft. Once you get established you can live absolutely anywhere federal Village laws allow you to live.

The Village laws work as follows: A Village is a region of 100 square miles that's dependent on a Village farm. (It's not really a farm, but a compact food-producing center that feeds the region's citizens. But more on that later.) Every ten years you renew your V-citizenship or apply to another Village, or—good luck—to a gated City (for subletting only). All this togetherness seems normal to you now, but 40 years ago, right before you were born, Village living was a radical idea proposed very sheepishly by California researchers trying to cure L.A.'s filthy congestion. Mag lev, light rail, monorail, bullet, subway trains? Not exactly. They decided that engineering was no longer the ticket (no money, no public willpower). **The only solution was discipline: grounding its citizens,**

22

Industrial American WABI artifacts preserved for tourists.

confining them to smaller circles; making them live, work, and recreate without driving too far (11) (not unlike your life as a teenager). Needless to say, the recommendations were shelved—that is, until the Sino-OPEC treaties blew gas prices sky-high. That's when the NAR erased state and province boundaries and divided the northern continent into six Climatic Zones administering a total of 150,000 Village Entities (VEs).

Micromanagement on this scale was unthinkable before the advent of commercial bureaucracies—highly digitized entities charging fees (not taxes) for local government services. You pay for what you use. Dispensing with elected officials boosted efficiency, cut costs, and created economies of scale. (You probably don't remember the 1990s, when you were a tyke helping me pull the election booth lever at city hall— quaint, right?) (12)

The advent of commercial government, nicknamed "home rule," made shopping much easier and cheaper by subsidizing warehousing and distribution instead of mass transit, etcetera. In fact it really made "shopping" disappear and, with it, all the costs of pro-shopping advertising (no need to harangue nonshoppers).

Instead of fumbling around, searching and schlepping by car and computer like we used to do, everyone chooses a consumer brand—a company that produces and distributes nonfood consumables—and signs a ten-year brand loyalty contract to buy pretty much everything from them. Once again, like a public utility. Software, Smart Skin, one-off clothing (you spec it), pharmaceuticals, anything you need replaced often—just about everything except cars and furniture, which people tend to keep forever.

There are three North American brands: TruTrust, Lifelong Products, and the Commitment Corp. Only the first two are owned by Wal-Mart, which now manufactures a lot of stuff in its own solar-warmed nation, the former Yukon territory—a safe, legal haven for political refugees, because employment there is guaranteed (13).

Instead of shopping you set up a brand-replenishment plan that covers what you want to replace when, and then stuff just appears in the public storage lockers or in your garage locker if you've got one. You remember how everyone was worried about freedom-of-choice competition and all that? Brand contracting delivered some new benefits. Things are cheaper because the three big brands can predict, demand and manufacture in huge quantities. Also they don't try to seduce you with expensive fluff—constant restyling, repackaging, advertising—because there's no physical marketplace, no store. Ironically the big brands are like co-ops: the more you buy the bigger your rebate.

No fluff means the brands get to spend more on research and development. So they're competing with real engineering, not smoke and mirrors. They test out new models by delivering freebies to customers who report back to the company about how the things work. The company's survival depends on customer satisfaction, which is measured by daily consumer polling. Every household has a suggestion box linked to brand hardware; this brings in trillions of comments per hour. In other words, people vote for products rather than people.

Not everything is bigger. Roads are smaller, because cars are tinier now that allowable travel distances are shorter. When you were a kid, you and your friends

25

were shuttled around in faux jeeps (SUVs)—so we all thought—to protect you from highway crashes. Now that highways are long gone and their roadbeds have been turned to soil by tar-eating microbes, there is no need for defensive vehicles. At first North Americans resented being forced to break up their famously smooth asphalt and turn their interstates into linear forests. But after the Fifth Kyoto Environmental Accords threatened more expensive measures as compensatory penalties for fouling the global atmosphere with excessive carbon dioxide, greening the highways seemed cheap and easy. In any case, it was less complex than planting millions of Kyoto-mandated trees on private property.

Food is smaller as well. When you were a youth, global agribusiness sent lousy food all over the world. (I can't believe what I let you eat: long-dead meat from doped-up animals, grotesque hybrids of mealy tomatoes, and so on.) **There was a big upheaval when meat was banned in 2007 (after several domestic animal scourges), and bacteriologists found that frozen food harbored a cancer-causing strain that multiplied undetected in cold temperatures. Now food is grown locally—very locally (14).** Each Village farm produces just enough fresh food to feed its residents. The farms are exactly what your parents envisioned way back in the 1960s: PV-heated and cooled solar greenhouses with thick forests of hydroponic veggies suspended over huge indoor lakes full of fish. They're really beautiful inside and out.

What we couldn't have predicted is the way things sort of reversed. When I was your age, cities were the centers of action—technology, culture, politics, religion. People talked about saving nature but trashed it beyond repair. Now culture revolves around agriculture. Each Village farm is the center of its little universe, a vital oasis. Kids grow up learning about natural processes, visiting farms and sort of worshipping the output. **I still can't get used to revering vegetables, but it's nice to have fresh produce (15).**

Kids are inducted to intern at farms like Israelis once had to serve in the military. That's usually their first exposure to the population we used to call the "underclass" or the "growing underclass" —people too poor, slow, arty, or old to keep up with technology. Only we don't call it "technology" anymore, in the same way I never told you to "heat your snack food in the electric microwave oven." It's life. Some people just fall out of sync. When they do, they become "foodists."

Foodists grow food. They live simply on the farms, run the educational programs, and maintain the grounds. They live simply. Students are taught to respect them, but there is some disingenuousness in the lessons. (Remember when you were in elementary school, and your class used to sing at retirement homes? Not your favorite community service.) And remember when retirement homes later became continuing-care facilities disguised as resort hotels and owned by Marriott? Cultural etiquette suggested that we treat advanced age as a vacation opportunity, a catered cruise getaway.

That's the mixed message. Yes, this is an attractive place with the noble purpose of uplifting one underclass while containing it. But it's not a place you'd aspire to. On the farm the implicit warning is drop out of college or fall behind, and you'll be growing fish someday.

Actually, it's not so bad. Fish are pretty fascinating, especially my trout. The farm looks like the most magnificent commune any former hippie could imagine. You should see it when the sunset reflects back and forth between the PV shingles and the greenhouse glass. When the fruit trees bloom, the perfume wafts throughout the compound. And everyone here is surprisingly interesting to talk to—we do a lot of that—because they've owned and read actual books, and done some thinking about them on their own.

I know you don't have much time to visit the farm now that you own Lambertville and compose your music. But every now and then switch on your ear appliance, press that Flesh-fone of yours, and give your mother a call.

Footnotes: Finding the Roots of the Future in the Past

1. 2000: Americans start believing global warming can happen to them. News agencies warn that Inuits notice more mosquitoes; the ecology of polar bears' hunting grounds change and they lose weight.

2. 1990s: British Petroleum produces and pushes photovoltaics. Advocates claim that price is the only thing preventing PV technology from taking over.

3. Late 1990: Driving cars becomes a privilege, not a right. "Road pricing" increases. Singapore installs a kind of EZ-pass system (electronic gates and car gadgets) that charges drivers' debit cards for entering downtown.

4. 1980s: Canadians complain that acid rain from the United States pollutes their quality of life. The United States complains that acids from Mexican battery plants are crossing the border. Emerging is the notion that one nation can ruin another's environment—gradually, unobtrusively, and legally.

5. Late 1990s: Industrial archaeology rises in Europe. The Germans and British turn their dead industrial sites into works of art and tourism: museums, concert venues, and landscape sculpture. The United States lags behind.

6. Mid-1990s: HUD demolishes low-income government housing projects. By 2020 the pendulum swings, and income-segregated housing (like artist and servant dorms) returns.

7. 1980s-90s: The United States uses music as offensive weaponry, blaring hard rock at armed strongholds to ferret out government enemies in Panama and Waco, Texas.
2000: New electronic receivers play music beamed from satellites, not radio stations. Public places are invaded by new private communication habits: beepers, cell phones, talking (voice-activated and responsive) laptops. Cell-phone use is linked to cancer. Sound is becoming ubiquitous—and insidious—in new ways. Silence takes on new meaning.

8. 2000: Napster puts music into the public domain; lawyers are flummoxed.

9. Mid-1990s: Electronic surfaces come alive. You can tell a computer what to do by touching places on its screen. You can make opaque glass turn transparent by flicking a switch that runs current through it. No big deal back then.

10. Mid-1990: The "invasive entertainment" trend begins with multisensory virtual-reality games at electronic arcades and theme parks.

11. 1970s-80s: Research from SCAG (the Southern California Association of Governments) and other entities predicts that L.A.'s congested freeway traffic will slow 20-40 mph by 2000. SCAG recommends that citizens live near their workplace—condense daily activities—to limit driving.
1990s: L.A. freeways are parking lots; new subway has room to spare.

12. Mid-1990s: Owners move into Celebration, Florida (a Disney-built, operated, and partially governed community), telling the press they don't need elected government because the trustworthy Disney company will "protect them."

13. 1980s-90s: Westerners learn about the devoted, lifelong, familiar relationship between large Japanese corporations and their employees. They wonder if that special bond—mutual loyalty—explains Japan's astounding productivity. Meanwhile Wal-Mart becomes a "category-killer," underpricing—and eliminating—neighborhood stores. Microsoft grows; the notion of benevolent monopolies becomes popular; antitrust laws are strained.

14. Mid-1980s: The Slow Food Movement, started by a famous Italian journalist, teaches people that good seasonal food, produced locally and consumed leisurely, can bolster world culture.

15. 1990s: In Japan, near Osaka, the city of Tondabayashi runs a municipal pick-your-own farm designed as an educational public park. No agriculture is more urban or local than the rice paddies and miniature farms occupying the empty lots between large commercial buildings in downtown Kyoto.

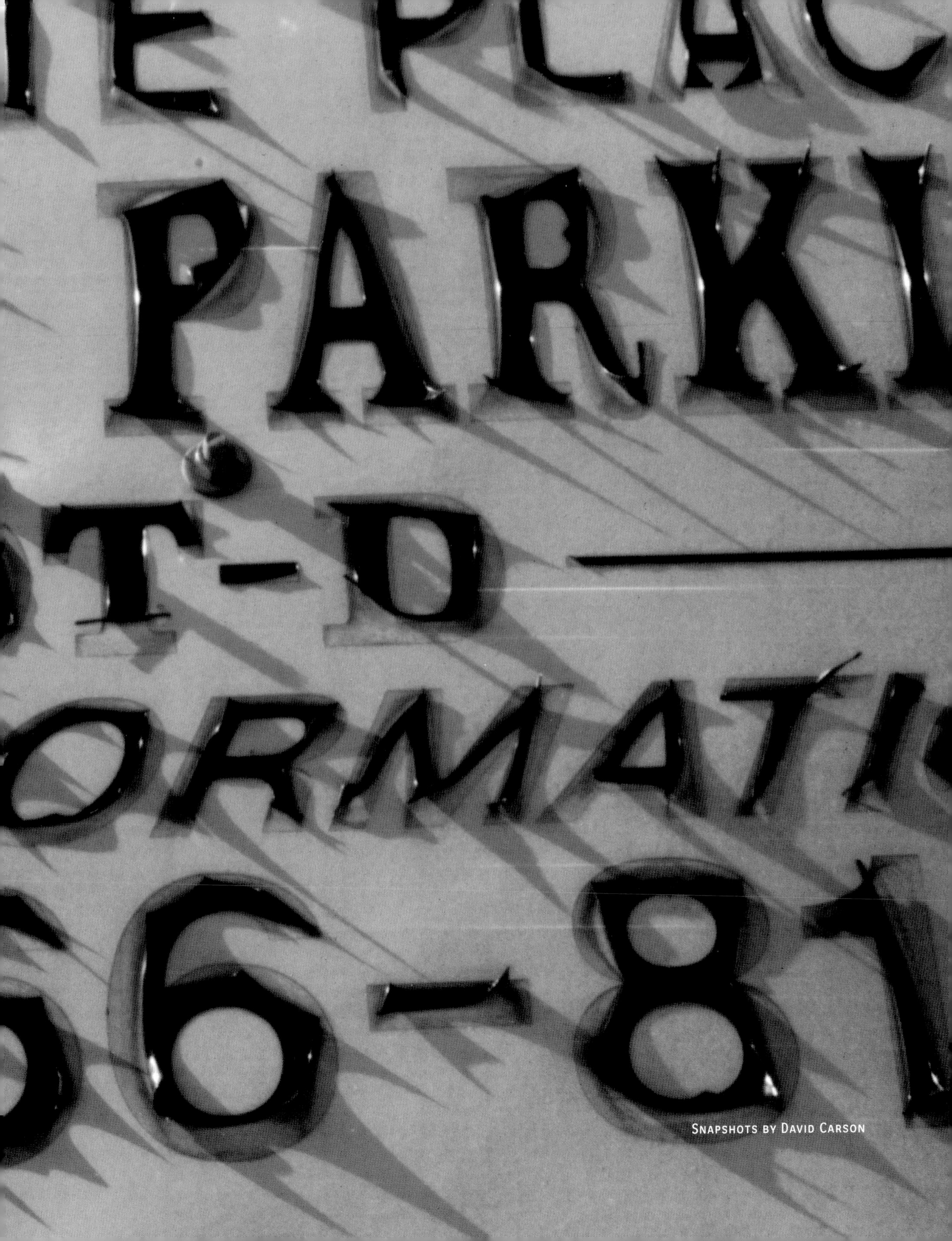

Snapshots by David Carson

That such things could occur during a time we call "The age of information" is both ironic and astonishing.

Photograph by **Criswell Lappin**

The occasion for collecting these views about design is the anniversary of a magazine. But as it happens, it is also the aftermath of a national incident of bad graphic design. During the 2000 presidential election, the butterfly ballot used in one county in Florida—with its confusing alignment of names—resulted in allegations of voter irregularity if not outright fraud. Then there were the questions of why the number of votes shifted so measurably with every count and whether a manual or machine count gave a more accurate tally. And so on. That such things could occur during **"the age of information"** is both ironic and astonishing.

Nevertheless such events also underline a conventional wisdom about design: well-considered, expressive design appears most regularly and prominently in the commercial realm. Market concerns drive design, whether it is the **packaging for a CD, movie poster, or Nike ad.** Designers are fond of pointing out that good design sells. What always takes longer is for good design to reach the places it is needed most—to bring clarity and efficiency to **census polls, ballots, or posters for the board of health.**

These are, after all, episodes of graphic design in the real world. It is not simply about packaging or signage or how to position type on a magazine cover to sell more copies. Rather it is about how we perceive, understand, and interpret—moment to moment—the information that governs our lives. METROPOLIS has always recognized the significance of such design: how words are positioned on a page, construction fence, computer screen, or ballot may not affect their meaning but it certainly affects how we comprehend their messages.

Which is why when Karrie Jacobs examines **a poster from the Metropolitan Transit Authority** that discourages subway passengers from giving money to panhandlers, she is looking closely at the most basic of human pleas—how people ask for help and under what conditions we hear them. Phillip Lopate takes on the metaphors of architectural discourse in an essay about how the moral language somehow manages to flatten the very real moral issues of overdevelopment. Richard Gehr ruminates on how the **electronic newspaper** will change the nature of how we receive news of the world.

Or as Veronique Vienne says in her critique of the **Benetton campaign of the late 1980s,** "We live in a time of great denial—if you don't like something, you just rename it." When to keep names, when to find new ones, how to spell them, where to put them, how to make them clear—these are the questions METROPOLIS sets out to ask. Akiko Busch

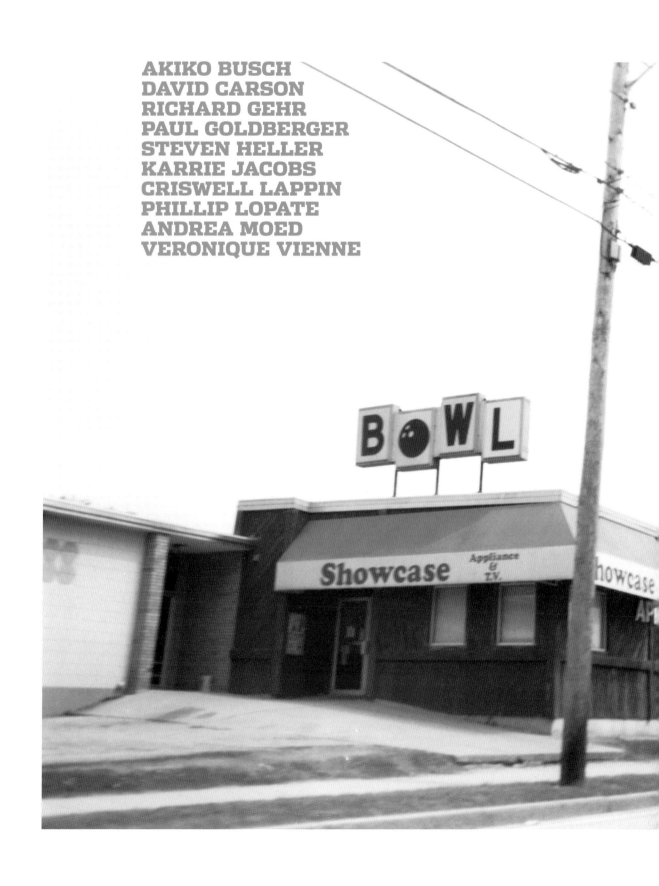

AKIKO BUSCH
DAVID CARSON
RICHARD GEHR
PAUL GOLDBERGER
STEVEN HELLER
KARRIE JACOBS
CRISWELL LAPPIN
PHILLIP LOPATE
ANDREA MOED
VERONIQUE VIENNE

YOU'VE GOT SPAM

During the dark days of the 2000 presidential election—the limbo period following miscast votes and dangling chads—the only bright light was on the computer screen. Internet sites and e-mail queues were flooded with GIFs, TIFFs, StuffIts, and JPEGs of digitally manipulated graphics skewering the presumptive president-elect for his intellectual, verbal, and even anatomical deficits. This energetic digital leafleting, or spam campaign (the distribution of e-mail missives), continued the tradition of satirical cartooning and protest-poster sniping that has long been a part of visual polemics. Owing to the widespread use of digital cameras, Photoshop software, and Internet distribution, a new era of graphic high jinks was launched with George W. Bush as its virtual poster boy.

The election may be over, but for a large percentage of the media map's "blue zone" (the states that went for Al Gore) Dubya's lack of a mandate is an issue that continues to prompt anti-Bush e-mail. These broadsides usually come in the form of forwarded attachments, as the e-mailers engage in a sort of barter relay. "The more you send to others, the more they send to you," says Nathan Felde, a graphic designer and sometime e-sniper. "I presume that people resend the ones they identify with most closely. It's like kids trading baseball cards."

There is no sinister conspiracy at work here—no dirty-tricks clearing house with a retinue of scheming propagandists. Immediately after the Florida butterfly ballot controversy, copies of the misleading form and a few homemade comic parodies hit the e-waves. It was quick but not orchestrated. The majority of virtual leaflets are in fact resolutely ad hoc; very few are produced by graphic designers. Given the availability of sophisticated software and the need to maintain a level of unpretentious simplicity, the professional and amateur approaches are usually indistinguishable. A missive designed by Felde (unsigned) and distributed a week before the inauguration is a wordplay that removes the last two letters in each of the stacked words BULL SHIT, resulting in the word BUSH. It was created on the spur of the moment with an untutored air about it. "I designed it for my wife, who needed a sign to take to the inaugural protest that succinctly expressed her feelings," Felde says.

Felde sent this e-flyer to 30 friends and acquaintances on his personal e-mail list. Thus began the chain. In addition to receiving Felde's original mailing, I also received the same attachment from two other sources not on his list, each showing between 30 to 50 names in the "send to" fields. Add to that the 40 or so names that I forwarded to on my "intimate friends" list. Considering that at least half of those are likely to forward it to their respective e-lists, the potential distribution over the course of a month (the usual time frame for saturation) is huge. Whereas some people merely get a momentary chuckle from what pops up on their screens, others print out and post the leaflet for off-line display.

The anti-Bush e-mail barrage tapered off after the Supreme Court decision, but the ones created since he was selected president are full of ridicule. David Vogler—a graphic designer and chief creative officer of Mutation Labs Inc., an Internet content-creation company—recently distributed a short QuickTime movie passed along to him by an anti-Bush pal in Los Angeles. The 20-second film, called GEO BUSH PICKS A RUNNING MATE, captures Dubya, then president of the Texas Rangers baseball franchise, sitting in the owner's box aggressively picking his nasal cavity with forefinger and pinky. The source of the original film is being kept a secret, but the invasive camera is a great political tool. "This is a nice demonstration of the power of iMovie and a Mac," Vogler says. "It's desktop video 'sniping' for the Web, wonderful guerrilla communication."

Of course, the "bushpic.mov," as it's slugged, like many other e-leaflets, is not in the same league as the artfully caustic graphic commentaries of nineteenth- and twentieth-century master caricaturists Honoré Daumier, George Grosz, and David Levine, but it does serve the same purpose: to "out" political folly by ridiculing those in power—the more venal the politician, the more biting the caricature.

Most digital leaflets are anonymous—the attacks hit-and-run—so tracking down the originators is usually futile. Nonetheless, repository sites for e-missives have sprung up, and one of the most inclusive is ilovebacon.com, a daily updated Web site for digital image postings. Founder Rob Glenn, a graphic designer who now devotes all his time to this site, says that he has no great mission: "It's just a place where you can find all the goofy crap that gets circulated around the Internet via e-mail." Glenn maintains that after the election he saw an influx of anti-Bush postings, but during the campaign the missives skewered both sides equally. Glenn edits the submitted postings based on quality of wit and other standards of acceptability. "We try to stay somewhere around a PG-13 to R rating," he says. People who have digital cameras "and notice weird stuff" create most postings, but he allows that anonymous professional image-makers contribute too, like Moe Bush at www.ilovebacon.com/jokes/012601.shtml. As for intellectual property rights, Glenn says: "I don't ask for exclusive rights. Some of the stuff, like jokes, are just retold and retold, and it's pretty much impossible to figure out where they came from."

Illegally wheat-pasting posters is still the confrontational activity of choice for many veteran graphic protesters, because poster sniping is ultimately an act of civil disobedience. Sniping on the Web is legal, safe, and free of consequence. Yet Robbie Conal, known for his "Art Attacks" in major American cities—with posters against Jesse Helms, Clarence Thomas, and anti-abortion advocates—has recently engaged in digital leafleting to augment his campaigns. "I used to be annoyed by e-mail leaflets," Conal says, "until my 18-year-old intern from USC taught me how to do them." After he learned how to do Photoshop "remixes" of conservative mainstream images and text, he says, "I got excited. It's like being a hip-hop DJ doing dance-party versions of standard tunes. We made a few of Bush and John Ashcroft. I started e-mailing them around to annoy my friends and enemies on the Internet. It works! Of course, the streets it ain't!"

Wall Street was long thought to be the source of topical jokes, which were then disseminated to the masses via fax. Today e-mail has become the purveyor of contemporary humor; in a matter of hours thousands of e-leaflets can appear on desktops nationwide. Internet technology has breathed new life into the venerable art of alternative satire. Digital sniping may not change the world, but it has opened a channel for Dubya opponents to exercise their democratic right to be indignant. STEVEN HELLER 06.01

ONLY MAKE BELIEVE

The word gesture in itself promises very little, which may explain why it is becoming
so indispensable in architectural discourse. Gestures need not ensure that the intended
communication is even received: one thinks of empty gestures or futile gestures. Some
are a bit more farfetched than others. I heard an architect speak of coloring his building
blue because, although it was located five long city blocks from the river, he wanted
to "refer" to the waterfront district. In the present climate of architectural guilt about
Modernist buildings not being sufficiently contextual, all this projection of gestural
activity onto stationary buildings shows a touching parental protectiveness, as though
buildings were autistic children who were not expected to relate much, but whose every
step in that direction must be celebrated.

A neoprimitive, mythologizing subtext is unmistakable as well in all
this gesture imagery. One reads in the journals about design gestures toward the earth,
the winds, the sky, the hills, the moon, the afternoon light, the ocean, the stars. Here a
building seems a sort of aborigine placating the gods of the elements and the spirits of
the site with its ritual dance. Avant-garde architecture, or at least one wing of it, seems
to have taken on the burden of reconnecting secular man to the cosmos. Quite an ambition. Might one also detect a flight from urbanism and its complicated responsibilities
in this mythologizing process?

"Earth, sky, divinities, mortals"—one hears the tom-tom beat of the
Heideggerian fourfold. Heidegger's influential essay (more so in architectural than philosophical circles), "Buildings Dwelling Thinking," with its keen advice, "The nature of
building is letting dwell" (from POETRY, LANGUAGE, THOUGHT), seems to have encouraged some architects to think of their discipline again as part of the eternal cycle.

Which is all to the good. Where it becomes comic—in the sense of the
distance between illusion and reality—is the sometimes misguided attempt to read pheno-
menological richness into banal, sterile industrialline products. It is one thing to talk
about the "presence" of an edifice mediating chapel-like between heaven and Earth, or of
a new suburban house in the woods recapturing the pious vernacular simplicity of a
forester's hut. But how often the description of a project's spiritual intent is subverted by
its accompanying photograph!

Moving from the spiritual to the moral-psychological idiom, we find
buildings judged as "narcissistic" or "self-centered," while others are approved of for having "responsible" lobbies or structural "honesty." Narcissism is a curious charge to level
against an artifact that was not only intended to be beautiful but is incapable of beholding
itself. Moreover, at a time when psychoanalytic literature has refined the concept of narcissism in an attempt to go beyond the simplistically pejorative, it seems jarring for a critic
like Paul Goldberger to continue to use it as contemptuous shorthand, even when his
underlying reservations against the particular building may be just.

Perhaps the most bewildering architectural moralism to an outsider
is the notion of "honesty." It would appear that if a building "expresses" its structural

41

elements, if the architect brings into the open its pipes, ducts, heating elements; if its facade reveals the interior division of floors; if its load-bearing columns are left exposed, it is somehow an honest fellow. Such a charming view of rectitude invites all kinds of charlatanism: a building may "unmask" the old Victorian decorum of backstage functions, with exposed pipes galore, while on deeper levels of integrity it proceeds to lie through its teeth. Even so, I can accept this technical/process concept of honesty more readily when it is sufficiently embedded in a larger recognition of the degree to which architecture must inevitably "cheat" as part of its being an art form.

In connection with "honesty," let us note the fancy rationalizations of one architect who had accepted a building commission in a large project (Battery Park City, New York), whose guidelines might be interpreted as encouraging "historical"
—i.e. postmodernist—solutions. In the statement accompanying his exhibit model, James Stewart Polshek wrote: "While the composition recalls the architecture of Amsterdam South housing in the 1920s, its effect is made by the manipulation of basic elements, not the superimposition of decoration. In so doing, the design remains true to the ethical core of modernism." I am fascinated with that smug phrase, "the ethical core of modernism." Would that all mortals could remain true to some ethical core in their daily struggle as easily, it would seem, as those in the architectural profession, who have only to eschew decoration.

I do not deny that there are serious moral questions implicit in architectural aesthetics; certainly there are profound problems of justice in the whole history of what gets built, and for whom. But these issues are often trivialized and deflected by a superficial moralism, which seems to have more to do with professional allegiances and careerist maneuvers. Just as fashion magazine writing always tries to introduce the newest stylistic artifice as a more "natural" look, so does much architectural discussion seem an attempt to elevate wrinkles of taste into moral imperatives. PHILLIP LOPATE 09.84

THERE IS NO CONTRADICTION BETWEEN DISCIPLINE AND FREEDOM, BETWEEN CAUTION AND CREATIVITY.

RENZO PIANO 12.92

A CRITIC ON CRITICISM

I think of architecture writing as the kind of criticism I want to read about film, music, or literature—all fields that interest me but with which I have no professional connection: I want my intelligence to be respected and a certain base knowledge assumed, but not the level of specific knowledge that a professional would have. I try to aim my architectural criticism in that direction.

To explain to readers what is difficult to comprehend is part of my job. Most architects fall apart when it comes to words. What's more important is to make it clear whether it's worth comprehending in the first place and why. When I examine a building I have a kind of unwritten checklist. Before I even go in I'm concerned about issues of context and urbanistic relationships: the connection of the building to its site, the appropriateness of the building to its program, its appeal as a pure aesthetic object, the manner in which it functions for the people who use it.

At risk of sounding mushy or indecisive, which I don't consider myself at all, I am not an ideologue. I'm concerned much more with fundamentals that go beyond and across various ideologies with the following issues: What makes a good plan? What makes good space? What makes a good composition? These are subtle and partly intuitive, as well as intellectual, judgments.

I think the position that critics should be architects is nonsense. It's a matter of individual temperament. I've made a point of not judging buildings as purely aesthetic objects, even though by training I am an art historian and journalist. I've argued that a building has to be evaluated in terms of the sociological, political, and economic climate that created it and in which it is used. I've covered issues of planning, urban design, zoning, economics, and architectural practice. Yes, architects are sensitive to these things, but you don't have to be an architect to be sensitive.

You ask why I've won the Pulitzer. I guess it's because of the breadth of the issues I chose to cover. In the course of a year I'll cover pieces ranging from aesthetics and the politics of preservation to the design of pure objects—years ago I did an essay on the paper clip. Architecture is social commentary as much as it is anything else.

It's also important to separate the enormous interest in architecture at this moment from the cult of the architect. They are different things that reinforce each other. Neither is wholly positive or negative. One is more positive than the other. Even tenth-rate commercial developers want an architect of note to do their buildings. Everyone talks about new architects. It would be cynical to the extreme to believe this public interest has not been a good thing. Otherwise I'd have no reason for being here.

Critics are somewhat responsible, but no one would have tried to manufacture plates by architects if they didn't think there was a market to sell them. They didn't sit down and say "Gee, I think we can get the press to write about these plates; therefore, they should be made." What they thought is that people would buy them. It's as wrong to overstate the power of the press as to understate it. It's strong and powerful, but it's not dictatorial, absolute, or immediate. PAUL GOLDBERGER 11.85

43

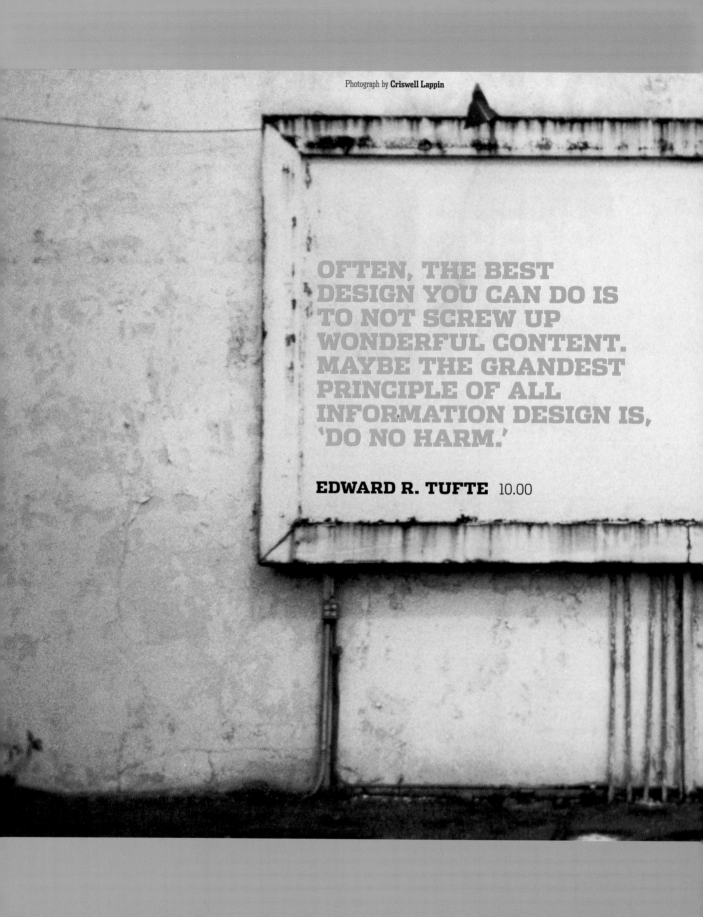

Photograph by **Criswell Lappin**

OFTEN, THE BEST
DESIGN YOU CAN DO IS
TO NOT SCREW UP
WONDERFUL CONTENT.
MAYBE THE GRANDEST
PRINCIPLE OF ALL
INFORMATION DESIGN IS,
'DO NO HARM.'

EDWARD R. TUFTE 10.00

ANGRY GRAPHICS

The construction fence at the corner of Prince Street and Broadway seems as though it's been there forever. It could, however, disappear at any moment, revealing a newly renovated facade. The one-story-tall sheet of plywood is completely covered with posters—layers and layers of posters. Most of them will not remain intact and visible for longer than two or three days. They all will get torn down or pasted over again.

The poster wall provides the best graphics show in the city. Not just this location—there are similar walls all over Manhattan—but this sort of location. These walls, called hoardings, have been used in this manner more or less illegally for at least a century.

They offer a highly visible, continuous graphics exhibition, one that is neither judged nor curated. It's a show that's hung and rehung nightly mostly by professional posterers, the pirates of the outdoor advertising world. The show's changing content is regulated by the peculiar Darwinism of "sniping," the repeated and methodical postering of a given location. The posters placed by the most skilled and persistent snipers will survive the longest.

Here multiple full-color images of Sri Chin-moy (dressed in a saffron robe) abut multiple black-and-white images of Andrew Dice Clay (dressed in a white T-shirt). A slick full-color poster for Spanish director Pedro Almodovar's new movie, which looks like a holdover from a perverse moment in the 1950s, shares space with a grainy black-and-white poster announcing an appearance of a band called Maria Ex Communikata at CBGBs.

On New York's construction fences, slick commercial posters for entertainment products share space with less commercial notices, including small, sloppy Xeroxed announcements for demonstrations, plugs for local bar bands, and broadsides for ideologies both obscure and commonplace.

Magazines and newspapers have standards that govern the appearance and content of the advertising they accept. The companies that lease outdoor and transit advertising space have rules about what is and isn't appropriate. But walls and fences operate beyond the forces of law and propriety. As a result, some of the strongest and most interesting graphics (as well as some of the worst) can be found in this setting.

The walls are also where groups and individuals take their political messages, where they try to reach people directly. At the end of April, on this particular wall at Prince and Broadway, there are a few political posters. On the top of the wall, there's a line of four or five "Happy Earth Day" posters, a photo of Earth from space against a background of magenta and violet, an image as threatening as a card from Hallmark. A set of posters that says "Stop the Drug Wars" with the word peace inset in the middle of a cartoon marijuana leaf, advertising a demonstration supporting legalization of drugs, is mostly torn to shreds. They're being squeezed out by posters for FURTHER MO', "the new New Orleans musical," and posters announcing a new magazine called MANHATTAN COMIC NEWS. Peering out from beneath the torn-off bottom halves of posters for the Elisa Monte

Dance troupe is a poster that had dominated many walls a few weeks earlier, a Barbara Kruger poster advertising a pro-choice art auction. "Your Body Is a Battle Ground," it says. Kruger lent this poster for use in promoting last year's massive pro-choice demonstration in Washington, D.C., but it reappeared this year advertising a National Abortion Rights Action League (NARAL) art auction.

One section of the fence seems to be given over almost entirely to homemade posters. There's a Xeroxed Earth Day notice in the cut-paste-and-scrawl style common to many street posters; it's a smudgy globe surrounded by slogans, hand-lettered or haphazardly assembled like a ransom note: "Boycott Styrofoam," "Stop Raping Mother Earth," and so on.

Less typical is a block of dozens of posters for a gallery show called Art Fux, featuring a crude figure that combines elements of the smiley face (without the smile) and a skull and crossbones. The poster carries the "Art Fux Manifesto": "We have arrived. We will not tolerate art for art's sake. We will not tolerate forced morality. We will not tolerate forced patriotism. We will not tolerate government censorship." Like many homemade posters, the only identification on it is a post office box address, in Jersey City.

Around the corner from the fence, on Prince Street, the postering is reduced to a trickle. There someone has repeatedly wheat-pasted a simple poignant message in crude black type on white paper: "My beloved was queer-bashed here."
KARRIE JACOBS 07/08.90

47

GREAT EUROPEAN DESIGN IS ALMOST ALWAYS BASED ON ONE AESTHETIC THEORY OR ANOTHER. GREAT AMERICAN DESIGN IS ALMOST ALWAYS BASED ON THE STUDIED DISREGARD OF AESTHETIC THEORY.

CONSTANTIN BOYM 10.92

AN AD CAMPAIGN THAT ALIENATES EVERYONE

"For us, just showing the product at this point would be banal," Luciano Benetton says. So instead of showing his cheerful and tidy collection of coordinated T-shirts and jeans jackets, the Italian clothes manufacturer chooses to flood the media with a nightmarish advertising campaign showing news photographs from this side of Hell.

If Benetton thinks that his merchandise is that banal, it seems that he should rethink it and improve its design. But we live in a time of great denial: if you don't like something, you just rename it. Companies with diminished profits are described as offering potential "growth opportunities." Cheap products are branded "deluxe." Handicapped people are called "physically challenged." Deny reality. Wear rose-colored glasses.

Benetton's innovation is to replace an inferior product with something even worse: an advertising campaign that is sure to alienate practically everybody. This fascination with the negative is a very European thing. I know this tendency too well. Born and raised in France, I always started my sentences with a nonaffirmative clause: "Don't you think," "Never mind," "I would not be surprised." To survive in the States, I had to retrain myself. I've learned the hard way not to expect the worst and to appreciate Optimism, Enthusiasm, and Hope—the great all-American values. So the first time I saw Benetton's apocalyptic campaign, I had to laugh—not at Luciano Benetton, but at myself. His gloom-and-doom approach to problem solving is a parody of a cultural attitude with which I am well acquainted, a caricature of my own existential native disposition.

From experience, I can pledge that Luciano Benetton and his creative director Oliviero Toscani are not trying to exploit our guilt feelings—they are just being practical. Benetton's hot pink, apple green, and turquoise shirts are old hat? No problem. You want news, we'll give you news: boat people—Albanian refugees hanging like human vines from a dilapidated ship; a modern Pietà—an emaciated, young man with AIDS dying in his father's arms; cannibalism—a black guerrilla soldier holding what looks like a human femur. Although not really newsworthy—many of the Benetton campaign's photographs have been published before—these pictures have a journalistic texture that evokes newsiness. And for Benetton, that's good enough. His casual clothes are not 100 percent cotton or wool. His idea of journalistic integrity and his philanthropic concern are not 100 percent politically correct.

Benetton's ambiguous contempt for his own merchandise is a subtle, intriguing, but annoying, message. For me, this lack of interest in the product is more disturbing than Benetton's controversial advertising campaign. Unlike the Gap or J. Crew, which treat their clothes with reverence and display their $10.50 tee or their $38 jeans as if they were museum pieces, Benetton refuses to waste his creativity promoting the value of his sportswear. That's too trivial and commercial for him. His bulky catalog, showing page after page of mix-and-match separates, does not even dignify the goods with a description or a price. Under the impression that a picture is worth a thousand words, Toscani has decided not to give us any words. It's a shame.

48

As demonstrated by the recent witty advertising campaigns of such companies as Barneys, Charivari, Kenneth Cole, Gap, and Nike, words are making a comeback. Rap music is reenergizing MTV's program mix. Big pull quotes combined with small mug shots are used in magazine stories to summarize situations. Catchphrases are becoming increasingly more popular in casual conversation. Someone should have told Mr. Toscani that tasteful aloofness is a dated communication concept.

That someone should have been Tibor Kalman. An idea man, a conceptual graphic artist, and an articulate designer, Kalman is the art director of INTERVIEW magazine. He has an editorial mind. That's why he was hired by Benetton to find and edit the news photographs used in its campaign. "We asked photo agencies for strong and graphically beautiful images of the human condition," he explained. "But nothing we liked turned up. So we did the research ourselves, investigating every journalistic venue available to us: photo annuals, competition entries, and various archives."

He chose six photographs, two of which were not in color. "I wanted to avoid the arty connotation of black-and-white photography, so we hand-colored the photographs of the boat people and of the young man dying of AIDS."

For each picture, Kalman has an anecdote: the Indian couple wading through a flood could not be located to sign a release; what appears to be a human femur is probably the bone of a gazelle; before releasing the picture of her son on his deathbed, Mrs. Kirby drove all the way to Columbus from her rural home in Ohio to check the quality of the Benetton stores; the picture of the boat people taken during the Albanian crisis is particularly painful for Luciano Benetton to look at—as a newly elected member of the Italian senate, he is ashamed of his government's handling of the refugees.

You wish some of this context were integrated into the photographs. Unfortunately, they run without captions. Like the clothes in the catalog, Benetton's flesh-and-blood subjects are deprived of their specificity and their identity. They become generic. Nameless, they lose their ability to move us and transform us. "We think the photographs are so powerful they speak for themselves," Kalman says. But it is the Benetton campaign that speaks for itself through them: it betrays a subliminal indifference toward images of human suffering.

Kalman is also editor in chief of COLORS, Benetton's publishing venture, an oversize magazine printed in five languages and distributed through its 7,000 stores worldwide. COLORS is nothing like Benetton's recent ad campaign: its clean-cut graphic approach, silhouetted images, and pristine photography are in keeping with Benetton's well-known youthful image. Its editorial content is fun, clever, and playful.

Celebrating differences between people, it delivers its multicultural message through poster-size layouts, and bold and colorful charts. Reading like a cross between an in-house magazine, a slick advertorial package, and a college newspaper, COLORS nonetheless never reaches critical mass. It looks too much like a portfolio piece, a candidate for an Art Directors Club award. Self-consciousness weakens its impact. In spite of its handsome design, Benetton's magazine is self-indulgent, and as such, it is perceived as junk mail.

49

No offense to Tibor, junk is probably one of the most important issues of our time, and certainly a subject of great concern for Benetton's young customers: recycling, garbage, pollution, lost causes, fallen heroes, former countries, trash-as-art. As it should, junk is a recurring theme in COLORS' editorial mix. I particularly enjoyed a story on junk food ("Salty, greasy, curvy, and seductive"), a photograph of a skier wearing a gas mask and slaloming down a garbage dump, and an inventory of things made of scavenged materials. The Benetton catalog itself, inserted in the magazine like a throwaway advertising supplement, reinforces the urgent "junk is relevant" message.

The Benetton campaign is shocking to maturing baby boomers but it is appropriate for the Ninja Turtles generation. Our kids see the world as temporary, transient, disposable. Species are vanishing. Natural resources are diminishing. The Earth is threatened. Tomorrow is a perishable notion.

You cannot blame today's youth for not endorsing our talk of returning to timeless values. Why should they trust our sudden concern for integrity? Why should they care about the difference between Benetton's "journalistic" advertising message and the NEW YORK TIMES' editorial point of view? And last but not least, why should they want clothes that last more than a season?

Benetton does not need to offer the quintessential pocket T-shirt—its customers do not believe in quintessential values. As a teenager said to me: "I like Benetton clothes because they self-destruct. They lose their shape as soon as I get tired of them, and my mother gives them away. She says I look like a bum." No kidding. Today there are more and more homeless folks who wear recycled United Colors of Benetton sweaters. You can tell by the cut, the look, the way the fabric wrinkles and shrinks. So you see, in the end, Luciano Benetton is fulfilling his altruistic mission.

VERONIQUE VIENNE 09.92

THE POSTMODERNIST THEORE- TICAL APPARATUS SEEMS TO LEAD TO A COMPLETELY HUMOR- LESS, STRAIGHT-FACED, AND LEADEN-FOOTED PERSPECTIVE OF THE PAST.

JAMES MARSTON FITCH 11.93

IDENTITY CRISIS

Logos. I've got logos on the brain. Everywhere I look I see logos and trademarks and symbols. Dead center on this very typewriter is Paul Rand's classic IBM logotype. No stripes, just those assertive serifs and hard right angles. My phone bill has become nothing but a venue for trademarks: Lippincott & Margulies's NYNEX with the wind whistling through the slices in the X, the stylized predivestiture bell and the AT&T banded sphere (referred to by AT&T workers as the "deathstar"), both by Saul Bass. And my morning carton of orange juice is, of course, a showcase for little Tropic-Ana, the incredible shrinking hula child. With round belly and knowing smirk, she dominated the juice containers until about two years ago, when a more aggressive marketing stance dictated a package redesign. Strategic packaging pro Alvin Schechter reduced Ana to Lilliputian scale, a pixie standing bravely in the shadow of an enormous oozing orange. Ana is the lucky one. Unlike other inexplicable but endearing trademarks, she has survived.

When I talk trademarks I start to sound like the archetypal museum reactionary, the twit who's always just down the ramp at the Guggenheim keening, "What on Earth is this supposed to be?" These devices aren't abstract art. They're communication, and often it's what they communicate about both designer and client that makes me steam. "What on Earth," I demand to know, "is this supposed to be?"

While ornament and historical reference have, for better or worse, made a comeback in art and architecture, corporate America's love affair with the heartless style it considers modern is deep and lasting. This romance is nothing new. Hardly. The first kiss? Maybe it was the Chermayeff & Geismar Chase Manhattan Bank logo from the early 1960s, the wreath formed by four trapezoids. A powerful and enduring symbol, it was a triumph of geometry over representation, of vague implications over specificity.

That new corporate symbols are almost always more abstract than the ones they replaced, that most are conservatively colored squares, circles, triangles, or swirls, scrubbed free of idiosyncrasies, doesn't mean that minimalism is a hot topic at board meetings. It simply indicates that less is more noncommittal. In the information age figurative logos carry too much baggage. They're reminders of the dark ages when American corporations wanted to be known for making particular things, for doing particular things instead of selling services and sending binary impulses careening around the globe.

Witness the name changes. Primerica is the American Can company that no longer makes cans. Navistar is the International Harvester company that no longer makes harvesters. Greyhound is still called Greyhound, but they no longer own the bus lines and it's only a matter of time before they change their name and ditch the dog.

The new names are in a computer-generated language, an MBA's Esperanto. Unysis. Trinova. Enron. Forget the Latin roots they offer for these electronically invented names. The message is the same. We don't make what we used to make. In fact we may not make anything at all. We own things. We buy and we sell. We are creatures of Wall Street. And we are very, very powerful. KARRIE JACOBS 09.87

51

COME ON, NOT ME, NOT ME

I feel as though I've been in this office before: Barcelona chairs, a big Roy Lichtenstein poster framed and hanging behind the desk, a graphic treatment of the letters NYC with the silhouette of an apple nestled within the C hanging on another wall. It is the lower Fifth Avenue office of Allen Kay, the chairman of an ad agency, Korey, Kay & Partners, but it could be the office of any number of ad agency executives or design firm partners whom I've visited over the years.

The people seem familiar, too. Kay, his account director, Robbie Finke, and Alicia Martinez, the director of marketing and corporate communications for New York State's Metropolitan Transportation Authority. All of them are bright, thoughtful people. They could be any of the designers, creative directors, marketers, or public relations people with whom I've spoken.

Always it is the same. There is a problem, a message that a client has to get across, an image that needs to be polished or transformed. And within the confines of this office, within the world of design, advertising, or marketing—where image is reality and concept is king—problems have solutions.

The problem, in this instance, is panhandling in the subways. In the stations and on the trains of the New York City subway system, there are often people asking for money. Sometimes they stand next to the token booth and plead as you're buying tokens. Often, as you're sitting on a train, someone walks in and says something like, "Excuse me, ladies and gentlemen, I don't want to bother anyone, but..." And what follows is a hard-luck story. "I just got out of the veterans' hospital and I've got nowhere to go. I just got out of jail. I was burned out of my apartment. I was robbed."

Always, you feel as if you've heard it before. If you ride the trains you've seen some of these people a million times. Their litanies of problems are often as practiced as the litanies of solutions you hear if you spend time among designers or advertising people. Everyone has their rap. Sometimes, in the subway, as in the pricey offices upstairs, the rap pays off. "Hell," you think, "maybe he is hungry. Maybe she needs baby formula." So you shell out a quarter and feel as if there is a possibility you've done some good.

Still, these routine confrontations are disturbing, in part because all you want is to ride the train in peace, but especially because they remind you of problems that you don't want to think about, problems that have no easy solution—at least not in the real world of the city, not in the real world of the subway.

Marketing studies commissioned by the MTA showed that panhandlers make subway riders edgy. This is not surprising. MTA chairman Peter Stangl is quoted in a press release saying, "Almost 90 percent of customers we have surveyed say that panhandlers are a serious problem in the subway, and more than half say that they are intimidated into giving to beggars at least occasionally." He goes on to say that the beggars contribute "to a pervasive sense of disorder and discomfort."

Alicia Martinez, the MTA's communications director, puts the issue this way: "When you're sitting in a subway car and someone is in your face, what do you do?

Aboveground panhandling is a First Amendment issue. In the system, you're really trapped."

The MTA has been addressing the problem of homelessness by having police officers and social workers doing outreach within the subway system, offering shelter or some type of treatment to people who live on trains, in stations, or in tunnels.

The panhandlers (who are not necessarily homeless) are a related but different problem. Early this year the MTA began a well-publicized effort to drive beggars out of the system by deploying plainclothes police, the "Quality of Life Task Force," to ticket or arrest them. But, they reasoned, the beggars would return as long as passengers were giving them money.

So the MTA awarded Kay's ad agency what Martinez characterizes as "the toughest assignment ever." They had to devise a poster that couldn't be honest.

"It's tough to say 'don't give' when their instinct is to be charitable and give," Martinez observes. "It's not like we're hardhearted cretins."

"The message is 'panhandling is illegal,'" Kay reflects, **"but how do you say that without being insensitive?"**

What Korey, Kay's creative team came up with is a black card that says the insensitive thing along the top in Helvetica: "Panhandling on the subway is illegal. No matter what you think." Then it says something less insensitive in a softer typeface, one with serifs: "Give to the charity of your choice, but not on the subway."

"These are the type styles of the MTA," Kay notes.

However, a white thought balloon containing what might go through a passenger's head when confronted with a panhandler dominates the black poster. This copy is set in perhaps half a dozen typefaces and weights, making it look like something that might be the work of an experimental typographer or the auteur of an underground political poster—but not an official pronouncement of the Metropolitan Transit Authority. The typography is deliberately nonauthoritative.

"This is the type style of the people," Kay explains.

And what are "the people" thinking?

"Uh, oh. Come on, not me, NOT ME. Oh Pleeeeeze don't come stand in FRONT of me ASKING for money. GREAT. Now the whole car's staring. What do I do, WHAT DO I DO???? I know. I'll pretend I'm reading my book. Look. I feel bad. I really do. But HEY, it's MY MONEY. And HOW do I know what you'll spend it on anyway? I DON'T. SORRY. No money from me."

When tested in focus groups, subway "customers" responded favorably. "People said, 'How did you know that's what I was thinking?'" Kay recalls. He says that group members were pleased to discover that they were not alone in having uncomfortable and perhaps less-than-noble thoughts when approached by a panhandler. "It felt like a bond," Kay says, "a lifting of guilt."

So the solution to the problem of panhandlers in the New York City subway system was solved in part by a poster that uses the typography of the people (as opposed to Helvetica) to let those same people off the hook. What this poster does—

rather effectively—is give New Yorkers official permission to shut out one more of the city's many problems.

In the context of design problems and solutions, this poster is a success. It will probably win awards. In the real world of problems and solutions, this poster signals a grave failure. The poster exudes the moral worminess that appears to be the new hallmark of public life in New York. This humorous placard unintentionally admits something truly awful: that we have no solutions to the problems of hunger, homelessness, poverty, drug addiction, and alcoholism but we are sick to death of having to confront them. Now we simply want the sense of "disorder and discomfort" to go away. "Come on, not me, NOT ME." That's all we have left to say. However, it's one thing to think these thoughts as individuals. It's another to have this sort of reaction sanctified and encouraged by public agencies and policy. The poster, clever as it is, is appalling because it is the voice of authority speaking the language of fear and confusion.

The MTA's anti-panhandling campaign has drawn fire from advocacy groups such as the Coalition for the Homeless, where legal director Lisa Daugaard characterizes it as "mean" and "insidious." She believes that the messages about outreach work and donating to charity are there to camouflage the cruelty of the MTA's policies. She says that the outreach done by the transit police doesn't necessarily give people the kind of help they need and that the line about donating to the charity of your choice is irrelevant. "Charities don't exist to supplant the appeal of individual human beings in need," Daugaard argues.

The activist organizations Out of the Shelters and Into the Streets and ACT-UP responded to the MTA's posters by doctoring them with their own thought bubbles: "Uh, oh. Don't arrest me. I'm just asking for money, trying to get by. Great. Our new mayor thinks I belong in jail," one version says.

My own response is simple. I ignore or donate to the panhandlers on a case-by-case basis. The ones who deliver a polished rap, I figure they don't need my money. They could get a job in advertising.

As for the MTA's anti-panhandling campaign (which also includes a straightforward leaflet and incessant announcements over subway-station PA systems), I can think, "C'mon, not me, NOT ME." But it doesn't do any good. As a subway rider and taxpayer, I've already made a contribution. I had no choice. In the system, as Martinez put it, you're really trapped. KARRIE JACOBS 03.94

54

ELECTRONIC NEWSPAPERS

Newspapers have always commanded more authority than television news shows because they are thought to have more depth in their reporting. Nicholas Negroponte, the director of Media Lab, believes this will soon change. He foresees an individual returning home at night to a receiver that has downloaded 15 hours of televised news. "What you would see would be summaries, not too dissimilar from the current type of news we get. But as you come across a story you're interested in, you could push the button that says 'tell me more' and it would elaborate in progressively greater detail."

And what about the concept of "the newspaper of record"? According to Negroponte, "The concept of a [single] newspaper or medium of record will not diminish—it will go away. Because that is only somebody else's opinion of what is newsworthy, and on top of that, it's a very abbreviated form of what is available. When you receive your newspaper in the morning, some stories give you much less than you really want, others a lot more than you really want, and some stories you don't get at all because they're not considered sufficiently newsworthy. The definition of 'newsworthiness' has always been in the hands of the news publisher and not the consumer. In the future, consumers will assume this editorial function, deciding for themselves what is or isn't newsworthy."

Ironically, though, there is a risk that if vast amounts of information are available at the touch of a button, nobody will access it because it will have lost its importance and immediacy—its newsiness. And in the same way that the population at large reads fewer books and watches more television, mainstream culture might assign less value to the depth and analysis offered by print—something that many would argue is already happening. To attract or keep their "readership," electronic news carriers may have to Nintendo-ize themselves, in much the way that newspapers around the country are copying the eye-grabbing four-color graphics of USA TODAY to survive.

The problem of access also looms. What happens when the poor can no longer fish a used paper out of the corner trash bin? But maybe electronic publishing won't really be so exclusive. Consider television. Once an elitist product, it has become the most populist of media. Roger Fidler, who heads Knight-Ridder, Inc.'s media development laboratory, believes that the price of a subscription to an electronic newspaper will be no higher than a newspaper subscription today. Of course, the actual hardware will be an added, although infrequent, expense. And it is the hardware that most concerns Fidler. He worries that "we will go off and build Betamaxes when what we really want is relatively ubiquitous hardware with consistent standards." For this reason, he believes the growth of the electronic newspaper will be necessarily gradual, though inevitable.

Fidler distinguishes between how we interact and communicate with information as newspaper readers and the way we use computers as tools for creating information. Because of this, he conceives of the electronic newspaper as something separate from personal digital assistants (PDAs) such as Apple's Newton (a handheld computer similar to, but much more sophisticated than, the tablets used by UPS delivery personnel).

librarians skilled in data preparation and presentation. Given the spirit of the enterprise, it is not surprising that SIBL's interior rather resembles that of an upscale restaurant.

The reading rooms are spare but formal, with light wood paneling, vaulted ceilings, and cupolaed entry halls. Under mellow, indirect lighting, ample wooden tables can hold several courses of data at once. At an elegantly curving counter, patrons will order from the library's 800,000-volume noncirculating print collection. Without leaving their tables, users will be able to sample any of the library's online catalogs, CD-ROMs, and databases, or access the Internet at desktop computers provided by the library or via laptops they bring with them. Reference books and directories will fill the shelves around the carrels. If they are not sure what to order, patrons will be able to consult with specialists in marketing chemistry, and other subjects at the central reference desk. CNN news and stock quotes will flow freely from a video array around the corner. This confluence of traditional and high-tech media and personal attention is what makes SIBL appealing. Even though the books and computers have not yet arrived, it's easy to imagine contented library users sitting here in their trendy Aeron chairs, devouring all forms of data.

I suspect that SIBL will be a somewhat intimidating place for many nontechnical people, with its volumes of quantitative and arcane information. Nonetheless, it can provide something of much broader value: the chance to use print and digital collections together, following one's curiosity across media from book to database to Internet and back. Bill Walker, the director of the NYPL's research libraries, claims that the library's goal is "seamless access," but it is the "seams" between formats that will make the access interesting. Because part of their mission is preservation, library collections are naturally full of seams; SIBL will contain microform cards from the 1960s as well as databases. Researchers may be just as likely to use a long-outdated machine as a new one.

This situation contrasts sharply with what communications companies tell us to expect of reading and libraries in the future. In an AT&T ad, a woman reads an image of an open book on a computer monitor. In advertising for CD-ROMs and online encyclopedias, words, images, sound and motion, the historical, and the new are enfolded in a single on-screen universe. As any librarian will attest, this is unlikely to happen with most library material. To "migrate" collections from one medium to another is costly; often it is done only when the collection is on the verge of becoming unusable. "We would never retroactively digitize our books," Walker says. Alternating between a book's page and a screen is a way of reading that has to be learned; it's a more difficult, disjointed process than either reading a book or using a computer alone. But both the usefulness of libraries and continued intellectual pluralism depend on it.

Meanwhile, back at the branch, the debut of computer access has a very different meaning from that of going online at SIBL. At neighborhood libraries, with their small and slow-growing print collections, the PCs are a much-needed new reason to stop in. Using LEO, a colorful, new computer interface custom-developed for the library, patrons can point and click to search the NYPL catalogs, other library system catalogs, the library's collection of databases, or the World Wide Web. Unlike SIBL and the other research libraries, however, most branches have had to install their computers at tightly spaced stand-up stations, sharply segregating electronic access from print access and discouraging in-depth online sessions.

What LEO offers branch users is autonomy—the chance for those who don't own computers to "play" with computerized information the way they cannot do at work, school, or in a store. People who feel computer-illiterate can try it out without fear of embarrassment. Autonomous use can also afford confidentiality to those who need it most: funded by a special grant, some of the PC terminals equipped with the New York Online Access to Health database are placed away from the library's main traffic flow, allowing users to get information about AIDS and other health matters in relative privacy.

The Web takes user autonomy even further, putting the library in the strange position of distributing material it has not acquired and authorized itself. For the first time, the library provides the means to look beyond its walls. Search engines let users hunt for names and subjects on the Internet the way they do with the library's electronic catalog, temporarily imparting the order of the library to the Internet. Elsewhere on the Web, "digital library" sites use the Internet to distribute information that already exists in traditional libraries. By allowing people to download public-domain literary and historical works such as the U.S. Constitution or ALICE IN WONDERLAND, they do what libraries cannot: their public collections can also be a permanent part of each user's personal collection.

If the Net can sometimes perform, or even outperform, the functions of public libraries, it's also true that the libraries become less public when they go online. In the library and on the Internet alike, we now have the ability to be in one place finding, using, and reproducing information that exists in another place, and thus to cross boundaries between public and private domains. Libraries themselves have been eager to provide access to computer users from their homes, as the NYPL has done since 1991. Susan Harrison, associate director of Technical and Computer Services for the NYPL Branch Libraries, predicts that people will eventually be able to access all the frequently changing portions of the library's collection from their homes, and that computers in libraries will exist mainly to "provide resources to people who will never have them at home."

But even if everyone had a home computer, the Net would still belong in the library. Libraries and librarians contextualize the Net as no other media institution can, serving as a public model for its use. In the course of their history, libraries have played a similar role in nearly every medium, whether in preserving access to banned books, expanding from book-only collections to include audio and video recordings, or having story hours, movie hours, and Web-navigating courses. "We need to bring some structure into it," Walker says of the notoriously unstructured Internet. "We need to show people how to wade through the advertising and evaluate it." Less obtrusively, libraries enable us to work in mixed media by furnishing a contemplative space: both the physical space of wide reading desks and comfortable chairs, and mental space, the interlude between media that allows readers (as well as listeners, viewers, and interactors) to draw back and gain perspective on often disparate materials. In the midst of info-glut, the presence of an ordered shelf of books provides a certain intellectual orientation—even if what you are reading is electronic news. ANDREA MOED 03.96

59

SNAPSHOTS BY DAVID CARSON

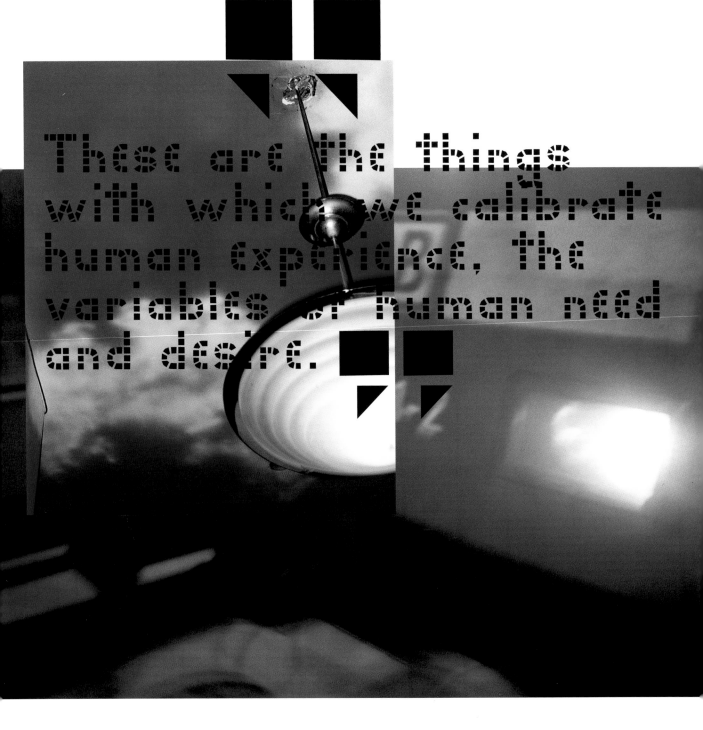

These are the things with which we calibrate human experience. The variables of human need and desire.

thank
god
its
monday

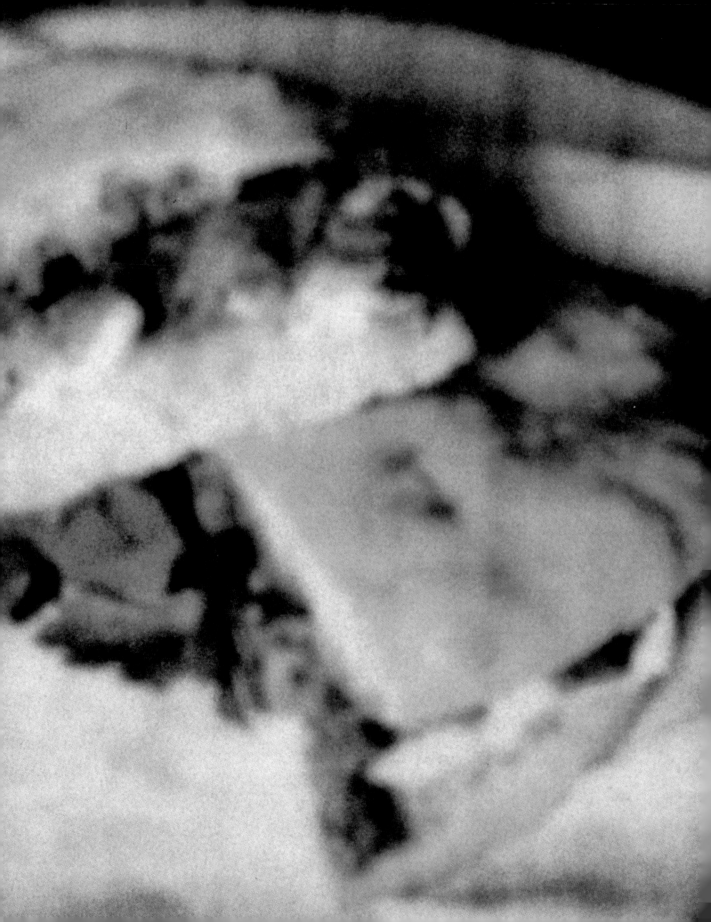

To many of us coffee—and the pots it comes in—represents pure deliverance. But to architect Aldo Rossi it is even more. In 1982 Sarah Bodine wrote, "Aldo Rossi's [design solutions] derive most directly from his own remembrances of Italian kitchens, where he spent hours sketching the strange shapes of enameled coffeepots. Today, he still often includes a coffeepot, the same one, over and over, in his drawings, sometimes at its own scale in a domestic environment, sometimes as the focal point of a composition, sometimes as large as the actual walls and towers of a town."

A coffeepot as big as a tower! But this is what designers do, after all. It's their job to calculate the correct scale of things, whether in the physical world or the popular imagination. It's also their job to imagine the value of physical objects, be it functional value or iconic value or any other kind of value. Objects acquire a presence in our lives, and these essays try to track why that is—why people make things, and why other people want those things in their lives.

It may be a lightweight, strong, easily maneuverable wheelchair that takes its cues from sports equipment and, in its ability to address the various needs of varied users, is the embodiment of all the principles of Universal Design. Or a yam pounder made in Japan and used in Nigeria: by displaying what happens when the manufacturer of one culture addresses the mealtime rituals of another, such an appliance reveals the multicultural mutations of product design. Or a coffee table that is the locus of American domestic ritual. Or a computer mouse with sensors that detect the user's emotional state.

All of these accessories help us to take measure of the world. They are the things with which we calibrate human experience, the variables of human need and desire. In the best of times what they show us is that there is grace in taking this measure, whether it is a 5,000-square-foot billboard, a miniature disk, or an immense coffeepot. In the best of all possible worlds it's what a deli server told photographer Sylvia Plachy: "Half a pound on the nose. It's my lucky day."   Akiko Busch

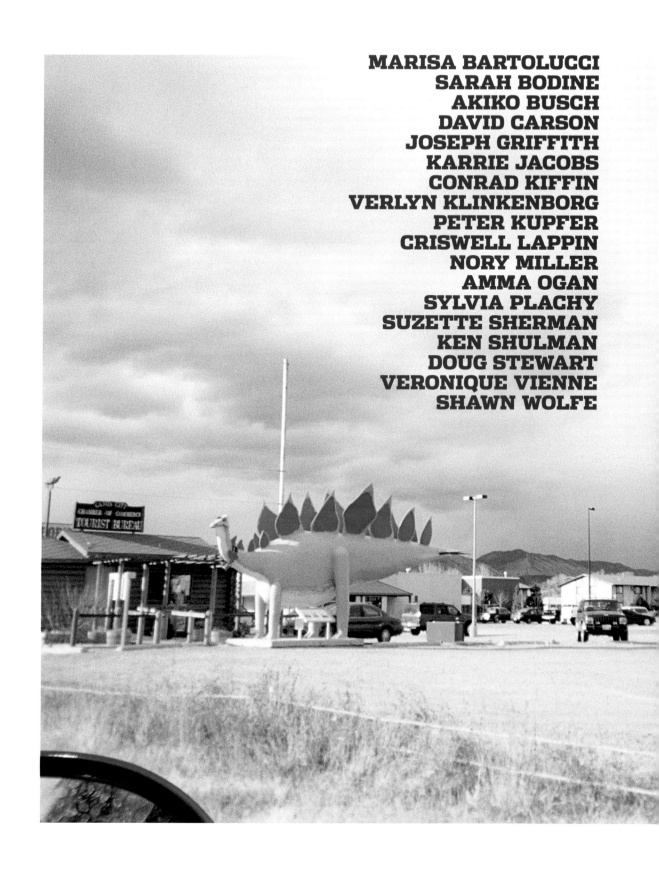

MARISA BARTOLUCCI
SARAH BODINE
AKIKO BUSCH
DAVID CARSON
JOSEPH GRIFFITH
KARRIE JACOBS
CONRAD KIFFIN
VERLYN KLINKENBORG
PETER KUPFER
CRISWELL LAPPIN
NORY MILLER
AMMA OGAN
SYLVIA PLACHY
SUZETTE SHERMAN
KEN SHULMAN
DOUG STEWART
VERONIQUE VIENNE
SHAWN WOLFE

A parrotlike device on our shoulder expands our field
of vision. Illustration by **Shawn Wolfe**

DESIGN IS **THINGS**

21 DESIGNS FOR 2021

When METROPOLIS started out in 1981, the issues facing today's designers—a global economy, virtual reality, bioengineering—were the stuff of science fiction. In reflecting on how far we've come, we started to wonder what developments another 20 years would yield. So we asked thinkers in many fields to contemplate the challenges that design will be meeting two decades hence. Some took the problems of the future seriously; others proposed fantasy schemes for a highly entertaining life to come. All responded wittily and well to our question:

Hella Jongerius, product designer, Droog:
"I'm looking forward to the year 2021 because everything will be designed for comfortable freedom. I won't need any keys for my house, motorbike, studio, garage, or school. I will have high-heeled shoes that will change into sneakers at the end of the day. I will have volume buttons for my ears, so I can turn the sound of the whole world down to zero. I will have children only on the weekend—during the week they won't exist. And business travel will not be necessary because our bodies will be transported virtually. I'm going to take a long nap now. Wake me up in 2021."

Mark Chow, Steve Harrison, Dale MacDonald, and Scott Minneman, Xerox PARC Research in Experimental Design Group:
"Words are everywhere: on billboards, T-shirts, appliances, signs, newspapers, toys, even fruit. Text is increasing in quantity and becoming more dynamic; there is no way we can attend to all of it. By 2021 we will need an agent, say, a parrotlike device on our shoulder, to expand our field of vision, catch interesting things we've missed, translate words from unknown languages, and notice things that have changed."

Bill Mitchell, dean of MIT School of Architecture:
"I want a building printer. First we had laser printers to produce drawings from CAD files, then stereolithography and deposition printers to produce small-scale three-dimensional models. Why not go to full scale? There is, of course, a bit of a problem with errors. With small-scale printers you can just throw away the spoiled output. It's not so easy with a half-completed building. The answer is an inverse building printer that devours rather than constructs. This would also provide an elegant way to demolish and recycle buildings when they've reached the ends of their useful lives."

Ben Rubin, artist and sound designer:
"It used to be easy to tell what was going on with the machines in our lives by listening to them chuckle, tick, whir, or ting—but no more. Now everything beeps. The elevator, the microwave, the Palm Pilot: beep, beep, beep. Twenty years from now, I would like to see diversity, complexity, and subtlety return to our personal soundscapes through the creative design of new sounds for electronic devices."

71

Natalie Angier, science writer, the NEW YORK TIMES:
"As we spend ever longer hours immobilized in front of computers, there is no 'natural' way to stay in shape any longer. Instead we must rally every gram of self-discipline we have to trudge off to gyms and engage in requisite periods of exercise. I would like to see some truly ergonomic office furniture: computer workstations that are also workout stations equipped with a variety of inconspicuous pedals and pulleys to allow people to use their bodies as well as their brains throughout the long workday."

Eleventh-grade industrial design class, Design and Architecture Senior High School, Miami:
"A microchip for mental enhancement, the C.U. Rx28, is implanted in the brain and produces waves that stimulate cerebral functions. The waves trigger the release of chemicals and hormones at key times to improve reflexes, stamina, strength, emotional balance—and to help the body cure medical disorders and illness."

Joseph F. Coates, president of Coates & Jarratt Inc., futurists:
"There would be great value in a headband with four lights that indicate emotional intent. The first would glow yellow if you lied. Should you not be listening, a blue light would indicate that you are spaced out. A red light, for hostility or anger, is in the tradition of the face flushed with anger. And an orange-brown light, signifying 'muddy,' would mark illogical thinking."

India Mahdavi, interior designer:
"Some of my best design ideas come to me in my sleep, but the details always seem to drift away as I wake up. I would love to have a dream recorder to capture these images as I sleep and play them back for me in holographic form in the morning."

Mary Ellen Mark, photographer:
"All of us are haunted by our dreams. Many we can't remember; we recall only glimpses of them when we wake up. It would be fascinating if there were a device that could read our brain waves, record our dreams, and translate them into a non-technical language. You could hook up to the device before falling asleep, wake up, and be able to read a text of your dreams. Each person would have a PIN number to access their dreams—there are certain secrets we won't want our friends, families, and lovers to know."

Eleventh- and twelfth-grade design studios, Architecture and Design Charter High School, Philadelphia:
"We'd like to see a power unit for a city bus fueled by garbage. The bus fare would be a piece of trash that each rider would deposit in the machine upon entering the bus—providing an immediate and constantly available energy source. Such an application would create self-cleaning neighborhoods. Imagine people fighting over pieces of trash and trying to get on the bus with three and four bags of household garbage."

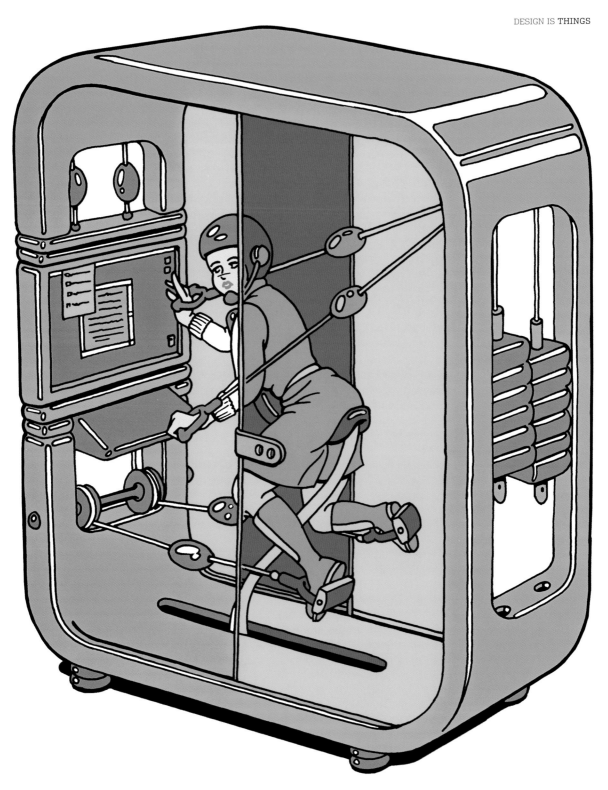

Saskia Sassen, sociology professor at the University of Chicago and London School of Economics, and author of THE GLOBAL CITY 2001 (Princeton University Press, 2001):

"It will not be long before we begin to experience the 'local' as a type of microenvironment with global span. Many of the things we represent and experience as local—a building, a household, an activist organization in our neighborhood—are actually located not only in concrete places but also on digital networks that span the globe. They may indeed be more oriented to other areas than to their immediate surroundings. We need to ask what it means for 'the city' to contain a proliferation of these globally oriented yet localized offices, households, and organizations. The city will reemerge as a strategic amalgamation of multiple global circuits that loop through it."

Murray Moss, owner, Moss store, Soho, New York:

"In 2021 I will want a device for supplying the equivalent of additional RAM to my brain as I now can to my computer. If an external device, most certainly Prada."

Simon Doonan, creative director of Barneys New York and columnist for the NEW YORK OBSERVER:

"There is too much stuff—too many tchotchkes, too many stores. I'd like a heavy-duty equivalent of a paper shredder to vaporize or eliminate stuff from the planet without damaging the environment. There are already too many objects. I'm a little bit like the design Grinch."

Momus, musician:

"I'd like a projector TV on which I could watch intelligent, experimental programs such as biographies of artists and original thinkers. They'd be well produced, have big budgets, and run 24 hours with no advertising and no repeats. There would be simultaneous real-time audio translation. I'd also like to be able to tune into an archive of all TV ever broadcast in the past and on other planets."

Von Robinson, industrial designer:

"In 2021 a cosmic perspective would provide focus for an emotional age to develop from the information age. Thus we'll need affordable space shuttles with plug-in interiors to convert from cargo to passenger vehicles, taking citizens to orbiting pieces of architecture. The advance will really be in human consciousness; the object is literally and figuratively just a vehicle. When we evolved to land we brought the sea with us in our bodily fluids. If we are to evolve into space beings, we'll need first to recognize and internalize the essence of being earthlings."

John Maeda, associate director, MIT Media Laboratory:

"I want a sticky blob of living thought. Not too big: small enough to fit in the palm of my hand."

Tim Brown, president and CEO of IDEO:
"I imagine a cross between an intelligence agent and a bathroom scale. It acts as your personal health adviser, discreetly following your weight and metabolism, and working off a drop of blood from a pinprick to track your nutrition and watch for emerging illnesses. It doesn't act like Big Brother—prying and scolding—but it suggests that you might want to run a little more or eat a little less to more closely approach your ideal condition."

Sheila Klein, artist:
"Good drugs have gotten increasingly difficult to obtain, but humans continue to want to get high—therefore we're going to start asking more of our environment. In the future we'll need mind-altering environments that will get us off, experiences that are designed to make us feel like children, spaces that simulate being in the womb, sybaritic spaces, places that smell like the earth."

Maira Kalman, artist:
"Considering the approaching age of my baby-boomer colleagues, what would be good is a mega-energy pill, a cure for jet lag, and a time expander—some gizmo that doubles the amount of time you have in a day. Then the energy pill would go a long way."

William McDonough, architect:
"I propose a horizontal chimney: turning smokestacks of fossil-fuel power plants into sinuous, water-filled, air-supported plastic greenhouses. Effluents and wastes would feed algae to make polymers and methane for powering the turbines. We would still use coal and natural gas, but we'd create solar carbon engines for future generations. This device would transform an intergenerational liability (airborne toxic gases) into intergenerational assets (nutrients or 'food' for industries), causing life instead of death. Waste would equal food."

Alexandros E. Washburn, director of the Diebold Institute for Public Policy Studies and faculty member at the Princeton University School of Architecture:
"For those of us who require the community of cities to live, we can lament that we have lost the art of how to grow. I want to rediscover how to grow by 2021. That means first how to lose our fear of the physical future, and then how to design, finance, and make politically imperative the desire for new infrastructures and the new community relations they will bring. For 2021, just give us a modicum of courage."

03.01

THINKING SMALL

The first computer was a marvel of portability: the ancient abacus could be carried in the pocket of a cloak. Five thousand years later, the most sophisticated calculator was the enormous ENIAC the Electronic Numerator, Integrator, Analyzer, and Computer. The size of a large room, the ENIAC contained tens of thousands of vacuum tubes, wires, and switches. Today the Macintosh Portable, no larger than an attaché case, surpasses the ENIAC in power and capability. Progress, it seems, comes in many sizes.

During the first half of the century, the wonders of technology loomed large, promising a brilliant new world for everyone—big cars, expansive TV consoles, even large alarm clocks. "There's a story about Henry Dreyfuss when he was designing alarm clocks in the thirties," says Donald Genaro, senior partner at Henry Dreyfuss Associates, the New York-based industrial design firm. "He had designed clocks that were lighter and smaller than the conventional models, and they didn't sell at all. One day he did a little research of his own. He went over to a department store and observed people buying these clocks. He watched them looking at the different clocks, then picking them up, and testing them as if they were melons. In those days, weight and size were equated with quality. The perception was if it's bigger and heavier, it's better."

Nearly 60 years later, the maxim "less is more" has become our mandate. We find ourselves not in a world of limitless frontiers, but of shrinking resources. When we think of technology's potential our thoughts are not utopian, but personal. "Miniaturization is a part of a more general personalization of technology," says Steven Holt, a partner in the industrial design firm Zebra Incorporated. "Things that used to be shared by a number of people can now be owned by an individual, such as a personal cellular phone or a handheld copier."

The beginnings of this "personalization" can be traced back to the invention of the transistor in 1948. In the thirties and forties, the radio was a large and fragile instrument. Planted on a table in the living room, it became a kind of electronic hearth, around which the entire family would gather in the evenings. Unlike the cumbersome glass vacuum tubes then being used in radios to conduct electricity, the transistor was small, compact, and virtually unbreakable.

Sony's introduction of the Walkman personal stereo in the late seventies launched the next great revolution in personal entertainment. Stereophonic pleasure was a headset away, and it now was not only solitary but insular. The eighties brought an onslaught of individualized electronic products: tiny televisions, CD Walkmans, even a portable VCR.

In our isolation, our relationship with our gadgets grows all the more intimate. Neil Taylor, a partner in Taylor & Chu, product design consultants based in San Francisco, sees the relationship as symbiotic. "There is an urgent desire to replicate our own senses in machines, and conversely the desire of Western medicine to revitalize our ailing bodies with artificial parts and processes," Taylor says. "To me, this is an extraordinary crossover of philosophies that was inconceivable before miniaturization.

MARISA BARTOLUCCI AND JOSEPH GRIFFITH 04.90

HOW ARCHITECTS DESIGN TEAPOTS

While Alessandro Mendini reasoned that a tea and coffee service would provide the architects with a comfortable group of interrelated shapes that could be viewed as the micro-urbanism of the tabletop, other designers preferred to break away from familiar cityscapes. Hans Hollein's tray, for example, looks in plan more like the tapered deck of an aircraft carrier, on one end of which winged forms with noses and rudders have alighted, awaiting take-off clearance. Kazumasa Yamashita nestled his simple rectangular shapes in a simple rectangular enclosure. Oil refinery-type tubing snakes around and seemingly through the shapes, forming here a handle, there a spout, and on the lids, in kitchen-canister style; the tubes form the first letters of the words for the substances contained: T, C, S, M. In one of Aldo Rossi's drawings, the sets are positioned in a kitchen cupboard, but the actual model of this has yet to be realized.

77

The first items that most of the architects designed were the tea- and coffeepots. Characteristically the Venturi office went directly to the vernacular, sketching page after page of leaning towers, Romanesque churches, and bargellos with applied handles and spouts. Knobs corresponded to flags atop towers, lids were fortress ramparts, and feet were classical columns. More significantly, however, they also studied English teapots, with swelling bellies and sturdy feet, traditional symbols of friendliness, and these were their true models. The Venturi teapot prototype reflects an awareness of a well-brewed pot of tea: the form, broader than high, gives a larger cross-section for the movement of the tealeaves during brewing. The generous tubular spout looks extroverted and is angled sharply enough to prevent dripping. The pot appears well balanced for lifting and pouring, and the lid opening seems wide enough for easy cleaning. The knob, while substantial for grasping, is still whimsical, and the lid, flush with the curve of the belly, retains the shape's simplicity. Following fashionable British tea-drinking style, although the prototypes do not reflect it, Robert Venturi's tea- and coffeepots will be highly decorated.

The coffeepot, by necessity originally taller than the teapot due to the need to let the grounds settle during brewing, drew a larger variety of design solutions because of today's methods of coffee filtering. A simple cylindrical coffee percolator was proposed by Rossi, and Hollein offered a Melitta filter version in which the unusual design element was an uneven blue winged top. Both Mendini and Venturi alluded to bird forms by lifting the round bodies of their coffeepots off the ground on legs or spindles. Mendini's handles even suggest vestigial wings, a motif that carries throughout his set.

Evident in the initial drawings and first prototypes was a tendency to overload a piece with too many elements, too many forced connections, and too many "meaningful" references. But in the more developed stages of the Venturi and Rossi pots, simplification through production restrictions, proportional relationships, and a familiarity with functional requirements seem to have strengthened the statements. Details are more easily changed at this scale than at an architectural one, and the architects are taking advantage of such newfound freedom. Michael Graves's latest prototype manages to reverse the process by becoming more complex yet at the same time more unified.

Although never having actually carried out a design for household ware in three dimensions, Graves and Rossi often have included these objects in their architectural drawings, which perhaps gave them a conceptual head start on this project. Graves's translation of his ideas for fortresses and bridgelike architecture come across strongly in his latest coffeepot, in which a simple cube is set on four columnar legs, the whole being visually integrated by colored balls at feet, handle, and lid joints. Although the handle attachments on other parts of this set, particularly the sugar bowl, seem sometimes forced and fussy, the whimsical addition of these colored balls imputes a charm and personality that render the piece lively and exuberant. These objects walk a thin line between sculpture and functional hollow ware.

Of all the design solutions, Rossi's derive most directly from his own remembrances of Italian kitchens, where he spent hours sketching the strange shapes of enameled coffeepots. Today, he still often includes a coffeepot, the same one over and over, in his drawings, sometimes at its own scale in a domestic environment, sometimes as the focal point of a composition, sometimes as large as the actual walls and towers of a town. It seems justified, then, that the circle be completed and that these coffeepots of his drawings should once again be transformed into three dimensions in the Alessi prototypes. They embody the clean, elegant, quiet shapes that pervade Rossi's perception of the world.

Not yet as fully developed but equally intriguing are the designs by Richard Meier and Paolo Portoghesi. Meier's application of Cubist space in three dimensions has some of the same double-take effect of Rossi's familiar two-dimensional forms, but they have yet to be transformed into metal. Portoghesi's hexagonal shapes remain distinct miniature buildings, their lids having knobs resembling roofs with chimneys, pleasant in their simplicity but still sketchy in detailing.

Although the architects' building styles are at first glance overwhelmingly apparent in these ideas for tea and coffee services, subsequent examination reveals progress beyond this superficial connection. Have they redefined the coffee- and teapot? Perhaps not, but they have produced the unexpected, and they have taken steps to understanding these most demanding of hollow ware forms. And although this design cross-fertilization may not produce 100 percent in terms of product, it has already paid off in new attitudes and fresh ways of seeing utensils in everyday use. SARAH BODINE 06.82

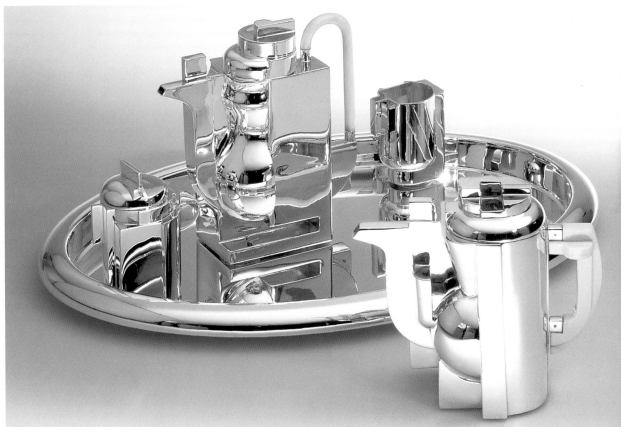

Robert Venturi's Grandmother Collection of jigsaw-cut and
dyed chairs, designed for Knoll International in 1984.
Courtesy **Knoll**

VENTURI AND HIS GRANDMA

Robert Venturi tells us that he has added symbols—specifically historical symbols—
to modern chair design. These are not "real historical chairs that are made in the old
way," he explains. "They are rather signs representing historical chairs." So far, so
good. No one would take these willowy cutouts to an auction at Christie's or look for
them at W & J Sloane. But what does the use of historical shapes in this particular way
symbolize? Symbol and sign are not words in a vacuum; they're information. For example, consider some of Venturi's own favorite precedents: the Long Island duck-shaped
building, highway signs, and suburban houses. The duck tells passersby what they
can buy within, whereas the two-dimensional billboards carry distinct messages, from
"Burma Shave" to "Holiday Inn 12 Miles," on which—it is hoped—people will act.

81

More abstractly, but decidedly to the point, the suburban ranch houses
decorated in historical details borrowed from English manor houses or Mediterranean
villas say something very specific to the Americans whose ancestors were generally serfs
or peasants in the countries in which such architectural detailing was associated with the
aristocracy. What is symbolized, consciously or unconsciously, is that a once-unattainable
goal has, after a fashion, been achieved.

Venturi describes the new chairs, as he has often described his buildings, as being "like Mark Twain's famous house, Queen Anne in front and Mary Ann
behind," adding that they are also "Alvar Aalto from the side." But why did Twain's example have a Queen Anne front and Mary Anne behind? It was presumably to put on airs,
a human frailty that it amused Twain to uncover. Are the Venturi chairs, then, about
showing up the silliness of pretension? Where is the chuckle? Are they, on the other hand,
using historical references to be pretentious? How intimidating can something be in only
two dimensions?

Or are the decorative shapes in fact historical symbols without meaning—in other words, form? And has Venturi, rather than adding symbol to modern design,
instead subtracted symbol from it? The moderns, after all, replaced historical imagery
with industrial imagery originally to present the vision of a progressive world free of traditional status distinctions. But what is the vision that Venturi presents?

Could it have something to do with nostalgia? "Grandmother" is not
often a name for plastic laminate. Is there some feeling for his grandparents and their
lives and times that is being expressed? "This doesn't have anything to do with my family
specifically," he answers. As it happens, his grandparents and father were all born in
Italy, but he feels, "Italian imagery is too special." The sofa and floral patterns, he says,
are just "old-fashioned and conventional, the kind of thing that would belong to a general
middle-class grandmother. All they stand for is something that modern architecture
threw out." NORY MILLER 06.84

SELLING BIG

Cluttered, self-defeating billboards are rare in Times Square, which is after all the mecca of big-time billboard design. Along with the Sunset Strip in Los Angeles, the stretch of Broadway from 42nd to 47th Streets is the home of the hand-painted "spectacular": huge, one-of-a-kind displays, often replete with neon and moving parts. (The industry standard, by contrast, is the "30 sheet"—30 strips of paper printed with ink and hung like wallpaper on 12-by-24-foot boards.) Elsewhere in the country, outdoor advertising may be considered a crime against nature, but in Times Square, in the words of the NEW YORK TIMES, they're "a spectacle as germane to New York as canals are to Venice." The city now wants developers planning new skyscrapers in the neighborhood to provide space for outdoor advertising as part of the package.

The people who take brush in hand to create this much-maligned art form are a specialized lot. Some people paint only heads. Others paint car bodies. Apprentices mix paints and do backgrounds or lettering, hoping to work their way up. Painting a board with a 40-foot head of Liza Minelli takes a lot more planning and coordination than hanging wallpaper does.

Still, it's an ephemeral art. A few months after Kusi, Gonzalez, and company finished up the Jeff Hamilton display, I watch from a rooftop across the street as a crew of painters methodically buries the debonair surf walker under 10,000 square feet of white paint. In its place another crew to the left has already begun painting a blue-and-white, 100-by-100-foot TV test pattern announcing "Fox Broadcasting." I ask Marvin Adelson, a painter working on a scaffold a few feet above me, if it bothers him to see so much work obliterated after so short a time. He glances across the street and shrugs. "We don't want our work to last," he explains, speaking for his brethren in the Sign, Pictorial, and Display Union, Local 230. "It would be less work for the sign painter."

He and Paul Chan, head painter for the Artkraft Strauss Sign Corporation, have been spending the past month painting a 59-by-96-foot billboard above Nathan's on 43rd Street. The board is part of an ad campaign for the New York Yellow Pages. It features an enormous full-color hand walking along a Manhattan sidewalk. The two fingers doing the walking are bandaged, and the hand appears to be staggering. (When they're through painting, real bandages will be stapled to the board.) From up on the rooftop, the hand suggests a monster terrorizing the streets of New York—a huge mutant oyster perhaps. The tag line, not yet painted, is "Use It. And Stop Working Your Fingers to the Bone."

"It's nice out here now," says Chan, a wiry, hardworking 45-year-old who's responsible for many of the billboards around us. "But when it's cold—20 degrees, 15 degrees—your fingers can't move, and the paint doesn't dry." Chan studied art in Hong Kong and then moved to the United States 18 years ago. Two years later he began painting billboards for Artkraft Strauss. A 5,000-square-foot billboard doesn't faze him. A few years ago, on a wall at 35th Street and Eighth Avenue, Chan painted a Michelob bottle that started on the 7th floor and ended on the 26th. DOUG STEWART 07/08.87

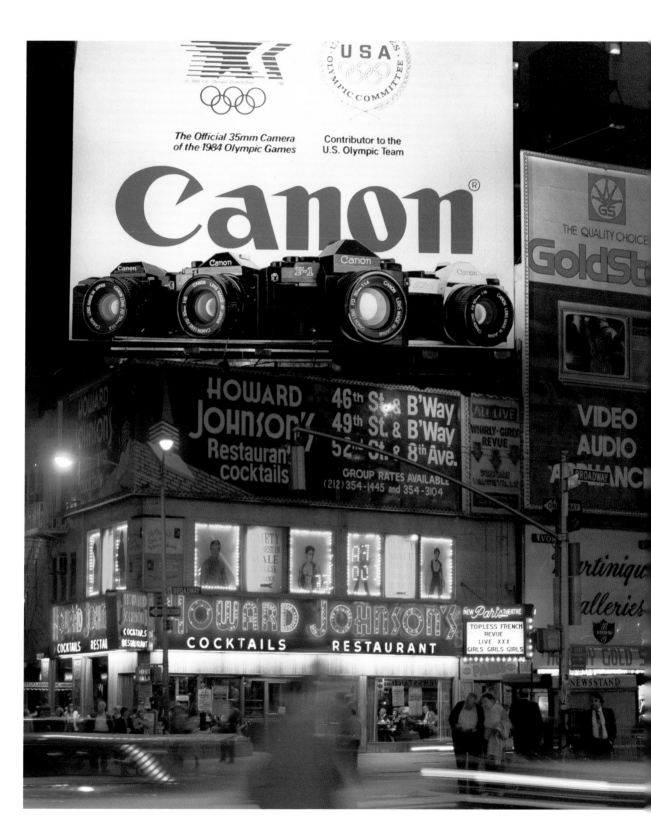

THE CODE

The strangest thing about the bar code, the striped two-tone slice of concrete poetry that's routinely applied to an ever-widening share of every single thing on Earth, is that we don't really see it. That is to say, we don't look at it. It's there; no other symbol—corporate, civic, religious, or political—has ever been so extensively or so proudly displayed. But because it is omnipresent, we will the bar code into oblivion.

The second strangest thing about the bar code is that if for any reason we resolve to see it, if we begin to notice it in all its permutations—from the Universal Product Code (UPC) to the codes used on magazines and books to the long codes used for tracking air-freight package—it becomes impossible to ignore. There it is on a soda can, rippling like a neon sign. There it is **on a glossy magazine cover** sitting at Jack Nicholson's heel like a well-trained pup. There it is **on the back of the paperback edition of THE BONFIRE OF THE VANITIES**, shimmering like a striped suit louder than any in Tom Wolfe's wardrobe. **There it is in our wallets. It's on our library cards, our employee IDs, and our health-club memberships.** The only surprise is that **there isn't one on the dollar bill.** Not yet anyway. The bar code embodies all the traits that corporate designers want in a logo: it is strong, simple, memorable, and easy to recognize. But **the bar code is not a logo; it's not even a piece of graphic design.** It's not intended as a symbol, though it's become one. It's not there to contribute to the design of any of the millions of objects on which it can be found.

The bar code is a little machine. It is a rectangle of unadulterated function, a zone allocated to the pragmatic. The bar code is a paragraph of information that we cannot read. It's not there for us. It's there for the reading pleasure of the computer: the computer at the checkout counter, the computer in the warehouse, the computer in the factory. A bar code is a visual equivalent of the binary language of computers. The varying thicknesses of the code's parallel lines represent numbers and letters to the computer. The scanner isn't reading the individual lines, it's reading the pattern: the black bars absorb light and the white spaces bounce light back to the laser eye.

To the human eye, the bar code is almost never decorous. At its most inappropriate, it's as out of place as a cash machine would be if installed in the lower left-hand corner of a Jackson Pollock canvas at the art museum. Most of the time, on most objects, the bar code is something that's just a little worse than everything surrounding it. Occasionally the bars are the best thing about a given design. What's unforgivable about the bar code is the simple fact that it is a common visual element, a seal representing the triumph of expediency over aesthetics on myriad items, most of which have no business sharing any visual elements at all.

In Dayton, Ohio, is the headquarters of the Uniform Code Council (UCC), the administrative organization formed by the grocery industry to assign UPCs and other codes. From this fountainhead of codedom they have issued some 55,000 manufacturers' five-digit identification numbers. Here's how it works: A manufacturer with a consumer product to sell joins the UCC and, for a minimum of $300 (the price goes up depending on sales volume), is assigned a number. On the familiar 11-digit UPC, the first digit is the product category—0 is assigned to most items—the next five digits identify the manufacturer (this is the number the UCC assigns), and the following five describe the product itself. A twelfth digit isn't part of the code but is a "check digit," which cues the scanner to verify its translation of the data. A special machine is used to transform these number sequences into a pattern of blacks and whites, the 0's and 1's of the binary idiom.

The Ad Hoc Committee on Random Weight Products of the UCC has recently developed a double-decker 24-digit code that will allow more detailed descriptions of variables like poultry and meat cuts, underwear styles and sizes, or wine vintage—get ready for twice the line count on your bottle of Pinot Noir. Actually, the consumer-product codes are discreet compared to certain industrial markings such as Code 39, an alpha-numeric code used by the Pentagon and the automobile industry, which can go on and on.

85

A friend who hails from the Bible Belt—and spent time in his youth as a missionary and still has a fascination with fire and brimstone—sees the proliferation of the bar codes not as a benign signal of widespread computerization but as a manifestation of 666, the mark of the beast. He reads from the New Testament's book of Revelation, 13:17: "And that no man might buy or sell, save he that had the mark, or the name of the beast, or the number of his name." He explains that you can't win. You starve to death without the mark, but those bearing the mark are ultimately subject to the wrath of God.
KARRIE JACOBS 04.89

OBJECTS COMMUNICATE IN REAL TIME. IT'S NOT TRUE THAT WHAT IS USEFUL IS BEAUTIFUL. IT IS WHAT IS BEAUTIFUL THAT IS USEFUL. BEAUTY CAN IMPROVE PEOPLE'S WAY OF LIFE AND THINKING.

ANNA CASTELLI FERRIERI 02/03.99

THE COFFEE TABLE

Some people remember the first time they saw the sea, the Statue of Liberty, or the northern lights. I don't remember anything of that scope, but I do remember the first time I saw a coffee table.

From a distance it looked like a thick piece of glass precariously propped on skinny chrome legs. As I moved closer to examine it, my perspective changed, and the clear slab became a mirror reflecting the living room upside down. Through this looking glass I could see a window framing a rectangular piece of the Manhattan skyline that appeared to be anchored to the thick carpet.

"I hate those fingerprints," said the woman who owned this strange object. As she kneeled, trying to erase some offending smudges with the edge of her sleeves, I sensed her utter devotion. Perhaps she was praying to the icons of Good Taste on this altar: the thick glass ashtray, the burnished pewter cigarette box, the three issues of HOUSE & GARDEN, and the small sculpture, a Henry Moore study of a reclining nude. Indeed, I too felt a religious fervor—and almost crossed myself—as I noticed Bad Taste lurking around us in the background: foil paper, plastic flowers in wrought-iron planters, and frilly pillows thrown on the couch.

I had arrived from Paris that afternoon, and this was my first visit to an American home. Driving into New York from the airport, I had the premonition that from now on anything could happen: a windswept newspaper had taken off vertically from the sidewalk and disappeared above the rooftops, streets were venting steam like fumaroles near a volcano, the facades of deserted-looking houses were covered with creeping metal stairs like ivy clinging to ruins. In this odd environment, people moved about like absent-minded creatures, oblivious to the phantasmagoric backdrop.

My first coffee table was part of this new American magic kingdom where things were either a little too new or a little too short or a little too tall. Invited to sit down, I sank far into the soft upholstery of a couch, experiencing yet another change of perspective as the horizon rose drastically around me. From this low angle, things looked simpler, more graphic, and more appealing. Maybe to understand America, I would need a new point of view, a parallel adjustment—maybe to appreciate this new culture, I would always have to sit 13 inches from the ground. VERONIQUE VIENNE 05.91

WHAT WE NEED IN CITIES IS FEWER GRAND SCHEMES AND MORE MOVABLE CHAIRS.

WILLIAM WHYTE 05.99

A PAIR OF MY FAVORITE THINGS

I do not own these. They are not what I would save in case of fire, nor are they the most valuable things in the house. They are not decor, not art, not furniture, and only barely fashion. They are a pair of my wife's flannel winter pajamas. She wears them; I admire them. They fit her the way winter pajamas are supposed to, like a fat man's suit on a wire hanger. They trap air. I like them because they depict breakfast.

On the tops and bottoms of my wife's pajamas, the foods of the American morning meal float wallpaperlike on a field of pale Naples yellow. They are life-size. Here is the menu, iterated across the flannel: coffee with cream, steaming in a blue cup and saucer, poured from a red graniteware percolator. Three sugar cubes, almost invisible. An egg, with too much green to the yolk, frying in a cast-iron skillet. Two strawberries, with juniper-colored stems and leaves. Another egg, upright in a blue eggcup. Two slices of streaky bacon, the fat vivid yellow, the lean carmine. Half a grapefruit with a maraschino cherry at its center, served on a blue plate. A piece of very light white toast, with an executive-dimension pat of butter sitting in its midst. The napkin is cloth, of course—brown check—and the silverware has Bakelite handles: red for the spoon, yellow for the knife, blue for the fork.

If it were real, this is the kind of breakfast you would eat if you planned to browbeat someone later. The man before whom this breakfast was laid every morning probably called his wife "Kitten." She ate the strawberries and the boiled egg and read the headlines on her husband's upraised morning paper. She was still deciding what to call her husband. These people lived nearly four decades ago, and they are as extinct as the dire wolf. Their breakfast has been fossilized on my wife's PJs.

I do not call my wife Kitten—her name is Reggie—and she does not make me breakfast. That has always been my lookout. Reggie does not eat breakfast, maybe just a piece of toast in the morning. She works too hard. I happen to like a little more starch in my breakfast than I see in the one on her pajamas. I like a little less fat. No egg. I like hot cereal or a bagel. And some juice. Black coffee. I try to think about my weight and my cholesterol.

But in the ideal meal on my wife's pajamas (or is it in them?), the bacon lurks without guile, the eggs beckon innocently. The butter hesitates before melting and seems to wink. The white toast boasts of its nutrition. The coffeepot is not only red, it is red hot. You can't get enough of a meal like this one. In fact you could eat it every morning and not get tired of it. When you were done eating, there would be no lipstick stains on the coffee cups, no dried egg yolk between the tines of the forks, no butter on the knives, no bacon grease congealing in an empty cat food can somewhere on the kitchen counter. No coffee grounds. No grapefruit rinds. No dishes!

When nighttime comes and my wife puts on these pajamas, I want to go downstairs and rustle around in the refrigerator. I want to start the day fresh. I want to vote Republican and pay a stack of bills with checks that will not bounce. I want to do push-ups and sing in the shower. I want to have breakfast in bed. *VERLYN KLINKENBORG 05.92*

87

STARS

In postwar Hungary where I spent my childhood, big red stars were perched on rooftops like predators, while tiny gold and enameled ones sparkled menacingly from the lapels of gray-suited, righteous men and women. Utopia promised by the posters was always years away: we had the three-year plan, then the five-year plan. The last one they dared to put a number to was seven years long. Meanwhile, my aunt and uncle were deported, and my father's small business was nationalized. "Everyone is suspicious who is alive," was an oft-quoted line in our household, part of a poem by Janos Arany. People often whispered or spoke in euphemisms; this was called "flower language."

88   When my parents and I first arrived in the United States in 1958, we were amazed and a little distressed to see the proliferation of stars. Stars were used for everything from political campaigns to Fourth of July sales, and as recommendation for movies and restaurants. There were 48 of them on the American flag. The sheriff had a silver star; Texaco's logo was a red star, and Texas was the Lone Star State.

Lately the stars of Central Europe are disappearing. First they were cut from the center of flags; then the big ones were destroyed or put in storage; what was left the tourists bought. Even the Hungarian Socialist Party has switched symbols. Now it too speaks flower language with a stylized red carnation. Only in Moscow do the concrete stars stand firm, because Stalin had the foresight to incorporate them into the architecture.

Two years ago I was at the Folk Art Museum in Budapest. When I looked through the heavy drapes that kept out the winter chill, I saw something familiar, a ghost from the past—a star made of light.   SYLVIA PLACHY 10.94

WE ARE NOW WITNESSING THE RISE OF A CLASS DISTINCTION IN DESIGN. EVERY OBJECT IS TRYING TO BE UPMARKET. THERE IS NO RESPECT FOR OBJECTS THAT ARE INEXPENSIVE.

TIBOR KALMAN 10.89

THE YAM POUNDER

Small mortars are used to mash vegetables, condiments, and spices like pepper or soup thickeners such as melon seeds. These rich soups, chockablock with vegetables, smoked fish, fresh meat, and sun-dried crayfish, cannot stand as a meal unless accompanied by a fufu, which the British colonizers in their befuddlement described as a "stiff porridge." Fufu can be made from a variety of grains and tubers, rice, cassava, or millet, but the king of them all—what most Nigerians would describe as the food of the gods—is fufu made from the yam. Soft, smooth, and white, good fufu has a consistency that is nothing like porridge, but draws just slightly. The drawing action is important—it means the yam has been well pounded. Nigerian fufu is eaten with the hands, not a knife and fork. You pull a morsel from the mound of pounded yam, roll it between the fingers into a bail, dip this into the soup—extracting as much meat or fish as you desire along with it—and pop it into your mouth.

92

The preparation of meals is a major preoccupation in Nigerian households, in part because Nigerian food should be eaten as soon as it is done. Preparation is a personal matter; you add just enough of this or that ingredient, and cook it till the consistency meets your satisfaction.

The "revolutionary appliance," as National Panasonic called its yam pounder, turned this very personal preparation into an automated activity. The technology was adapted from the company's automatic rice-cake maker, and employed a blade rather than a pestle. It came boxed with a set of instructions, five parts, and four accessories. It stipulated a cooking time of 30 minutes and a pounding time of five minutes. "Within only 35 minutes," the brochure read, "you will have a delicious pounded yam." This procedure knocked an hour off the time it takes to prepare fufu with mortar and pestle.

Having modeled the machine on its rice-cake maker, National Panasonic didn't expend further effort on adapting it to fit the Nigerian lifestyle. For example, the appliance produced enough to feed four adults moderately, enough by Japanese standards perhaps, but Nigerians have large families, with sometimes as many as 20 members, and mealtimes are an open invitation to anyone who happens to be in the house. Nigerian housewives, nevertheless, worked around this snag, all too appreciative of the time and effort the yam pounder saved.

But other factors made the clinical features of this modern implement seem out of place in the organized jumble of Nigerian life, quite apart from the fact that it was designed to make life easier. Nigerians distrust automation, preferring something they can manipulate and watch in action. Something that won't be rendered inoperable by a surge in electricity, that won't lie idle during a power cut. When you are pounding yam in a mortar, you can see it; you can poke it to check the consistency; you can graduate the addition of the yam, add water when necessary, and pick out lumps.

These are nuances a machine cannot perform. What's more, yam is more than just a vegetable; it is invested with much symbolism and ceremony. Nothing like the sweet potato of the same name in the United States, some varieties of yam can grow to three feet in length and look like giant gnarled phalluses. It is the dominant crop of the Igbo farming regions, with the New Yam Festival—the equivalent of harvest time, Thanksgiving, and New Year's—marking the most important event of the Igbo cultural year. Coming-of-age ceremonies and a whole slew of rituals of thanksgiving and rebirth follow the arrival of the year's first yam crop, the richness of which in olden times would determine the health of the community for the next 12 months. It was—and still is— taboo for anyone to eat new yam before the elders in the community have declared the day of the festival and carried out the necessary ceremonies.

Nigerians were, in fact, the first to introduce a mechanical yam pounder. In 1976 Professor Makanjuola, a Nigerian agricultural engineer then at the University of Ife, conceived a version that was actually a high-speed automated mortar and pestle. The Nigerian company Addis Engineering commercialized Makanjuola's invention, with the design help of Adolphus Ojobo, a chemical engineer. It could pound enough yam for four people in 20 seconds. In five minutes it could make enough yam for 20 people. Its cumbersome design, however, made it far less "woman friendly" than the Japanese machine, but then that was no surprise to Nigerian women, who were used to Nigerian-made products.

Reasonably priced at what would have been about $350 at the time— and less than half the cost of National Panasonic's appliance—it was popular with restaurants and as wedding gifts. So popular, in fact, that Addis Engineering never had to advertise, because it was always out of stock. But then the company manufactured only 200 machines a season, in keeping with the rhythm of the yam harvest. Despite the demand, the company couldn't produce more because it had to import the motors for the locally manufactured machine from Italy, and it had only a limited amount of foreign currency with which to do so.

Import and currency restrictions of one kind or another arising from the country's political instability have plagued Nigeria's industry for years. In January of this year Addis itself became a casualty; it was forced to halt production of the yam pounder altogether, having run out of all of its foreign currency. Ten years ago National Panasonic stopped exporting its automatic yam pounder to Lagos. Like so many other foreign companies, it had become fed up with Nigeria's ever-changing rules and had decided the business wasn't worth the hassle.

Recently Addis Engineering has come up with a scheme it believes will solve its foreign exchange problems. The firm hopes to receive foreign funds through the Nigerian Industrial Development Bank to manufacture yam pounders for export to Nigerians in America and Europe. This way the company can establish an independent source of foreign currency so that it can again produce yam pounders for the local market. In the meantime Nigeria's housewives have returned to their ever-dependable mortars and pestles. AMMA OGAN 10.94

93

NEW MATERIALISM

It's dark outside. You are startled awake by the sound of clanging metal and smashing glass. Car break-in? Danger looming at your door? Only if you don't recognize this obstreperous intruder as a recycling truck making its rounds.

      Collection trucks may be relatively new, but recycling is not. It used to be known as peddling, without the connotations "recycling" implies today. That was when gathering and reusing cast-off materials was key to the economic infrastructure. It was, in fact, a fairly lucrative venture for such Colonial eco-entrepreneurs as Benedict Arnold, who more than supported himself by peddling used woolen clothing, and Paul Revere, who when not making a name as one of the Sons of Liberty made a living as a metalsmith, reusing scrap metals.

      For the next two centuries—and particularly after the onset of the Industrial Revolution—America nursed a considerably optimistic view toward production and consumption, flexing its manufacturing muscle until 1962, when scientist and poet Rachel Carson knocked big business off its pedestal with her book SILENT SPRING, chronicling the environmental destruction wrought by indiscriminate use of toxic chemicals. By the early 1990s recycled anything wasn't just back in style, it was all the rage. Coffee filters, toilet tissue, greeting cards, you name it—if it was flecked with visible proof of a previous life, it was sure to turn up in your brand-new stretchy string bag. But in truth, most of the consumables riding the "Earth friendly" wave—the coarse linen sofas and sisal rugs, the unbleached cotton bed sheets and muslin clothing—were not made from recycled or even recyclable materials; they were merely evocative of nature's raw, unrefined bounty.

      More than an eco-aesthetic, the media marketed recycling as the feel-good solution for environmental responsibility. We thought we were doing the right thing simply by placing a few recyclables at the curb for collection. And so, for a while, the single issue of recycling became the sole issue of environmental stewardship. Now we're beginning to understand, as Paul Hawken discovered while researching his book THE ECOLOGY OF COMMERCE (HarperCollins Publishers, 1993), that such thinking is a recipe for disaster. "The rate and extent of environmental degradation is far in excess of anything I had previously imagined," he writes. "Recycling aluminum cans in the company cafeteria and ceremonial tree planting are about as effective as bailing out the TITANIC with teaspoons."

      Hawken offers a bleak perspective of recycling within the larger scope of our ecological woes. "Approximately 80 percent of our products are thrown away within six to eight weeks," he points out. "This means that 98 percent of the materials we use end up as waste within two months of production." Add to this the fact that the U.S. represents merely 5 percent of the world population but produces half of the planet's solid waste—all of which leads Hawken to argue that, along with refining and devising new systems to recover and reuse our municipal garbage, we should work to eliminate waste from industrial processes so that none or very little is produced to begin with. This would save resources outright, he says. It would also rearrange "our relationship to resources from a linear to a cyclical one."

Nevertheless, waste exists; product lives will expire. But a broad-based approach to recycling could have a substantial impact. This is documented by a 1989 report from the U.S. Office of Technology Assessment, FACING AMERICA'S TRASH. Aside from yard and food wastes, the study reveals, 70 percent of our municipal solid waste can be recycled. Here's how it breaks down: containers and packaging account for 31 percent; nondurable goods (newspapers, commercial paper), 25 percent; and durable goods (major appliances, furniture), 14 percent. Together they yield the not-so-raw materials designers and manufacturers could be working with. Their very existence provides an unprecedented opportunity for us to rethink the way products are designed and made, to explore a new aesthetic derived from a holistic realization, a synthesis of beautiful form in harmony with the natural world. As we implement new methods, we may be able to move away from our present one-way course of production and consumption—and move beyond the lip service of all that questionably eco-sensitive paraphernalia of a few years back.

To design holo-aesthetically requires not only reverence for form but for material sources and legacies. In this approach, three fundamental strategies can be used in conjunction with one another: the design of recyclable products (utilizing a virgin material and allowing for it to be subsequently recovered); the reuse of materials (taking castoffs directly from the waste stream and reemploying them without altering their state); and the use of recycled materials (grinding, shredding, or crushing waste to be melted, heated, or otherwise reprocessed into a new material).

Plastic soda bottles are easy enough to recover. Wellman Inc., for example, began recycling soda bottles at its Johnsonsville, South Carolina, plant in 1980. Today the fiber producer recovers some 2.4 billion bottles annually—made of polyethylene terephthalate, or PET—that is then used to make everything from thermal jackets to blankets. But most products are not made from only one material, and must be "designed for disassembly." By consolidating the number of parts and employing compatible materials and two-way, snap-fit fasteners in place of bolts or glue, the components of durable products can be separated out and reused once their useful life is over. Design for disassembly, however, may be more placebo than panacea, because its success depends upon a sophisticated recovery and refabrication network as well as the creation and cultivation of a demand for recycled materials.

"Large appliances, furniture, and automobiles have been recycled by scrap processors for ages, and disassembling a product [not designed to be taken apart] hasn't stopped a scrap processor yet," points out Lenny Formato of Boulder Resources, a large marketer of scrap metals in New York. Scrap processors like Formato, though, are now having to deal with the advanced polymers being used in place of metals in everything from cars to bicycle frames to refrigerators. Unlike the existing scrap metal infrastructure (auto manufacturers were historically huge contributors to the recycled steel industry), currently there are no viable collection or reprocessing systems for these plastics. The shift from metals to polymers may mean more high-performance goods— carbon-fiber composites, for example, are lighter and stronger than any metal—but it also means that a host of appliances and products that were once recycled now end up in

Photograph by **Criswell Lappin**

THERE ARE VERY FEW THINGS IN THE WORLD THAT ARE REALLY NEW OR ORIGINAL. THAT'S BECAUSE FOR MOST IDEAS, MAN DID A PRETTY GOOD JOB THE FIRST TIME AROUND.

DIETER RAMS 10.90

A MATERIAL WORLD

The increasing availability of new industrial materials suggests that the objects of the future will look very different from the objects of 2001. Why? Material innovation often leads to formal innovation. With that in mind, METROPOLIS gathered a small group of designers and architects at New York's Material ConneXion—a resource library of the most innovative materials being produced today—and asked them to examine a specially selected collection of materials. They were captivated by the look and feel, the strangeness of some, but everyone was concerned about environmental effects. How sustainable are they? What will they do to our air, to our water, to us?

"It's like the diaper versus linen thing. If you're really concerned about waste then you think disposable diapers are a poor choice. If you're worried about energy and water consumption, you think that they're a great solution. In fact, that's what's not arbitrated. So it has nothing to do with money or desire. It's that there are philosophical and environmental issues that aren't properly arbitrated." JAMES BIBER

"I think the challenge for us as designers, and as teachers of the next generation, is the idea of confluence. If you are careful about what you select and about designing the application, there are enormous opportunities for using materials appropriately, for contributing solutions to very severe problems that face us environmentally. For me the key is computing, the Internet, the availability of information. I think that when you look at the computer as a design tool and as an information-gathering tool, as complex as these problems are, there are solutions." MICHAEL MCDONOUGH

"I think scented plastics are just an interesting idea of integrating a sense into materials. The examples are horrendous—they usually are. It doesn't have to be on the cheesy level of aromatherapies or display applications." LIAT MARGOLIES

"I think you don't have to have new fruit, you can just have a new recipe for the old fruit. And I think it's great to see aluminum in sixty different new versions or sintered or gelled—that's taking a new form. So to me the form change is much more productive and prolific than material change, because frankly we are running out of elements." MICHAEL MCDONOUGH

"We tend to feel more comfortable with materials that have some basis in nature. It makes us feel more comfortable, and we believe it's more sustainable. It may or may not be." MARGARET HELFAND

"Soybeans are potentially extremely toxic. That's why, for example, tofu has to go through several layers of processing before you can eat it. The first layer of tofu is nearly fatal." MICHAEL MCDONOUGH 2000

WHEELCHAIR DESIGN

In recent years, some wheelchair users have begun participating in a new kind of occupational therapy: wheelchair sports, including basketball, racing, tennis, and volleyball. Participation in sports helped to heal the wounded sense of self so characteristic of the disabled. But wheelchair sports could not be played easily with the standard chrome hospital chair. What's more, the chair represented the very pathology and dependence from which its users longed to be liberated. Physical activity and competition so empowered these wheelchair users that a number of them started modifying their chairs themselves with saws and welding tools to make their vehicles better suit their athletic needs.

102

Their adaptations led to a new concept in wheelchair design: the sports chair. It was easier to maneuver, weighed less than 20 pounds, and had, so unlike the typical wheelchair, a bit of dash. Several of these mavericks—some of them engineers—went on to set up their own manufacturing companies and revolutionize the industry.

They were successful because the needs of wheelchair users were finally being addressed. Until then no one had seriously studied the wheelchair as an orthosis, examining how users interacted with their chairs. Research into such issues as how much of a task could be assigned to the user and how much to the chair had never been conducted. Yet this kind of information was vital to developing efficient and versatile equipment. By incorporating the knowledge from their personal experiences into their own models, these disabled designers created sports chairs that were vastly superior to the traditional ones; in fact, many of their customers selected them for everyday use.

Among the sports chair's many innovations was its ability to be adjusted to the individual user, to her frame and carriage, to the way he propelled the chair. Also it had a more durable frame—rather than chrome tubing, it was made out of painted aluminum, titanium, or high-tech carbon fiber—to withstand impacts, jarring drops off curbs, and the wear and tear of traveling over outdoor surfaces. The rear wheels were often cambered, which had a number of advantages: the chair was more laterally stable; the bottom of the wheels made contact with objects like doorways first, protecting the user's hands; the hand rims were positioned ergonomically for a more natural arm stroke. Armrests were eliminated—an unnecessary feature in a chair meant for action. Unencumbered at last, the user became the focus of attention rather than his wheelchair.

Over the years the sports chair has brought about dramatic changes in the design of "everyday" wheelchairs. Although the chrome hospital model continues to be the standard in hospitals and nursing homes—where people are too sick or too old to complain—elsewhere, "sporty" versions in black, red, or multicolor metal tubing proliferate. Wheelchairs now look more like vehicles than pieces of medical apparatus.

MARISA BARTOLUCCI 11.92

ELECTRONIC PETS

You can say a lot of things about technology, but you're seldom moved to call it adorable. And so it was a mystery to me why anyone would want a virtual kitten, the whole point of kittens being their flair for the adorable. Replace the fur with injection-molded plastic, and there isn't much point to being a kitten. But this being the nineties, my kids were fixated on getting a virtual pet, and once we considered the escapee snake living in the attic, along with the brain-damaged Siberian husky and anorexic lizard in our familial past, it didn't seem like such a bad idea. And indeed, her brief residence with our family was a lesson in human attachments, evolutionary electronics, and the emotional relationships we insist on having with technology.

If Nekotcha, the brand name for our new kitten, skipped adorable, she went directly to pure efficiency. Her flair was for growing instant body parts. Properly fed and cared for—which means her owners had to guess precisely what buttons to push when she beeped—she obediently responded by growing ears, whiskers, a body, legs. Most miraculous, perhaps, is that she was equipped with five hearts, any number of which might appear on the tiny display monitor when this pet had been satisfactorily nurtured and fed.

But we soon learned that such body parts could disappear just as quickly. In fact, we discovered that the kitten was adept at negotiating her way in and out of the shadow realm with disquieting ease. Earlier generations of these pets had a single life span. But too many children, on going to school or soccer practice, were forced to abandon their little pets at home, where they perished. Taking a cue from evolutionary biology, Nekotcha and her electronic peers have adapted accordingly, and are now capable of another enviable feat: should she cease to exist, she can be brought back to life with a convenient reset button.

For nine days Nekotcha came and went in our lives like a tiny virtual Buddha whose capacity for rebirth suggested a miniature psychic acrobat. She was the perfect New Age pet, collecting past lives at a clip that Shirley MacLaine might envy. You may think there would be spiritual lessons to be drawn from this ability for constant regeneration, but having five hearts was not indicative of having a soul. Relinquishing existence was just something else to do, an alternative to eating virtual fish, drinking a bowl of milk, playing with a piece of ribbon, going to the bathroom, or going on dates with Beautiful Cat or Ugly Cat.

There is something charming about watching little boys exchange tips on nurturing—a confederacy of mini-parents, affectionate, protective, wavering between being slightly competitive and purely generous, a lot like new moms comparing notes on how their babies are teething. If the rest of us are trying to get in touch with our inner child, kids are naturals at tapping into the parent within.

That said, after five days of responding to Nekotcha's arbitrary demands, my sons became exasperated. "This is one messed-up screwball," I hear one of them mutter. And it occurs to me that Nekotcha is not so much a virtual pet as a virtual teenager.

103

Top: Flux lamp, by Jan Mellis and Ben Oostrum of FMO;
bottom: Solitaire easy chair, by Alfredo Haberti for Offect.
Courtesy **Totem**

OBJECTS OF MEANING

There was a time, as recently as 20 years ago, when the universe of American design
was fixed and easy to navigate. One bought affordable, repetitious home furnishings at
the department store. Or purchased monolithic, mass-produced office furniture from a
major supplier. An extremely small elite had access to the upper echelons of design, but
only at exorbitant prices, and almost always through the intercession of a decorator—
a half-divine being who often supplemented the design fee with markups slapped onto
objects obtained at discount from decorator-only stores. The mass media, which fawned
over designers of shoes, dresses and handbags—items whose effective life spans could
be as short as a season—seemed wholly uninterested in the people and industries creating objects made to last for decades. The only consistent window normal folk had for
truly innovative or classic design was through the glass of a museum display case.

"My European friends often tease me about Americans having poor
taste," says David Shearer, creator of Totem, an iconoclastic design enterprise that functions as showroom, retail outlet, design forum, talent incubator, virtual gallery, furniture manufacturer, didactic center, and budding media empire. "The truth is, we haven't
had access to good design, either domestic or imported. I believe if people have access
to good design, they will buy it."

Born in 1958, Shearer had always felt an inexplicable attraction toward
design. During college he spent hours at salvage stores and attic sales seeking out objects
of American design from the 1930s, '40s, and '50s—a period he still sees as this country's
golden age. One of these safaris led him to the Salvation Army in St. Paul, Minnesota,
where he found a tubular, triple-arm chrome sofa by Norman Bel Geddes buried beneath
a pile of books and clothes. He bought the piece for $25 and ended up selling it to a
Chicago dealer. In 1986, after several years working in the interior design department at
BWBR Architects in St. Paul—and studying everything he could find about midcentury
American design—Shearer opened his first gallery, Geometrie. There he held bimonthly
shows of contemporary design, events that coincided with the exhibition schedules
of neighboring art galleries in the downtown warehouse district of Minneapolis. Shearer
also organized several design competitions, including one sponsored by Timex and the
Industrial Design Society of America for watches. He continued his zealous independent
study in design, supplementing reading and research with regular trips to Europe. In
1990 Shearer moved to New York where he worked at Cappellini Modern Age; he founded
Totem in 1997.

For Shearer, Totem is just as much mission as business. His intention,
he says, is to make design accessible, both aesthetically and economically. Shearer's
activity encompasses almost every aspect of design, blurring boundaries between sales,
production, design, education, and publicity that the industry once thought inviolable.
The entrance to his Tribeca store—a former textile warehouse on Franklin Street—is a
Plexiglas vestibule that funnels visitors into an open interior space where they can
examine—and touch—such things as a lacquered acrylic screen by David Khouri; a

106

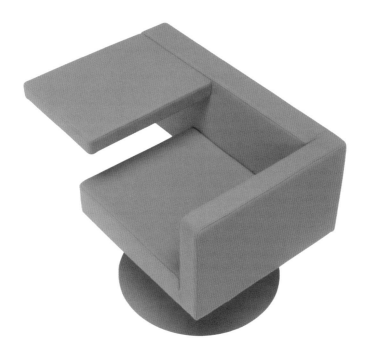

birch-topped, steel-legged table by the Swedish triumvirate Claesson Koivisto Rune; and light sculptures by Britain's Jeremy Lord. The experience is a metaphor, leading the mortal customer through a museum vitrine and directly into the realm of sacred objects.

The idea of appealing directly to the design public—shattering the glass wall between object and viewer, purveyor and purchaser—was certainly not Shearer's. New York's Cappellini Modern Age store, where Shearer was a manager, first eliminated its designer discount in the 1980s. Today that store, along with other high-end New York stores like Moss and Troy, consistently displays fine design for retail customers. Although Modern Age may have been ahead of its time 20 years ago, the democratization of design is paying aesthetic and economic dividends today. Most designers agree that the American public is now far more discerning—and willing to spend more—than at any time in the past.

"In the old days, you would have to have an expert, a decorator or an architect, tell you where the resources were and how to put together a room," says Melissa Barrett Rhodes, a collaborator at the advertising agency Baron & Baron, and former design editor at HARPER'S BAZAAR. "There wasn't an awareness of product or industrial design infiltrating all the areas of our lives. We're now surrounded by images in the media. We have well-designed objects like Palm Pilots and cell phones, the VW Beetle, the iMac."

It is difficult to gauge the role Shearer and Totem have played in the current design explosion. Easier to chart, although still tricky to define, is Totem's almost cataclysmic expansion. What just four years ago was a wholesale distributor representing four Swedish companies is now if not an empire certainly a confederation of city-states. Shearer is adept at discovering young designers, whose work he features in his store. Many of these designers see their objects manufactured by the company and distributed to more than 300 U.S. stores under the Totem Products label. Shearer is also known as a nurturer of talent. His relationship with Gaston Martincorena dates back to their collaboration at Modern Age. Totem produced Karim Rashid's vinyl desktop landscape collection, and will soon be coming out with furniture, lighting, and tabletop objects by the designer. Shearer is also responsible for the creation of the so-called "(G7)," a group of designers that includes Nick Dine, Ross Menuez, Mike Solis, and Christopher Deam.

Last year Totem opened a second store, in Santa Monica, California. In 1998 Shearer published the first issue of DSGN, a flashy quarterly magalog that featured articles and photos covering many of Totem's products and designers—but which Shearer promises will be almost exclusively editorial in future issues. Totem's Web site (www.totemdesign.com) features a plethora of design information as well as a virtual tour of the Tribeca showroom. The site logs more than half a million hits per month. Even more ambitious is Shearer's plan for a regular television design show—a 30-minute pilot, culled from more than 60 hours of documentary footage shot by Shearer and a crew at last spring's Milan Furniture Fair, is almost completed—that would bring the products, processes, and parties of once faceless designers into the living rooms of mainstream America. "People want to learn about the people who design the objects they live with," says Barrett Rhodes, who will host the TV show. "Especially designers with big personalities and crossover appeal. In Milan, the Fendi sisters held a reception for Marc Newson to celebrate the debut of the 021C car he designed for Ford. It was just like going to a party after a fashion show."

Although Totem's hybrid commercial and media activity has popularized design, it doesn't seem to have made it vulgar. The items sold at Totem may be economical compared to those available at Modern Age or Moss. But the design, which reflects Shearer's erudite, refined—but ultimately intuitive—taste, is almost always inventive and engaging. If anything, bringing design to the people has inspired consumers as well as the trade. "David puts forth options and possibilities that I don't see anywhere else," says Brad Zizmore, a partner at A+1 Design Corp., in New York. Zizmore frequently uses Totem as supplier and resource when creating office spaces. "He's always coming up with the extra element that can make a difference in the overall space."

Shearer's efforts have even drawn praise from scholars and curators. "What a Store like Totem does is help us reach the young audience—the one that for us is the least accessible," says David McFadden, chief curator at New York's American Craft Museum. "People who see finely designed objects at Totem will definitely be more inclined to come to the museum."

In an age when movie studios own television networks and magazines sponsor tennis tournaments, Totem's merging of the commercial with the creative makes perfect sense. But from an economic perspective, Shearer's insatiable expansion is curious. Totem's business plan clearly is driven by passion, not profit. It's not just a question of how many hats one man or company can wear, but also what sort of return this hyperextension could possibly generate for Totem. "If I were to look at this strictly as a business, we wouldn't do a lot of the things that we do," Shearer says. "For me, it's still a mission. Ultimately, I think what we put out there will return to us in one way or another, whether it's people coming into the store to buy something or simply learning more about design. It's not just about buying and selling design. Of course there is the bottom line: we've got to make money or we can't do these things. But we're also sharing things that we truly love with people, trying to make their lives better. If I were in it purely for the money, I'd probably be doing something else." KEN SHULMAN 11.00

SNAPSHOTS BY DAVID CARSON

Design curator **Paola Antonelli** tells us that **Achille Castiglioni** has established the following principles of practice: "Start from scratch, stick to common sense, know what your goals are and what your means are." **Danny Abelson** says, "Paradox and irony are the natural habitat of the rebellious. A great deal of the work **Tibor and Maira Kalman** and company created explored the tensions between the expected and the actual, the rich and the poor, the professional and the amateur, design and un-design." Of his own work **D. J. DePree** says simply, "I realized that making something for the American home was a worthwhile thing to be engaged in."

You wouldn't argue with any of them, and yet clearly all of these people are driven by profoundly different concerns. The last 20 years have been a time of tremendous energy and innovation in design—perhaps exactly because of this diversity of belief, motivation, and desire. **Alessandro Mendini** is inspired by the paintings of **De Chirico**. Gaetano Pesce likes to have a lot of empty bottles around: "Beer bottles, mineral water bottles, black wine bottles. All these bottles." Monoracial societies make **Ingo Maurer** claustrophobic. Such are the preferences and prejudices that make up the human face of design. They are also what animate the objects of the physical world and—when things go right—give them their sense of humanity.

The profiles excerpted here attempt to identify what compels these designers to believe in what they believe in and to work the way they work; and to track the petty irritations, exasperations, and furies that sometimes generate new work. One senses that there is little shared ideological ground. On the other hand, when **Charlotte Perriand** tells us, "I married my epoch," it is, oddly enough, a personal confession that any one of these designers easily could have made. Akiko Busch

DANNY ABELSON
PAOLA ANTONELLI
MARISA BARTOLUCCI
SYBILLE BRANTL
AKIKO BUSCH
DAVID CARSON
SARAH DUNCAN
RICHARD HORN
JANE JACOBS
JAMES HOWARD KUNSTLER
CRISWELL LAPPIN
JANE MAYBANK
SYLVIA PLACHY
PENELOPE ROWLANDS
TATIANA SAMOILOVA
FERN SCHUMER
PHILIPPE STARCK
CHRISTOPHER WAHL

WHAT'S WORRYING JANE JACOBS

Toronto always gives me the strange sensation of being in a parallel universe, one in which I might be in a great American city—say, Detroit, St. Louis, or Cleveland— if only we had not gone through the cultural convulsions of the postwar era and tossed our cities into the dumpster of history. Hollywood constantly uses Toronto as a set for Anycity, USA, but the truth is that it is in much better shape than almost any American city. Toronto is alive. Its downtown streets are teeming with people who actually live in the city center in apartment buildings and houses, and the sidewalks are jammed until late at night. The public realm, where the buildings meet the sidewalk, is active.

    Jane Jacobs—the renowned urbanist and author of THE DEATH AND LIFE OF GREAT AMERICAN CITIES, CITIES AND THE WEALTH OF NATIONS, THE ECONO- MY OF CITIES, SYSTEMS OF SURVIVAL, and other books—lives here. Her house is in the Annex neighborhood on a serene residential street off Bloor, the main drag of the University of Toronto, which resembles Eighth Street in Greenwich Village—where Jacobs so famously lived and wrote years ago.

    Jacobs still looks like that famous photo of her taken in the White Horse tavern in the West Village more than three decades ago (a cigarette in one hand and a beer mug in the other). Her hair is the same silvery helmet with bangs, and her big eyeglasses emphasize her role as the ever-penetrating observer, with an impish overlay. She still likes to drink beer, and worked on a bottle of some dark local brew while we talked.

    The daughter of a doctor and a nurse, Jacobs grew up in Scranton, Pennsylvania. She worked briefly as a reporter for the SCRANTON TRIBUNE and then went to New York City in 1934, where she plugged away as a freelance writer. She landed a staff job with ARCHITECTURAL FORUM in 1952. The job gave her a privileged perch for observing the fiasco of postwar urban renewal and all its evil consequences. A decade later she seized the imagination of an otherwise extremely complacent era when she declared so starkly in THE DEATH AND LIFE OF GREAT AMERICAN CITIES that the experiment of Modernist urbanism was a thumping failure. Jacobs urged Americans to look to the traditional wisdom of the vernacular city and its fundamental unit—the street—rather than the planning gurus. This was the first shot in a war that has been ongoing ever since.

    Jacobs suffered the opprobrium of the architectural and planning establishment for decades. They never recovered from her frontal assault—especially the sinister Robert Moses, who fell from power not long after he tangled with Jacobs on his proposal to run a freeway through Washington Square. One can say pretty definitively that she won the battle and the war.

    By the mid-1960s Jacobs's interests and writings broadened to take in the wider issues of economics and social relations, and by force of intellect she compelled the cultural elite to take seriously an untrained female generalist—and wonderful prose stylist—who had the nerve to work out large ideas on her own. Naturally her books are now part of the curriculum. During the course of our conversation we were seated at her dining room table. JAMES HOWARD KUNSTLER 03.01

JHK: In THE DEATH AND LIFE OF GREAT AMERICAN CITIES you wrote: "It may be that we have become so feckless as a people that we no longer care how things work, but only what kind of quick, easy outer impression they give." What was your state of mind back then? Were you ticked off at American culture? What was it that was getting under your skin in those days?

JJ: What was getting immediately under my skin was this mad spree of deceptions and vandalism and waste that was called urban renewal. And the way it had been adopted like a fad. People were so mindless about it—and so dishonest about what was being done. That's what ticked me off; because I was working for an architectural magazine, and I saw all this first-hand—how the most awful things were being excused.

122

JHK: You must have already been acquainted with things like Le Corbusier's "Radiant City" and some of the schemes from the 1920s and the Bauhaus?

JJ: Yes, but I didn't have any feelings about these things one way or another. I didn't have any abstractions about American culture. I had no ideology. But I'll tell you something else that had been worrying me. I liked visiting museums that showed old-time machines and tools. I was struck with the way these old machines were painted. They were done in a way that showed you how they worked. The makers cared about how these things were put together. I used to go to the railroad station in Scranton and watch the locomotives. I got a big bang out of seeing how those pistons moved the wheels, and then the connection of that with the steam inside. In the meantime, along came these locomotives that had skirts on them. Suddenly you couldn't see how the wheels moved, and that disturbed me. It was supposed to be for some aerodynamic reason, but that didn't make sense. And I began to notice how everything was being covered up, and I thought that was kind of sick.

JHK: So the whole streamlining thing bugged you?

JJ: That's right. So I remember very well what was in my mind when I wrote, "We have become so feckless." It was those skirts on the locomotives I was thinking about and how this had extended to "we didn't care how our cities worked anymore." We didn't care to show where the entrances were in buildings—that's all I meant. It was not some enormous comment on American society. I just thought this was a real decadence.

JHK: How were the proponents of urban renewal dishonest?

JJ: Well, I talked to an architect in 1958 who helped justify the destruction of the West End of Boston. And he told me that he had had to go on his hands and knees with a photographer through utility crawl spaces so they could get pictures of sufficiently dark and noisome spaces to justify that it was a slum. Now that is real dishonesty.

JHK: But isn't that the whole tale of the mid-twentieth century? That scores of architects and planning officials went along with something that was really pernicious?

JJ: That's right. And how did they justify it? Urban renewal was a greater good, so they would bear false witness for this greater good. Why was this a greater good? Because slums were bad. And I'd say, "But this isn't a slum!" They didn't care how things worked anymore. That was part of what was making me so angry. They also didn't seem to care what part truth and untruths had in these things. And that's part of how things work too.

JHK: Did you ever meet the infamous Robert Moses?

JJ: No, I saw him only once, at a hearing about the proposed road through Washington Square, which was to lead to an entrance ramp to the lower Manhattan expressway. He was there briefly to speak his piece. But nobody was told that at the time. None of us had spoken yet, because they always had the officials speak first and then they would go away and they wouldn't listen to the people. Anyway, he stood up there gripping the railing, and he was furious at the effrontery of this. I guess he could already see that his plan was in danger, because he was saying, "There is nobody against this—NOBODY, NOBODY, NOBODY—but a bunch of, a bunch of mothers!" And then he stomped out.

JHK: Why did you move to Canada in the late 1960s?

JJ: We came in protest of the Vietnam War. We had two draft-age sons. Both preferred going to jail to going to war. And my husband said, "You know, we didn't raise these boys to go to jail." In any case we didn't like the war. We sympathized with their antagonism to it, so we decided to come to another country. We were just not cut out to be citizens of an empire.

JHK: It must have been very disruptive.

JJ: It would have been disruptive if we had thought of ourselves as exiles. People who think of themselves as exiles, I find, can never really put their lives together. We thought of ourselves as immigrants. It was an adventure, and we were all in it together.

JHK: But you were leaving quite a lot behind.

JJ: Yes, but we discovered another thing when we got here. Americans don't think that other places are as real as America. We were leaving things behind. Well, we were coming to other things that were just as real, just as interesting, just as exciting. And people would ask me after we'd decided to stay, "When are you coming back?" "We're not." "Oh, but you can't just—you've got to come back to real life." And I would say, "It's just as real." This is very hard for Americans to understand. I think that may be the biggest difference between Americans and people elsewhere. Canadians know that there are places just as real as Canada. This self-centeredness is a very strange thing. I came here for positive reasons; we stayed for positive reasons—we liked it. Why did I become a Canadian citizen? When I became a Canadian citizen, you couldn't be a dual citizen—now you can—so I had to be one or the other. But the reason I became a Canadian citizen was because it seemed abnormal to me not to be able to vote.

JHK: How many years did it take you to compose your classic, THE DEATH AND LIFE OF GREAT AMERICAN CITIES?

124 JJ: Not very long. I started it in the fall of '58 and I finished it in January of '61. But I had been thinking about it for a long time. And although I didn't know what I was gathering information for, I was gathering information for it.

JHK: What are your thoughts on what has happened to American cities?

JJ: It's a tragedy—a totally unnecessary tragedy. Nothing has really changed. Talk has changed, but regulations haven't; lending systems for these things haven't changed. The notion—and I tell you this one even worries me that it extends into New Urbanism—the notion of the shopping center as a valid kind of downtown has taken over. It's very hard for architects of this generation even to think in terms of a downtown or a center that is owned by different people with different ideas.

JHK: But that's one of the other directions the New Urbanists are going in. I think we're leaving the age of the megaproject.

JJ: Here's what I think is happening. Look at the end of Victorianism. Modernism started with people getting infatuated with the idea of "It's the twentieth century—is this suitable for the future?" This started happening before the First World War, and it wasn't just the soldiers. You can see it happening if you read the Bloomsbury biographies. It was a reaction against Victorianism; there was so much that was repressive and stuffy. Victorian buildings were associated with it, and they were regarded as very ugly. Even when they weren't ugly, people made them ugly.

JHK: You were particularly harsh on Ebenezer Howard and Patrick Geddes, and the Garden City movement. It was in some ways another one of those really bad ideas that a lot of intelligent people fell for—including Mumford, who got sucked in really big.

JJ: What was bad about the Garden City movement was the idea that you could take a clean slate and make a new world. That's basically artificial. There is no new world that you make without the old world. And Mumford fell for the whole "this is the twentieth century" thing: the notion that you could discard the old world completely. This is what was so bad about Modernism.

JHK: Were you friendly with Mumford, or were you adversaries?

JJ: As far as I was concerned we were friendly. It was very funny: he was furious at THE DEATH AND LIFE OF GREAT AMERICAN CITIES—absolutely furious. He thought— and I never gave him any reason to think this—he thought that I was a protégée of his, a disciple. Because he thought that all young people who were friendly must be his disciples.

JHK: And he was furious that you turned on him?

JJ: I think that's what he thought. I first met him when I gave a talk at Harvard in 1956. I was substituting for my boss and had awful stage fright. But I gave a speech in which I attacked urban renewal. It was a real ordeal for me. I just went into a trance and recited this thing that I had memorized, then sat down. And it was a big hit. Nobody had heard anybody saying these things before. This is why Holly Whyte got me to write that article for THE EXPLODING METROPOLIS—because of this speech. Anyway, Mumford was in the audience, and he very enthusiastically welcomed me, and we shook hands. I'd hypnotized myself, but I had apparently hypnotized them, too. I met him some more times, and everything was amiable. I had my doubts about him, because we rode into the city together in a car and I watched how he acted as soon as he began to get into the city. He had been talking and all pleasant, but as soon as we got into the city he got grim, withdrawn, distressed. And it was so clear that he just hated the city, and hated being in it.

JHK: I'd like to turn to economics. It seems to me that the American living arrangement, the "fiasco of suburbia" as Leon Krier calls it, is approaching a point beyond which it might be difficult to carry on. All that's necessary is a mild to moderate chronic instability in the world oil markets to throw places like Houston, Phoenix, San Jose, Miami, Las Vegas, and Atlanta into terrible trouble.

JJ: Well, I don't know whether it will happen because of the oil markets. I do know things won't go on as they are now. But people who try to predict the future by extrapolating in a line from what already exists—they're always wrong. This is a continuation of what I was saying about the revolt against Victorianism. I think what's coming is one of these great generational upheavals. Not simply because people care about community or even understand it, or because of the relationship of sprawl to the ruination of the natural world. They just don't like what's around—and they will be absolutely ruthless with the remnants of it.

JHK: In your book CITIES AND THE WEALTH OF NATIONS you talked about "the master economic process called import replacement"—the idea that a city and its region would prosper over time only if it started to furnish for itself many of the goods or services that it formerly imported. With the so-called global economy, it appears that import replacement is no longer significant given that the overwhelming majority of the products sold in the United States are made elsewhere. Is this a dangerous situation?

JJ: [Chuckle.] I think a more dangerous situation is the standardization of what is being produced or reproduced everywhere—where you can see the same products, in the same malls, in the same chains, in every city. This goes even deeper than the trouble with import replacing, because it means that new things are not being produced locally that can be improvements. There's a sameness—this is one of the things that's boring people. But this sameness has economic implications: you don't get new products and services out of sameness. This means that somehow there's no opportunity for these thousands of flowers to bloom anymore.

126

JHK: The million flowers are now blooming in China. Every product I pick up is made in China. I'm not against the Chinese, but it makes you wonder how long we can go on having an advanced civilization without making anything anymore. Can we?

JJ: I don't think so. But you know we aren't complete dolts in all of this. For example, we don't manufacture our own computers. They're made mostly in Taiwan, but they aren't designed in Taiwan. Is it more important to design computers, or more important to manufacture them? It's vital to do both; it's fatal to specialize. All kinds of things show us that the more diverse we are in what we can do, the better. But I don't think you can dismiss the constructive and inventive things that America is doing—and say, "Oh, we aren't making anything anymore. We are living off of what the poor Chinese do." It's more complicated than that. Look at Detroit. Look what happened when it specialized just in automobiles. Look at Manchester when it specialized in textiles, in those "dark satanic mills." It was supposed to be the city of the future.

JHK: We have an awful lot of places in America that don't specialize in anything anymore. In the region where I live, which is a kind of a mini-Rust Belt in upstate New York, one town after another has practically vanished. There is no more Utica, New York, really. No Amsterdam, New York, or Glens Falls. Economically they're gone. Is the rest of America going to be like that?

JJ: Never underestimate the power of a city to regenerate. And things everywhere are not as bad as you are picturing it. For example, Portland.

JHK: I'd say Portland is in pretty good shape compared to lots of other American cities—but it ain't France.

JJ: No, it ain't. But there are lots of things about America that are better in their own way than France.

JHK: Are there other countries, other parts of the world, that you particularly love or admire?

JJ: I am very fond of the Netherlands. I like the immense variety of it on a very small compass. The human scale of the whole thing and the density are far above what we are used to in North America, or anywhere. They prove that high density and human scale are not incompatible at all.

JHK: The Europeans seem to have a higher regard for city life than we do, and to do better with it. How do you account for that?

JJ: Well, you have to go back to something I don't understand and can't explain, which are these planning hysterias that went over America. I guess different kinds of hysterias swept over Europe.

JHK: They get Adolf Hitler, and we get Ed Logue.

JJ: So we are lucky. But something else amazes me about the United States versus Europe. When we are faced with the task of fixing up a riverbank—and many American cities are on rivers—we have to put in theme parks, ballparks, aquariums, all this stuff. In Europe they make granite embankments with a ramp or stairs down to the water, and it's beautiful.

JHK: You've left urbanism behind somewhat and moved on to economics. What are you working on now? Is there an idea you're galvanized by these days?

JJ: I am interested in the question of why time is such an enemy in American neighborhoods—what specific things does time threaten—and how time can be made an ally.

JHK: Are you suggesting that American neighborhoods don't regenerate themselves?

JJ: No. I think they have a very poor track record with regard to time.

JHK: When I was a kid, Brooklyn was like another planet. Now it's where a whole generation has moved to in New York City.

JJ: Parts of Brooklyn are now, you might say, the outliers of my old neighborhood.

SOCIETY IS SO AGGRES-SIVE. IT'S VERY IMPOR-TANT TO FIND A MORE SPIRITUAL WAY OF LIVING. WHAT I CAN DO PERSONALLY IS TO INSIST ON AN ARTISTIC APPROACH TO DESIGN INSTEAD OF THE HIGH-TECH APPROACH OR THE FUNCTIONAL APPROACH, SO THAT MY OBJECTS HAVE A LITTLE BIT OF RELIGION, A LITTLE BIT OF SOUL.

ALESSANDRO MENDINI 10.98

Executive seating designed by Charles Eames for Herman
Miller and used by Bobby Fischer for World Chess
Championship in 1972. Courtesy **Herman Miller, Inc.**

D. J. DEPREE'S CONCEPT OF SIMPLICITY

When Bobby Fischer challenged Boris Spassky for the World Chess Championship in
1972, the match was postponed for days. The reason: Fischer refused to play unless he
could sit in a specific chair.
    It sounds like a lame excuse, but this was no ordinary chair. Fischer,
infamous for his idiosyncratic nature, insisted that for the long hours of sitting through
the 25-game match, his behind deserved a swivel chair manufactured by the Herman
Miller Company. (Remember, one move took Spassky 55 minutes.) The chair, shipped
from New York to Reykjavik, Iceland, contributed to Fischer's game and ultimate victory.
    Why did Fischer insist on that particular chair? The publicity-shy
chess champion has never explained; however, it is generally accepted that the incident
was not only a ploy to unnerve his opponent, but a testimonial to the design of the chair.
    The last thing on Fischer's mind during that tournament, of course, was
how his chair came into being. But there is a man behind that chair, a man who is to contemporary furniture what Bobby Fischer is to chess.
    The retired chief executive officer of Herman Miller Company, Dirk Jay
(D. J.) DePree, a distinguished-looking man of 91 with clear blue eyes, is credited with
changing the look of the American home. He introduced mass production of modern furniture into the country in the 1930s. His concept is simplicity.
    "The most interesting thing in a home is not its furniture, it is the
people who live there," DePree said recently, while gently rubbing the leather of his own
Fischer-Spassky chair in a conference room at the Herman Miller headquarters, in
Zeeland, Michigan. DePree was echoing the sentiment of his first designer, Gilbert Rohde,
who joined the company in 1930.
    Original Herman Miller furnishings, like the Charles Eames-designed
Fischer-Spassky chair and the more famous Eames lounge chair, continue to sell well.
Bobby Fischer's chair is notable for the depth of its seat, which supports the full length of
a man's thigh; its padded arms; and its firm but not overstuffed upholstery. The Eames
lounge chair, revolutionary when it was introduced in 1956, is made up of three separate
leather cushions, each with a curved plywood back. The separation of interchangeable
parts made it possible for the first time to mass-produce a chair as soft and deep as the
English "club chair." It offered old-fashioned comfort in a contemporary design.
    The lounge chair is the hallmark of the Herman Miller Company's
design philosophy and reflects DePree's Calvinist beliefs. "When Rohde first proposed his
simple designs we were still making eighteenth-century English-style furniture and imitat-
ing ornate period pieces," DePree recalled. The "providential" decision to abandon the
manufacturing of period furniture in favor of Rohde's Modernism, he said, was influenced
by a couple of events. The Depression had taken its toll. In 1930 the company DePree had
bought with his father-in-law, Herman Miller, only six years earlier was just a year away
from bankruptcy. DePree realized he had to come out with something different.

FERN SCHUMER 04.84

131

ALESSANDRO MENDINI'S HOUSE

Mendini intends his discomforting works to be used in the most comforting places of all, the home, which he feels compelled to examine in light of postatomic realities. Home to him is a place of controlled disorder where the standard spatial divisions of living room, kitchen, bedroom, and bath make little sense. These outmoded areas could be replaced by "swimming rooms, vegetation rooms, discussion rooms, reading rooms, et cetera. The primordial function could be absorbed, as subproblems, by the more sophisticated ones. One could eat in the swimming room, cook in the vegetation room, wash in the discussion room, or sleep in the library," Mendini writes.

132

Home is also a place without hard angles and rigid definitions. Each room is softened with its own peculiar decoration. (With this, Mendini gives a taste of his somewhat muddled feminism; he equates "hard" architecture with the male, "soft" decoration with the female; designing with men, simply living life with women.) Mendini's unconventional attitude toward interior design goes along with his idea that his furniture can be used anywhere. He sets down no rules. It's up to each person to figure out how and where these adult, yet childlike, pieces will work.

As a child Mendini lived in "a protective and restraining system of objects," he confesses. "Furnishings in my father's room were forbidding, hostile, realistic, and uninviting like those in a museum, owing to the unquestioning respect demanded for the 'never to be touched' household antiques." He contrasts this grim setting with his grandparents' country home, which was full of "romantic scenes that set one on flights of fancy and consisted of cats, attics, courtyards, washtubs, and a waste of staircases and kitchens—all spelling mystery, delighted senses, and large dimensions."

This same sense of liberation is present in Mendini's furniture and interior designs. In them he seeks to accentuate "those finer points lost in the depths of time, those sensations felt by man in a remote past, which we are very badly in need of: the deadened sounds, the half-shadows, the odors, the memories, the cloths, the whirligig, the fluids, the hiding places, the flowers, the grilles, the cobwebs, the delicate colors, the glass balls, the tiny things," he writes. And so he shows that the great disorder seemingly weighing down his work is nevertheless uplifted by lyrical poetry.

RICHARD HORN 04.87

Clockwise from top right: Alessandro Mendini's Sirfo Goose table; Calamobio Commode; Papilio tempered-glass coffee table; Zabro folding table. Courtesy **Zanotta**

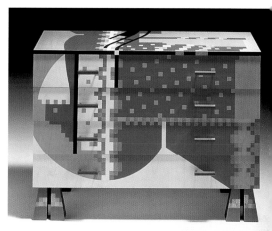

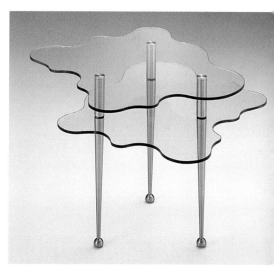

THE TALENT OF ACHILLE CASTIGLIONI

"Any device made for lighting can be considered a proper exercise of industrial design only if the fixture-object is subordinated to the effects of light it produces," Achille Castiglioni told an interviewer ten years ago. This austere statement appeared in DESIGN SINCE 1945, the catalog for a show at the Philadelphia Museum of Art in 1983 that featured a dozen or so Castiglioni lamps. Although the quote is a synthesis of the designer's straightforward approach, its absolute flatness is deceiving: missing are Castiglioni's endearingly animated gestures, as well as the complexities of his thinking.

Asked to talk about the famous Arco lamp, which he and his brother Pier Giacomo designed in 1962, Achille replies: "We wanted to know—could we make a hanging lamp without drilling the ceiling? So, thinking of street lamps, we took a piece of marble as a counterweight [his hands model the lamp's elegant rectangular base in the air], we drilled a hole in it so that two people could carry it around with a broomstick [he sketches the scene on a piece of paper], and we launched the light source, see? [his arm sweeps the air in an arc-like movement that mimics the lamp's overscaled stem] with a steel arch that puts the light right in the middle of the table. You can sit and eat, and someone can walk around and serve you food; there's enough room to stroll around [he strolls]." Clearly, the Arco lamp's design, like many other works from Castiglioni's 50-year portfolio, is about much more than an adherence to function: it's about memory, curiosity, observation, wit, a willing client, experience, manipulation, perfectionism, luck, and, of course, talent.

The Castiglioni design office in Milan occupies a huge mezzanine apartment in a building that faces the Sforza castle. Opened in the late 1930s by Livio and Pier Giacomo, after the brothers graduated from the architecture school of Milan's Polytechnic University, the office became known for its designs of interiors, furniture, and objects. Among Livio and Pier Giacomo's early works is the highly innovative Phonola radio, one of the first radios that wasn't encased in heavy cabinetry, which they designed in collaboration with architect Caccia Dominioni. By the end of World War II, when Achille, the youngest, joined his brothers as a licensed architect, the office had a reputation for forward-thinking work. And although in 1952 Livio set out on his own to design lighting and sound installations, and Pier Giacomo died in 1968, the office is as it was when the three worked together. It still doesn't have a name; the huge reflecting lamps still hang from the ceiling over the giant desk shared by the three, and Achille still uses an old black telephone with a rotary dial and big white buttons. Even the brothers' infamous "trompe l'oeil," a floor-to-ceiling mirror set at an angle to multiply the space and to enable them to see the office without moving from their desks, is still there. To the designer-architects' lasting amusement, generations of visitors have bumped into the mirror in their efforts to try to go beyond it.

The Castiglioni sense of humor and delight in experimentation is easy to detect in the "125, I think...maybe more," objects Achille remembers designing. These include some 60 lamps, in addition to the stools, bookshelves, electrical switches, cameras,

134

ONCE, THERE WAS A CAT LOOKING AT ME WHILE I WAS PUTTING ON A WARM JACKET IN WINTER. THE CAT WAS LOOKING AT ME, AND I REALIZED HE WILL NEVER KNOW WHY I'M PUTTING THIS ON BECAUSE HIS BRAIN IS NOT ORGANIZED ENOUGH FOR THIS KIND OF THING. I'M IN THE SAME POSITION WITH THE SKY."

138

ETTORE SOTTSASS 12.97/01.98

LETTER FROM LENINGRAD

6 March 1989

My name is Tatiana Samoilova. I'm an industrial designer and a member of the board of administration of the Society of Soviet Designers.

I was born in Leningrad. My father and older brother were both naval officers; there were no designers in my family. During my last year in school (the 10th grade) an uncle took me to an artist he knew. After he looked at my drawings, some copies of Christmas cards, this artist accepted me as a student. When many years later I asked him why he took me on, he said, "I looked into your eyes, not at your drawings."

140

Between 1956 and 1962 I went to the Leningrad Fine Arts and Industrial School. Those were the Khrushchev years. Design began to be talked about in the Soviet Union, and our school's design department switched from teaching applied arts to design for mass production.

Those years at the Leningrad school were unusually creative. As students we were inspired by the spirit of search and change as well as by the exciting new field that we were about to enter. But our teachers had a difficult time of it. To fit the school's new focus on industrial design, faculty members [many of whom were trained as architects] were required to devise new lecture programs by improvising as they went along, often in the classroom. We were a highly motivated group of students, grateful to our teachers and glad to have an opportunity to enter a useful and interesting new field.

Our class was graduated in 1962. That same year marked the formation of the USSR Research Institute of Industrial Design. [This government bureau, known under its acronym VNIITE, was sponsored by the USSR State Committee for Science and Technology. Its first members came from the fields of architecture, engineering, art, and art criticism. No industrial designers were among them, since no Soviet school had an industrial design department until the 1960s.] I was among the institute's first apprentices in the Leningrad division, where Yuri Soloviev was the principal director, and has been for 25 years. During this past quarter of a century he has had a key role in shaping our state system of design. [The "system," until the recent reforms, has been a centralized, government-run organization of designers—6,000 people forming 1,500 design teams in 330 cities and towns throughout the Soviet Union. VNIITE members were often kept busy with conceptual projects since factory managers showed little interest in innovating.]

After graduating from the institute, I worked in the Department of Heavy Machinery Construction for three years. While there I collaborated with V. Pakhomov on a tractor-trailer in 1964. Our design is still being used at some logging sites. When my colleague and I were working on our tractor-trailer we went to the factory up north where these heavy machines were being produced. Before our arrival there, no one in that factory had seen a live industrial designer. And so when the managers looked at our first sketches, they were somewhat skeptical, if not disappointed. "You are showing us an ordinary tractor. We expected something special, something like a pumpkin," they told us.

Ten years later I gave up designing heavy machinery and turned my attention to smaller scale. Since then I've been designing consumer products like lamps, door handles, massage and manicure sets, watches and clocks, as well as electric razors. And I've found that I like working with objects that are close to people and make their home environments beautiful. But my designs have as yet to be used by many people.

None of my designs were produced between 1972 and 1986, and much of my work is still in model or prototype form. In looking for reasons why this was so, I began blaming myself, particularly my poor knowledge of technology. Then I noticed that the same thing was happening to most of my colleagues. While we had orders to design new products, industry wasn't able to produce them. Though we were grateful for having had the work—in addition to designing, we published articles and prepared models for exhibitions—these were our years of stagnation. As a mirror of our industrial development, product design was clearly vulnerable to the events that shaped our world.

Then around 1986 there was a change, and one after another I saw my designs put into production. My massage and cosmetic kits, as well as my manual sewing machine, can now be bought in some shops. This development gave Soviet designers some cause for optimism, but our most interesting work is still in prototype form.

I've been at the institute for as long as VNIITE has been in existence. During those 25 years I have done research on large and complex projects, designed individual objects, and worked within the creative collective. And I've had an opportunity to observe what each new group of young designers is doing. I've attended seminars in Norway (1979), Armenia (1985), and New York (Worldesign 88), where I could compare my work with that of others. Such meetings also helped me understand that of all the creative fields, design is perhaps the most international one—that it has no boundaries.

Here in the Soviet Union there's been no competition between products, and the designers who have been successful tend to be the theoreticians and researchers, not the practitioners. Soviet designers have always studied foreign experience with great respect and curiosity. We know the work of Charles Eames, Raymond Loewy, Ettore Sottsass, and Dieter Rams. And I hold special admiration for Mario Bellini's sense of form and use of modern materials, as I respect Kenji Ekuan [known for his work for Kawasaki as well as his soy sauce bottle that pours from both sides]. Now some of our own people, like Dmitry Azrikan, are good enough to compete with the best of them on world markets.

Perestroika has brought considerable changes into our lives, including a new demand by our markets for more and better-quality consumer goods. In 1987 a long-awaited event took place. The Society of Soviet Designers was formed, and with its help we are taking the first steps to having our work realized. It has become possible to open an independent design studio. My colleague I. Chuprun (he and I designed several electric razors together) and I are waiting for funds and space to become available for a studio. And we're hoping for a free exchange of ideas with designers from other countries as well as with companies to produce our work.

My trip to New York and Worldesign 88 showed me how much goodwill there is between people.

141

JOHN HEJDUK: ORACLE WITH A BRONX ACCENT

Interviewing Hejduk is like going to Delphi. **Thrown into silhouette by the window behind him, he has a voice that seems to emanate from the darkness, like an oracle with a Bronx accent. Hejduk has made no effort to rewrite himself. Encountering an idea that interests him, he pounces and his caterpillar eyebrows spring to life. His eyes sparkle with amusement and speculation.**

Hejduk is adored by his students, from whom he demands and gets some of the most rigorously crafted work produced by any architecture program in the country. He does not dictate the direction of their work but beguiles them with allegories—a method that gives his teaching persona the aura of a mystic guru, and raises some eyebrows. Are these allegories a way to get to the essential questions of architecture or, like the smoke and mirrors used by the Wizard of Oz, are they empty masks?

His independent nature has led Hejduk to a lifetime of practicing on his own terms, producing architecture, drawings, models, furniture, and poetry that make up a compelling body of work. Often the context is poetical and allegorical. Hejduk's architecture has more to do with character and spirit than with problem solving. The bulk of his work is uncompromised by the constraints that gnaw away at the visions of other architects. This is its great strength and, some would say, its weakness too: While his ideas are expressed with unique force and clarity, they are frequently criticized as being something other than architecture.

His determined resistance to compromise is something that Hejduk imparts to his students. When asked if they might not be surprised by what's expected of them once they leave the Cooper Union think tank, Hejduk tells the following story: "I just came back from an interesting experience. I saw the Russian show for the first time [an exhibition of Constructivist work at the Guggenheim Museum in New York]. The thing that struck me is that the architectural drawings are quite overwhelming, fresh, authentic, alive—tons of them. I say tons: many, many tons' worth. The fact of the matter is that all that activity was tremendous: the beauty of it, the significance of its thought. There aren't even four [Russian Constructivist] buildings built, and yet the impact of that thought upon the world of building has been immense. And there's the point: it was an idea; it was a mission. I make no separation. A drawing, a building, a model—it's all equally meaningful."

JANE MAYBANK 06.93

Petit Jour (#57) glass bowl, designed by Gaetano Pesce.
Following spread: photograph by **Criswell Lappin**

GAETANO PESCE'S EMPTY BOTTLES

"When you work with this gun, you work with a lot of heat, so we drink a lot, so we have all these bottles around," Pesce says. "So we start to think about what we can do with all of them. Beer bottles, mineral water bottles, black wine bottles. All these bottles."

Out of all these bottles came Pastis, a new technique that involves heating intact or broken glass bottles to varying temperatures to form them into large plates or broad, flat bowls. The bottles are either placed by themselves in the mold and heated until they flatten and melt, or they're placed between panes of ordinary window glass and heated to two-dimensionality. Either way they end up looking like what you would get if you put bottles on a railroad track to be run over by a train—if the glass didn't break. "Again, it is an evolution," Pesce says, "and the result is personalized. We put the bottles in the oven; it depends on the heat how much they melt, but they keep their shape. I said, look, we can use simple, inexpensive, banal materials, and get something very personalized."

The individuality of each piece is a matter of great importance to Pesce. The glass objects are idiosyncratic and distinct, despite the fact that they are created by an industrialized process. The Pastis series includes broad platters of different color bottles fused together in an indistinguishable mass; brown bottles overlapped with clear in a near plaid; watery green bottles solidified in a luminous mass like a piece of a creek going over rocks; inky expanses of shiny black bottles like oil slicks on a dark river at midnight. There are large bowls with fragments of bottles suspended in clear glass that are supported on thick metal stanchions. SARAH DUNCAN 11.93

145

NO ARCHITECT HAS ANY POWER. BECAUSE THE DEVELOPERS HAVE IT—OUR CONTROLLERS—JUST AS THE ARCHBISHOPS DID IN THE FOURTEENTH CENTURY.

PHILIP JOHNSON 11.98

THE MOST E

OPERATING

DESIGN IS T

INDIVIDUAL

I STICK TO

MORE I LIKE

NIELS DIFFRIENT

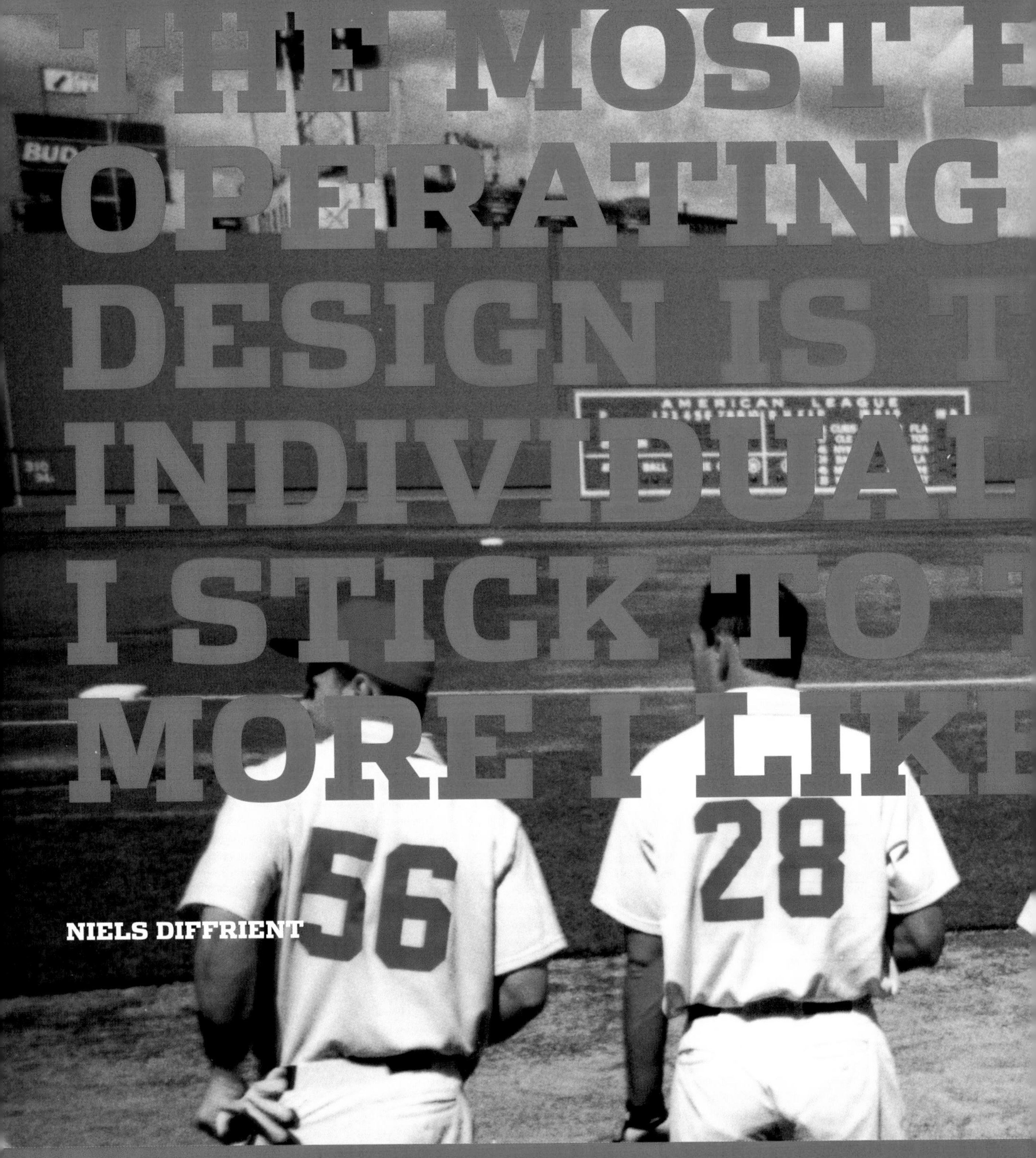

FFICIENT
SYSTEM IN
E SINGLE
THE MORE
HAT, THE
IT.

FRANCE'S HOWARD ROARK: JEAN NOUVEL

Formidable is the word—intoned as the French do, with its syllables stretched out in all their grandeur and menace—that seizes you when you first encounter him. Amidst the cerebral bow ties and languid aesthetes who populate the club of world-class architects, Jean Nouvel is another breed altogether—a savage savant. Tall, powerfully built, and dressed entirely in black, with a massive, nearly bald head and Mephistophelian eyebrows, he is France's version of Howard Roark, played this time by a punk-style Yul Brynner.

Unlike so many of his peers, who have made careers theorizing about architecture, Nouvel has concentrated on building, and his structure may be the most daringly imaginative to define the modern landscape. When he does theorize—and this is a man of tremendous intellect—he draws on the realms of contemporary cinema, art, philosophy, and physics, putting forth ideas that are as provocative as they are startlingly original.

He believes, for example, that the practice of architecture must be radically rethought because the explosion in communication technologies has irrevocably transformed the way we live, think, and interrelate. Architecture can no longer be based on cultural models of the past (he calls such attempts a "scourge/a symptom of the disintegration of architectural thought") but must instead express the emotions and senses, the images and signs, of the times. And so Nouvel's mysteriously luminous, sleek black opera house in Lyon resonates with sci-fi imagery: the pitch-hued armor of Darth Vader in STAR WARS and the ebony monolith in 2001: A SPACE ODYSSEY. And his miraculously transparent Fondation Cartier in Paris, which from certain vantages seems to disappear into its surrounding parkland, plays with current philosophical notions of boundary and virtuality.

Nouvel insists it is not just contemporary culture that is changing but, more important, the very framework for its ideas and structures: the city. "What has happened in our century is that we have lived through a kind of urban cataclysm [due to] the population shifts in the industrialized countries and the demographics of the Third World," he says. "It is almost as if a geological stratum has broken over the cities of the planet. There are five or ten times more people than before and no existing design for any order." Because of this, the city has been "blown wide open. [It] has become an urban cosmos, a multicentered nebula ... where things are perpetually forming and dispersing." For Nouvel this implies "the end of formal planning, general rules, and zoning."
MARISA BARTOLUCCI 06.94

BREATHING FREEDOM WITH
CHARLOTTE PERRIAND

Here in Paris, Perriand, the designer best known as a collaborator of Le Corbusier, takes me on a tour of her apartment, which she recently doubled in size by buying a neighboring unit and having the wall between them torn down. For years she lived in a tiny flat housing the library-study where we sit, a bedroom just off it, and a Japanese-style kitchen—complete with a Japanese cook—upstairs. She's playfully competitive about her space, challenging me when I say that my Paris apartment is even smaller.

"But doesn't mine look much larger?" **Perriand asks.** It does, remarkably so. The key to clean, modern living, she says, is to keep possessions to a minimum. Storage is a favorite fetish—"There must be a space to put everything away"—every wall seems lined with cupboards and shelves. She believes firmly that less is more, decrying "consumer society" and constantly coming back to the importance of simplicity, even for kids. "I've seen children playing with dolls made of rags more happily than they would with all those Barbies," she says. "The more they have, the less they'll be happy. That's why I'm for limiting things. So that we can breathe freedom."

If Perriand's design philosophy is nicely housed in her old apartment, the new addition—which is all polished wood and smooth lines—seems to take it a step further. Perriand softens a bit on the tour. She's whimsical at times, and I notice that she's wearing brightly colored ribbons wound in her hair: "Don't you think I'm in an adorable environment?"   PENELOPE ROWLANDS 01/02.96

149

WE'VE BROUGHT MORE
PUBLICITY TO MEMPHIS THAN
ELVIS. HE DIDN'T CALL HIM-
SELF "ELVIS MEMPHIS."

ETTORE SOTTSASS 07/08.85

ETTORE SOTTSASS: TRY TO BE NICE

About his glass vases, Sottsass once said he was trying to create the sense that there was "a uniquely strange object in the room." They are indeed extraordinary, brightly colored hybrids of sculpture and laboratory glass with such names as Black Hole and Sacred Asparagus—but this comment could apply to his other work as well. His creations are unique, and therefore they endure. Even long obsolete machines designed by the master linger in the hearts of those who care about good design. David Kelley raves about Sottsass's mainframe. "His computers were so human. They had mouths and faces." MoMA curator Paola Antonelli describes Olivetti's Valentine typewriter as "little, sexy, fun, witty"; Paolo Polledri recalls the fine design frenzy of typing his application to architecture school on one.

For Polledri, Sottsass's investigations have an intellectual edge. "It's his relentless pursuit of going back to the essence of things, never taking anything for granted, never ceasing to question what his work is about. It's easy to take what he does as an artistic statement, but if you look at it, it's a sort of investigation about forms and materials and about the place of objects in our lives."

That investigation continues for Sottsass in his ninth decade. Age doesn't seem to have changed his life much: besides his work at Sottsass Associati, he continues an active freelance life and still spends time traveling the world, taking photographs almost everywhere, particularly in India and China. What has changed is his assessment of his own place in the world. "I feel this nonsense in everything around me," he tells me more than once. "Young people are very aggressive and very presumptuous, and I was one of them. I thought I knew everything. Now I know I know nothing."

He describes his approach to life as "one that's been developed over a thousand years by Vedic thinking." His advice to the rest of the world, "Try to be nice. You know life is so funny—and so stupid. Give up, and know every minute of your life that the whole system is nonsense. Metaphysically it's just nonsense." He sits back from his desk, as inscrutable as a cat, and I notice for the first time that all the pencils in a cylindrical holder on his desk are colored ones, and only in shades of orange or yellow. The reporter in me seizes on this tiny fact, determined to wring some meaning, however minuscule, from it. But then, Sottsass-like, I let it float away. Across from me, the most famous designer alive falls quiet for a while, then asks politely but firmly, "Can we stop now?" We do.
PENELOPE ROWLANDS 12.97/01.98

WHEN PHILIPPE STARCK WAS A FISH

I shall tell you about when I was a bacteria. Perhaps not a bacteria. Perhaps when I was a fish. Very young. And when I was a fish, everything was okay because my wife made eggs. She loved to do that. One time the eggs went away with the stream. No problem. Sort of like caviar. That's why a lot of us big fish eat our caviar. We don't have really serious relationships with these eggs. After, I became a little older, and we became sort of like frogs. We went on the ground, and things were less simple. There was a small problem because, like every year, my wife made the caviar, but the caviar stayed on the beach. And she saw the eggs and she said, "Wow, it's so beautiful. I never saw eggs like that." Me too: I love caviar. And she said, "I love this egg so much, I want to protect it." Yes, okay, I said, you can make a box like this with elastic around it. "No, not like that. I want to protect it. I want it to get better. What can you do?" I said, Me, I don't know. I know nothing about how to protect an egg. Me, I am a hunter. I hunt whales. T. Rex. Enormous monsters and things like that. PHILIPPE STARCK 10.98

152

MICHAEL JACKSON WAS BOTH THE HIGH POINT AND THE LOW POINT OF THE EIGHTIES. HIS MUSIC IN THE EARLY PART OF THE DECADE, LIKE 'BILLIE JEAN' WAS REALLY GREAT. BUT THEN HE TURNED INTO A PIECE OF PLASTIC. HE SYMBOLIZED THE WHOLE SHIFT IN THE EIGHTIES FROM REALITY TO HYPERMARKETS.

TUCKER VIEMEISTER 10.89

INGO MAURER'S VERY PRIVATE DIALOGUE WITH LIGHT

"Day and night, they rise and fall on silent wings. Pure soundless miracles." These are not the lines of one of the Metaphysical or Romantic poets, but of the German designer Ingo Maurer, trying to describe his obsession with light in all its manifestations. Lyrically inspired lighting fixtures like Don Quixote, Ya Ya Ho, and Tijuca have made him one of the field's foremost creators. It is because of his reverence for light, he explains at the start of our conversation, that he is so deeply bothered by "light pollution," the wanton use of illumination in urban life.

What he means by this is "the unholy alliance of light and power." Maurer adds, "Just think of the wealthy firms all over the world, how they illuminate their buildings. What irritates me is not the way light is used. That, of course, may look brilliant and wonderful. It's just the ulterior motive of self-representation and power, the lack of decency, modesty, of humanity, vanishing into nothingness. It's the dreadful attitude of 'Big Brother is watching you' from George Orwell's 1984." For Maurer this is the abuse of light's myth: "Going back into history, you'll find that dictatorships—for example, the Third Reich—were very aware of light's mystical and religious connotations and how to misuse them for their own doubtful purposes."

Tall and charismatic, with longish gray hair curling around his face and warm, deep brown eyes behind his small, frameless oval spectacles, Maurer is all open-minded friendliness. He was born in 1932 on the island of Reichenau on Lake Constance, in the southwestern-most region of Germany, known for its mild climate and abundant flowers, fruit, and vegetables. It was here that Maurer first became captivated by light's complex qualities. "The reflections of light on the sea, on water, impressed me very deeply," he remembers. "Already as a little child I found myself watching the light reflections on a boat or on a wall." This experience of communing with light and shadow deepened with the years. "I have a very private dialogue with light. When I see something outside in nature that has to do with the sun—a beautiful reflection on a wall or on the leaves of a tree—I sometimes thank God for all the beauty there is."

Early in our conversation he mentions what he considers the guiding principles of his soft revolution in lighting. First and foremost the work should be evocative—you should see more than there is. But Maurer wants to go beyond mere illusion: "I am interested in transforming the so-called vulgar into the sublime, the spiritual. It's the tickling of fantasy that attracts me. You can look at an object just as something plain or as a miracle." Or as the Russian painter Kasimir Malevich put it, "For the poet, the sun isn't always the sun." SYBILLE BRANTL 04.94

153

TIBOR KALMAN'S GOOFINESS AND INTELLIGENCE

To those of us who cared for Tibor Kalman and care for him still, his death, at the absurdly young age of 49, represents a deprivation that will be keenly felt for some time. His significance for METROPOLIS readers, most of whom are involved in design and architecture, will almost certainly be lasting.

Tibor was not merely successful and uncompromising: he was a moralist. He devoted real time and effort to articulating a coherent set of beliefs about the activity of design. Although there are many practitioners of design, and almost as many theorists, Tibor was a prolific creative director who delivered an ongoing commentary about what design is and should be. The fact that his presentations and pronouncements were often outrageous and funny did little to disguise the thoughtfulness and depth of feeling he brought to the subject.

Like Victor Papanek and Buckminster Fuller, **Tibor began with the assumption that design matters.** Or to put it differently, that if it doesn't matter, designers have no one but themselves to blame. Unlike many others who frown on fashioning baubles for the wealthy or manufacturing diversions for the stylish, Tibor was capable of being utterly absorbed by album covers and music videos and restaurant interiors. He just refused to limit himself. One of the reasons why he was able to wander far from the confines of the politically correct—despite being a passionately committed activist—was that, more than anything else, he loved the excitement of the new.

Moving to Rome to edit COLORS magazine, directing a television commercial for Subaru, developing a line of watches: these were leaps into the void for Tibor. If he had suddenly taken up mountain climbing or marathon running his colleagues and collaborators would have been mystified. There is little need to battle heat exhaustion sprinting through the desert or to test the limits of endurance on Himalayan ranges when you seek out such huge challenges during regular working hours.

In what he did as well as what he said, in the way he ran his company and the way he celebrated and delighted in his status as an outsider, he exhorted others to resist the comfort of easy certainties and received opinions. Of course, no one who worked with him would ever have been inclined to sink into a relaxed, predictable or boring routine.

The collaborator who wasn't a little intimidated was simply not paying attention. It wasn't just that Tibor had a formidable brain or that he had extremely good ideas. It was that he disregarded the rules, to brilliant effect. This resulted in a natural and sometimes all-too-visible impatience with the conventional and the lazy.

Collaboration was both a blessing and a curse for Tibor. It enabled him to make progress as an artist and designer—and frequently caused him frustration bordering on anguish. As anyone who worked with him will attest, he was fiercely opinionated. He lived with the tension that inevitably arises when a creative director propelled by the force of his own ideas has no taste for compromise.

154

A few years ago, over lunch in Rome—I had come to write for the AIDS issue of COLORS—Tibor expressed his irritation about an important piece of the introduction that we were struggling with. I told him that he was not allowed to give me that why-didn't-I-get-someone-else-for-this-job look. But I knew well, after our long history of friendship and collaboration, that once Tibor had a certain kind of belief in you, nothing he said needed be taken personally. He had enormous affection for all of the people who made up his staff. As a colleague and office mate of many years, I spent a lot of time with this evolving family uptown and down, and I count myself fortunate.

There was another way to earn Tibor's trust. Be Maira. Tibor's enormous faith in his wife's ideas and creative instincts isn't just an important part of his biography. It would be absurd and presumptuous to offer an explanation of why Maira was more his partner than his muse or sounding board. There was something about the way that Tibor referred to Maira as an artist, some years ago, that made a lasting impression. I had the idea at the time that he was talking about her ability to remain true to her creative instincts. She had then, as she does now, the playfulness and originality that drives a very specific type of person—an artist—to continuously rearrange and re-create the world. And as everyone who knows her can attest, Maira is profoundly funny.

This was true of both Tibor and Maira when I first met them. We were all just out of college, and what is remarkable to me now is how much Tibor was already the person who would later go on to influence so many others. He combined an outsize, enthusiastic goofiness with a sharply focused intelligence. Part of his considerable appeal came from this unlikely combination, which was expressed in a relentlessly ironic humor.

But then paradox and irony are the natural habitat of the rebellious. A great deal of the work Tibor and Maira and company created explored the tensions between the expected and the actual, the rich and the poor, the professional and the amateur, design and un-design. And it was all done in a consistently witty, distinctive Dadaist language. In an industry plagued by pomposity and self-importance, much of their work managed to be funny and charming. A cornerstone of their style—the silly-clever magic of Maira's books may be its purest expression—was the refusal to take themselves too seriously.

DANNY ABELSON 08/09.99

WE TOLERATE TOO MUCH. AND I THINK IT HURTS US.

BILL STUMPF 11.86

SNAPSHOTS BY DAVID CARSON

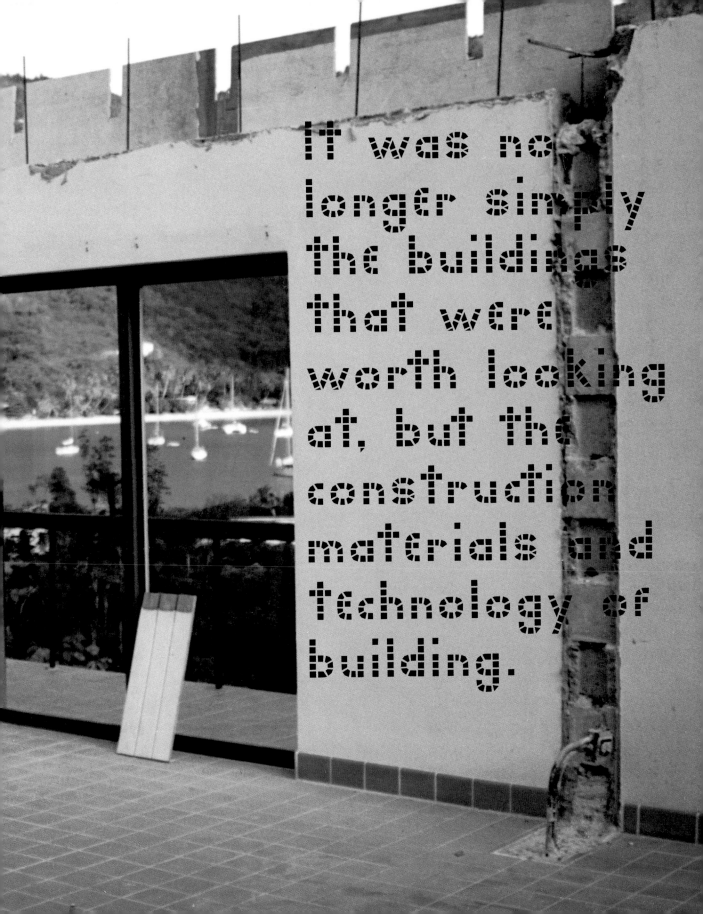

It was no longer simply the buildings that were worth looking at, but the construction materials and technology of building.

buildings

Writing in the first issue of METROPOLIS (July 1981), John Pile observed that New York City was an open-air museum of the history of architecture. For several years following that we concerned ourselves with the sense and seriousness of how the "museum" considered future acquisitions, be they assorted museum additions and expansions, Donald Trump's proposed 150-story TV City, or the conversion of the old Fillmore East into the Saint, a club with a dance floor enclosed in an immense white eighty-foot-diameter dome. In an era of unmitigated spending, questioning the social, economic, even moral circumstances of such building seemed a valid enterprise.

Not surprisingly, this period of extravagance was followed by sober introspection. Since then the questions have extended themselves to a much broader landscape. It was no longer just aesthetic considerations but construction materials and technology that came under scrutiny. It became clear that buildings could suffer illnesses with the same intensity that people do. As "sick-building syndrome" became a familiar phrase and questions about sustainability in architecture emerged, toxicity of materials, air pollution, energy conservation, and the more general life cycle of materials were all recognized as legitimate concerns of the design and construction industries.

No less important was the social environment of building: Does a 47-story mixed-use apartment building with a gym, a pool, a post office, and ten movie theaters bring new amenities to a neighborhood or does it simply deplete its city block of street life, energy, and services? Sometimes the questions seemed tinged with absurdity. For example, how can the 4.2 million square feet of retail space in the Mall of America be designed to seem more intimate? Looking ahead into the new millennium, Alexandra Lange asks whether and how the urban rooftop can serve as a viable building lot.

Of course, all of these questions can be asked in a variety of ways—through words, photographs, and drawings, even cartoons. But regardless of how the ideas are conveyed, writers, photographers, and artists approach their subject not so much as professional critics who speak with an arcane jargon, but as users, participants, fully engaged inhabitants of the modern landscape. Introducing the work of several architectural photographers, Luc Sante suggests that they "have turned their empathetic lenses on the physical world as humans have redefined it." The same might be said for the articles, drawings, and photographs included here, because consistent in all these pieces—whether it is about a mosque in uptown Manhattan, a casino in Connecticut, or a Tribeca rooftop—is the recognition that buildings exist in a wider landscape, structures that both reflect and influence the environment around them. Akiko Busch

164

AARON BETSKY
AKIKO BUSCH
THOMAS J. CAMPANELLA
DAVID CARSON
NOAH CARTER
JAMES MARSTON FITCH
VICTORIA GEIBEL
SEAN HEMMERLE
KARRIE JACOBS
BEN KATCHOR
JOHN KELLY
ALEXANDRA LANGE
CRISWELL LAPPIN
PETER LEMOS
HUGO LINDGREN
WILLIAM MITCHELL
NINA RAPPAPORT
KIRK SEMPLE
JULIUS SHULMAN
MICHAEL SORKIN
ANTOINETTE LE VAILLANT
JOHN VOELCKER
JIM ZOOK

THERE WAS NO WAY TO MAKE IT BLEND IN.

JOSEPH VANCE 2001

Rooftop addition, designed by Joseph Vance at Warren
Street and West Broadway, in New York.
Photograph by **John Petrarca**

DESIGN IS **BUILDINGS**

CASTLES IN THE AIR

Since the early part of the twentieth century architects have had their eyes on the sky.
The promise of the skyscraper, it seemed, was to create an alternate urban landscape
30 stories up. Luckily for the agoraphobics among us that vision never became reality.
Instead New York divided into a city that seems to be topped by a suburb.

Exhibit A sits—perches, if you're a friend, looms, if you're a foe—on
the corner of Warren Street and West Broadway, at the southern edge of Tribeca, one
long block outside the protected historic district. It is a four-and-a-half-story addition
to a five-story 1860s edifice. Now that all traces of its industrial origins have been
replaced with new wooden windows, a new corrugated awning, and new stucco stories, it
will be known as the Munitions Building. "There was no way to make it blend in," says
its architect, Joseph Vance. "With the zoning setbacks, it was an asymmetrical envelope
to start with—on top of an Italianate building that was nicely done and very symmetri-
cal. So we decided to make it sculptural and abstract."

One man's sculpture, however, is another man's eyesore. Talk to anyone
who looks to the rooftops of Tribeca, and they will complain about 60 Warren Street, with
remarks ranging from "ungainly" and "sad" to "nightmarish." "They reinterpreted the laws
of the building department," says Carole De Saram, a longtime member of Community
Board 1 and a member of the team that got Tribeca's cast-iron facades and Rococo rooflines
landmarked in 1992 to ensure that new construction would not destroy the character of
the neighborhood. She says, "The whole city has run amok; there are signs everywhere. It's
wrong." In the case of Exhibit A, there were emergency meetings and threats of lawsuits,
but now the single condominium unit has been sold to one very lucky family—they don't
have to look at their new home.

Historic districts are defined by the Landmarks Preservation Commission
as having a "distinct sense of place" because the architecture typifies significant periods of
city history. In Tribeca buildings are generally low and chunky, faced with red brick or marble and tall windows. Although many are former factories, they are now being reborn as
million-dollar lofts, more reminiscent of Renaissance palazzos. And although all proposed
building in the area must pass a design review by the commission, it is the vagaries of such
reviews that often engender controversy.

"The neighborhood has reacted to it as a true sin," says John Petrarca of
Guenther Petrarca Architects. He walks by 60 Warren Street every day en route from his
Tribeca home to his Tribeca office. Petrarca is amused by the current flap, but hardly surprised. "I think this thing was the point when someone built something that was so large
and out of character that the neighborhood finally woke up and said 'My God, what's that?'"

The rooftops issue is a microcosm of fears of overdevelopment across
the city: in Tribeca one developer wants to build a hotel on a 25-foot-wide lot; on the Upper
East Side Woody Allen successfully contested a high-rise apartment building that was to
be built on top of a two-story Citibank branch. There's a sense that no space is too small or
too odd to be renovated into housing. And in neighborhoods with a surplus of century-old

167

three- and four-story industrial buildings, it is the rooftop that often seems the most inviting building lot. The roofscape of Tribeca is serving as a testing ground that may help to determine whether rooftop acreage can induce new, innovative building for much-needed space or whether it is simply another venue for architectural ostentation, congestion, greed.

Since the early 1990s Petrarca has been tracking his neighborhood's building boom from the perspective of the sky, watching as the first generation of rooftop structures—quaint architecture-without-architects, greenhouses and Astroturf lawns of Tribeca's artist-pioneers—have been replaced by boxing gyms and landscaped gardens. The scale of building has changed as well, with small, one-room additions giving way to more expansive structures that are out of scale with both the building and neighborhood below.

Petrarca and partner Robin Guenther have participated in the boom by converting former office buildings into lofts (in one case cutting scores of new windows into what had been a light-free refrigeration facility). Working on these projects, Petrarca gained access to some of the neighborhood's highest places, as well as a clear view of what was essentially the second front in the developers' war for square-footage.

In 1995 a change in the zoning laws made it possible to add one or more stories to many of the former manufacturing buildings, as long as they were not built to their maximum permissible volume. Such additions needed to receive approval from the landmarks commission, but usually, with a sufficient setback from the front facade of the building, they remained invisible from the street, thus easily gaining a "certificate of no effect."

"Most of a developer's profit is in the penthouse," Petrarca says, "so economics dictate getting the maximum number of apartments up high." The usual method is to carve out a courtyard from the middle of the building and add that donut hole back on top. Sometimes the donut turns into an extension of the building, seemingly pulled straight up; other times, it's a smaller multistory box, like a building on top of the building. Unless you were privileged to own an apartment on the third floor or above, you might never have noticed there was a whole city being built behind the parapets.

Petrarca started taking pictures for a proposed book, HIDDEN TRIBECA, about the community's rooftop acreage. He joined the community board, serving as chair of the landmarks committee (but quit last year to spend more time with his kids). And he formed the Lower Manhattan Designers League with landscape architect Nancy Owens, to try to start a discussion not just about what rooftop structures look like, but about what they should look like. Not that he envisions any strict guidelines or edicts about rooftop structures; Petrarca recognizes the urban rooftop as an aerie landscape that, by nature, invites innovative building. Yet when such innovations are out of scale, the entire neighborhood suffers. What he is hoping for most may simply be some loose community consensus—and awareness—about what gets built on the roof.

"When I started taking pictures, most of the roofs looked like that," Petrarca says, pointing to a six-story building on Franklin and Church Streets. "See that, with the Astroturf and the kids' toys and the raised deck with a cute little umbrella table? This was the Tribeca roofscape circa 1990." We are on top of one of his firm's latest conversions, the former city office building at 90 Franklin Street. (Although the building is finished, having been its architect seems to give Petrarca permanent rooftop access as far as the doorman is concerned.) They added a petite zinc-sided addition that is not visible from the street. Half of the structure is a gym with a stellar southern Manhattan view, the other half is a private quarter-circle aerie now owned by Mariah Carey. "She hasn't moved in yet," Petrarca remarks dryly. "She's on her fourth decorator."

Three doors down from the umbrella table is another of Petrarca's favorite pre-1995 sites. "There's the little suburban house with shingles—which is totally illegal; you're not allowed to have shingles in New York City," he says. "It looks like they brought two trailers and put them together up there. It has a cathedral ceiling—it's straight out of New Jersey. "

Petrarca may mock these suburban pretensions, yet he'd prefer that there be more pitched-roof cottages, Argentinian cabins (a pianist who rebuilt his childhood home), and 1970s beach houses. In his view these idiosyncratic structures at least offer visual interest. Less acceptable are the myriad yellow, taupe, and tan stucco boxes—bland, unobtrusive structures designed to get a "certificate of no effect" from the Landmarks Preservation Commission and thus a quick approval. Although they offend few, they also seem oblivious to the rooftop tradition of innovation and wit; the rooftop is, after all, a place where one expects more earthbound restrictions to be loosened. Implicit is the idea that rooftop building can manage to fit in and be innovative. Petrarca's zinc box, for example, with its unusual sheathing material, manages to blend in with the charcoal roofing material ubiquitous elsewhere on adjacent rooftops.

"We tried a number of public forums to convince people that the landmarks commission was more open to this sort of stuff," Petrarca says, pointing to his favorite structure of all: a petite glass box with a roof deck of its own, accessible via a steel spiral staircase. The folly—a cafeteria for a small company—is toylike, lightweight, and above all else, fun. "A lot of them remain extraordinary interior spaces. So you can't see these by inches from the street, but go anywhere else in Tribeca—go up into your apartment, go into anyplace else—and you can see these things. The landmarks rule is that you can't see them from public right-of-way, so as structures they have been driven into this fairly generic nothing. More interesting things that you could see a little more of would be better."

On the community board, Petrarca couldn't push his own definition of "interesting" too strongly, but it is clear where he's coming from. Trained at Carnegie Mellon and the Architectural Association in London, he's dreaming of Rem Koolhaas's DELIRIOUS NEW YORK, or Coop Himmelblau's steel creepy-crawlies. That hasn't happened yet, and Petrarca's not quite sure how it could, barring open competitions or more public design presentations.

His most successful outreach effort was a public meeting, at local restaurant Capsouto Freres in spring 1998, that brought together neighbors, members of the Landmarks Preservation Commission, and local architects and developers involved in building the penthouses. At the meeting Petrarca gave his rooftop slide show, commission

169

chair Jennifer Raab spoke, and landmarks consultant Bill Higgins discussed the contextual framework for Tribeca's architecture. By all accounts it was a success.

"Since [Raab's appointment] it has become clearer that landmarks is willing to be intellectually engaged," says architect Harry Kendall of Byrns, Kendall and Schieferdecker. "They are not a regulatory agency that sees their role as preventing disaster. They are trying and succeeding in the very difficult process to demand good design." Kendall's firm is responsible for one of the largest visible additions to have been approved by the commission on its aesthetic merit: a three-story addition to the Fisher Mills buildings on Greenwich Street. Another positive sign, from the architects' point of view, is the approval of GDM Project's six-story ribbon-windowed building for the corner of Laight and Hudson Streets (designed by Dana Sottile). "I applaud them for allowing it to happen," Petrarca says. "Whether it's the perfect example of what you want can be debated."

170

Most other Tribeca architects tend to agree with the first part of his statement: the more modernity, the better. No one wants to see a repeat of the Tribeca Grand (just outside the landmark district's lines), a newly built hotel that is a thin, cheap-looking attempt to copy the look of a warehouse. "I live down by the World Trade Center, and one of the things I used to love to do with my kids was to go to a telescope on the World Trade Center and look at the amazing play of architectures across the rooftops of the city," says Peter Wheelwright, an architect and chair of the architecture department at Parsons. "It is another world up there, and it is a place where I think unfettered creativity can take place out of the governing purview of a lot of Manhattan zoning-code issues."

Still, what constitutes "unfettered creativity" remains open to question. Even Munitions Building architect Vance's rhetoric is almost identical to Petrarca's: "The tendency a lot of people have is to put up a nondesign, nondescript stucco box that is monochromatic and formless," he says. "We have all these beautiful buildings in Tribeca, and I wonder what are we contributing that people 100 years from now will consider worthy of saving?"

Vance seems unlikely to win the public relations battle. Although he says he's gotten more positive comments than negative ones, after speaking with me, he calls back and leaves a message asking that the building not be photographed in its unfinished state. "Now it looks like a big gray blob, but the final colors were very carefully honed and selected, breaking down the apparent mass. It's going to be a collection of geometries."

Obviously the fight has yet to be won. "Every time I come up here I see fewer of the old style," Petrarca says. A perfunctory check of the Landmarks Preservation Commission Web site confirms the impression that there are more penthouses to come. What are now ghostly volumes of orange construction webbing protected by brilliant blue tarps will, real estate market willing, be some family's dream apartment in six months.

Now that he's no longer on the community board Petrarca has been able to take professional advantage of local projects. He's designed and developed five new eco-conscious townhouses on Reade and Greenwich Streets (one for his own family) that he hopes will be completed by the beginning of 2001. The luxury properties—with geothermal heating and cooling, radiant floors, and nontoxic glues and paint—all sold immediately to families with three-plus children. "We marketed the energy efficiency as an amenity," Petrarca says proudly. In addition, he's got his own rooftop project before the landmarks powers-that-be: a two-story, highly visible addition to the Eagle Transfer warehouse on Laight Street, north of the wide-open space that marks the entrance to the Holland Tunnel. He's proposed a crisp, almost crystalline glass-and-steel box not unlike a supermini-malist (even Gwathmey-esque) house. "I had to put my money where my mouth was," he jokes, nervous about coming before the commission he spent so much time convincing other people was open to the twentieth century.

But of course the question is how industrial building stock from the nineteenth century can best be put to use in the twenty-first century. And the rooftop land-scape of Manhattan Island, defined on all sides by its rivers, has become a lab of sorts for these questions. But there are other cities bound by geographic boundaries that may man-date building up—consider San Francisco, already bursting at the seams. What the Tribeca roofscape may offer is not a model of strict guidelines and codes for such construction, but rather a prototype landscape that demonstrates both the risks and rewards of going through the roof. ALEXANDRA LANGE 2001

I THINK OF HOUSES IN TERMS OF SKELETONS, THE PLUMBING AND ELECTRICITY AS NERVES AND BLOOD VESSELS. THE WATER-TOWER MIGHT BE THE BLADDER. OR PERHAPS THE TEAR DUCTS.

RACHEL WHITEREAD 06.98

172

I'M JUST BOTHERED BY THE BASIC ATTITUDES ABOUT THE WAY PEOPLE DEAL WITH THE WORLD. IT'S OUT THERE TICKING AWAY REALLY NICELY, AND PROVIDING ALL SORTS OF GOODIES THAT PEOPLE SEEM TO IGNORE—THEY'RE TOO BUSY BUILDING THINGS SO THAT THEY CAN SAY 'I BUILT THIS!'

TERRY GILLIAM 09.91

THIS AIN'T NO PARTY

Some of the most expensive architecture in this city is invisible. In the most popular and profitable nightclubs of New York, the stuff that goes into making walls, ceilings, and ducts disappears. Clubs are architectural laboratories, places where designers are inventing new ways of ordering our environment. The $1 million or more that is necessary for the building of such a space goes toward creating the illusion that neither you nor the physical space are really there. Instead there is a fantasy world in which music is the only structure, lights the decorative scheme, the stage the only function.

A club can be put anywhere. Views are not important, and neither is location. The neighborhood must be preferably anonymous and industrial. The first step in the design of almost all of these clubs is to paint everything in sight black, or cover all the surfaces with mirrors, wrenching the space out of its location and structural limitations. The club turns inward, away from reality, toward a separate world pasted on the walls.

The fantasies created differ from club to club. Putting on the Ritz is easy in the East 11th Street club of that name, because there was some flashy material there with which to work. A converted 1930s movie palace, the club floats in waves of gold-painted board and pastel flowers attached with gilt imitations of ropes. The theater has been cleared and is inhabited only by a large, glittering hung column that contains all the material necessary for the light show.

At Interferon, a brand-new club on West 21st Street, the straight walls of a manufacturing loft have been covered with oblique walls and slanting buttresses. The sense that one has been dropped inside a military gray German bunker is enhanced by the gun-turret-like projection that serves as a sound booth.

The ultimate in illusionary design has been reached by the $3 million conversion of the old Fillmore East into The Saint. The dance floor here is enclosed in a huge white dome, a Buckminster Fuller-like creation 80 feet in diameter. Neon lights wash the dome from below, spots play off the curved surfaces, and a glittering ball spreads colored dots across the dome. But when the star projector (the same kind of device used in a planetarium) is turned on, the whole globe becomes a universe—an endlessly rotating vision of space in which one dances one's way through the stars.

The variable that disciplines and controls the range of spatial possibilities in these clubs is the music itself. Music has always had the ability to change one's spatial experience and mood, but here it determines when the lights will change, when the curtains will rise, and when the video image will flash. The music does tend to create a trip: a buildup of kinetic energy in which the space becomes increasingly smaller, more compact, and abstracted as the dancers work themselves into a rhythmic trance. Often the climax will consist of dull thuds and a continuous synthesized howl zooming through black or strobe-lit space. If the total design of the club—the decorations, lights, video, and music—is successful, the grand finale of the spatial experience is the disappearance of the club into abstract, hypnotic illusion. AARON BETSKY 08/09.81

GROWING PAINS

Michael Graves has long been known for his painterly penchant. During the past decade he has successively purveyed the iconography of classical and Renaissance art and architecture in his own work. In fact, to bolster his argument for his original plan of New York's Whitney Museum of American Art addition, Graves intentionally compared the overall building composition to a Renaissance annunciation painting. In that 1985 scheme he likened the role of his central cylinder to a connecting space in a Piero della Francesca diptych. Both act as hinges to connect yet divide the scenes on either side of them. But unlike the Renaissance composition, Graves's scheme, even as newly revised, exudes a sense of static conflict, not serene coexistence.

Even with the modified changes, Graves's new scheme for the Whitney recalls an image more recently recorded than the political or religious rituals of Renaissance art, that of Cubist fragmentation. By placing a ziggurat-shaped alabaster window on his building's red granite face (in line with the angled window of the original building), Graves has created an overall composition that registers as much discord as Picasso's fragmented female in the 1939 painting WOMAN WITH A BLUE HAT. With one eye horizontal, the other vertical, Picasso's woman is an image of schism, of the personality divided. In the revised addition to the Whitney, Graves's window (no longer a triangle, as in the original plan) is meant as a conciliatory gesture—a grudging acknowledgment of the presence and authority of the Marcel Breuer original built in 1966. The Graves building, however, does not submit readily to any notion of the Breuer building's supremacy. This is conflict held in check, antagonism sustained and not suppressed.

To Graves, this palpable tension is the inevitable result of two different sensibilities at work, a sign of the gulf "between Breuer's age and our own," he says. More than the effects of two different eras are at work in the Whitney scheme, however. This is a plan that encapsulates two polarities within those divergent periods. If Breuer epitomized one architectural camp in the 1960s, then Graves today symbolizes another. Juxtaposing the two is like placing competing rivals next to each other on an awards dais. Appropriate niceties are publicly exchanged, but neither is too happy about such close, tense, and provocative proximity.

As his recent career rise shows, Graves is an architect with the conviction of the converted. He has embraced postmodernism with a passion only a former Modernist could muster. (Though it's true his interest in historical references does not extend to Brutalism, the rough-concrete building style ably expressed by Breuer's Whitney.) Graves is not lackluster in his use of the postmodern palette, nor is he diffident in the expression of his beliefs ("I would do it again in a flash," he has said of his decision to accept the Whitney commission).

Such speedy enthusiasm, however, hit a snarl last year when community outcry and critical outrage pummeled his plans. In the face of that protest, Graves, as he explains, "nipped and tucked" his building. Slightly more exhibition space has been added in the internal plan. However, the auditorium, library, restaurant, museum offices, and

175

Clockwise from top right: Whitney Museum, Scheme One; Whitney Museum, Scheme Two; Whitney Museum, Scheme Three. Photographs by **William Taylor**, courtesy **Michael Graves & Associates**

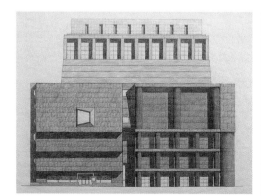

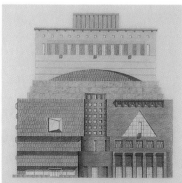

building operations have all been reduced, and the space for the study and storage of works on paper has been cut in half.

Gone is Graves's single most outrageous gesture: the "eyebrow" window on the extended top that would have spanned both the old and new buildings. The top still persists, but it has been reduced in size. It is now 47 feet lower than in the original proposal and set back 20 feet on the corners of the rear facade; this change was made possible by moving the elevators from the back to the center of the building. By lowering its height and inserting setbacks, the new top will be 60 percent smaller than it was in Graves's original proposal.

Also eliminated from the new plan is the 74th Street entrance. The restaurant, previously planned for the top floor, has been moved down to its old familiar site below grade (intended to be across from the new auditorium). For the first time all the galleries are to be contiguous. In the previous scheme, they were divided by a mechanical level placed between what were then the fifth and seventh floors. The mechanical level has now been moved to the top of the building, which has been scaled down from ten floors to eight. In all, more than 30,000 square feet in gross area have been eliminated from the original design.

Though practically every aspect of the building has undergone adjustment (except the price—$37.5 million), the hallmarks of Graves's initial imprimatur are still in place: the classical vocabulary and the prominent cylindrical column, intended practically as gallery space and subliminally as the "hinge" to link and demarcate Graves's design from Breuer's.

But more than just the visual vestiges of the old design remain. Also persisting is a lingering sense that this building carries the mandate to '"monumentalize" the Whitney's image. Like many a museum pleading spatial impoverishment these days, the Whitney needs more room. Less than 1 percent of its permanent collection can now be displayed. With the revised addition, that number will increase to only 3.6 percent. (This means that 275 paintings could be added to the 75 now on display at the site. The Whitney's various satellite museums, in staging rotating shows, do not keep works from the permanent collection on view indefinitely.) The motives for change, then, cannot be measured merely in spatial requirements. What is at stake here is something more subliminal, less quantifiable than straight square footage. One can only conclude that what the Whitney wants is to enlarge its scope and status within the national and international art communities.

No longer content to crouch behind the magisterial might of the Museum of Modern Art, witness to the Guggenheim's own snarled struggle to expand, chary over the Metropolitan's increasing encroachment on its traditional turf of American art, the Whitney is struggling to strike an image the public won't soon forget.

The Whitney is a museum that's willing to be ferociously of the moment, to exhibit the work of such media darlings as David Salle. As the Whitney's director, Tom Armstrong, has said, the museum's role lies in making "initial judgments about the merit of current work."

Interpreted at its most idealistic, Armstrong's comment reveals his museum's desired self-image as a critical force that sifts through prevailing sensibilities to define what work will inform the course of fine art. But in this period of pastiche, the Whitney has been criticized for pursuing the path of fashion more often than following the arduous course of adopting artists whose reputations are still to be made.

What better way to attract attention than with an architect who's unquestionably fashionable, who's unerringly "in" with the taste-making set? Graves's recent commissions, whether built or soon-to-be, attest to his popularity with the purveyors of art, architecture, and fashion. Witness the completed Diane von Furstenberg shop on Fifth Avenue, the planned Sotheby's condominium, the private winery in the Napa Valley, the current expansion of the Newark Museum, and, of course, the Whitney.

The question is not whether the Whitney chose the "wrong" architect. For the museum's purpose, Graves is exactly right. He's an architect accorded great attention by the media, a personality who projects well in public, an artist who conveys his ideas in engaging drawings that attract top prices—all in all, a highly marketable package. And in this moment when both art and architecture make for hot properties, Graves provides the Whitney with the means to achieve the high profile it so eagerly desires.

It is naive to think the Whitney should, or would, have left the Breuer building alone. If Graves had refused the commission out of righteousness, another architect would have accepted. And Breuer himself was no Boy Scout. In 1968 he proposed a 55-story tower intended to rise above Grand Central Terminal, no matter that the terminal had been designated a landmark only a few years earlier. He was also quite adamant in disdaining the "dumpy" look of the brownstones next to the Whitney.

Given the Whitney's resolve, it is no longer worth debating whether the Breuer building should be altered at all. The concern now is whether the revised scheme makes the most of much pent-up ambition and many built-in constraints (the site practically forced Graves to consider building up, since he could only build to the end of the block, the perimeter of the Whitney property). Sadly this is a scheme where schism is now entrenched, where stylistic division is now deeply rooted in the external design. In a composite photograph that presents the proposed addition superimposed next to Breuer's building, in a view looking south on Madison Avenue, what Graves calls his "mediating" cylinder juts out beyond Breuer's boundary wall, presenting a defiant and discordant parade of architectural styles. Neither the starkly brutal Modernist monument nor the seductively decorative postmodernist proposal for the late 1980s makes a connection to the neighborhood, which is in the Upper East Side Historic District. (Current zoning laws, it's important to note, no longer permit a stepped facade like Breuer's, should Graves even have wanted one. Buildings now must meet the sidewalk's edge.)

It may be some time before the Graves addition is built. For in the uproar and outrage that has pursued this project from the start, there is another factor that has often been overlooked in the critical controversy: to expand, the Whitney must convince a handful of stalwart tenants in the neighboring brownstones to move. So far 13 residential tenants are staying put, despite the Whitney's cash-laden entreaties for them to take off. As long as these people stay, the Whitney addition will remain no more than a model display. And so the human factor once again brings a lofty debate down from the ethereal clouds of critical review to the realm of reality. The conflict between the museum and its neighbors serves as a reminder that built architecture, unlike fine art, does impact on people's lives. In addition to relocating its recalcitrant neighbors, the Whitney still must move through the "Monopoly" game, including channels of city government approval.

Today, though, there seems something curiously fitting about the Whitney's choice of architect and its endorsement of the revised plan. For in its cloak of historical references and its resulting clash of context, the Graves building seems right at home on Madison Avenue. Like the parade of ultra-trendy, utterly self-conscious boutiques, bistros, and galleries that gaily line the street, this addition announces that it too partakes of the premise that fashion is the final arbiter of taste in these fickle times. **179**
VICTORIA GEIBEL 05.87

MARCEL AND MICHAEL (AND PHILIP)

Since announcing its expansion plans last spring, the Whitney Museum of American Art has advanced a number of intriguing arguments in support of its controversial plan to wrap a new addition designed by Michael Graves around its original 1966 building designed by Marcel Breuer. One frequently used line has been what might be called the "evolving museum" argument, which holds essentially that because museums must grow, museum architecture is by necessity often impermanent and expendable.

It's a sound enough argument. The problem is that one highly unlikely partisan recently came forward to deliver it: Philip Johnson—the same architect who at one point considered breaking his long relationship with the Museum of Modern Art (MoMA) because of the way Cesar Pelli's recent expansion impinged on his earlier additions, most notably on his sculpture garden.

Speaking in support of Graves's addition at a special public meeting held this summer by the New York Chapter of the American Institute of Architects, Johnson recounted his own experiences with MoMA, "which I have added to and have been added on to for some 50 years." Using every bit of his considerable charm to convince the assembled architects that all is forgiven and that, in essence, all is forgivable, Johnson reminded them that he "was the first villain that covered up a good deal of Mr. Goodwin's original excellent building. I took the cheese holes out of the roof," he noted. "The only man who was sad about that was Alfred Barr. Then I had to add a garden, which turned out to be a very pretty garden, but it did destroy the garden that was there. Again the only mourners were one tree and Mr. Barr. Then we come down to the present and Mr. Pelli, who faced much of what Mr. Graves has to face. The trustees did let him take a good bite out of what I considered to be my private garden. Again there was only one mourner, and that was me." PETER LEMOS 10.85

Top: Miller House, Palm Springs, California, by Richard Neutra, circa 1939; bottom: Mar Vista Development, Los Angeles, California, by Gregory Ain, 1950. Photographs by **Julius Shulman**

180

JULIUS SHULMAN SHOWS US HOUSES THAT WERE ONCE YOUNG AND BRASH AND RAKISH, SET TO INHERIT THE EARTH. THEY WERE THE OFFSPRING OF THE MARRIAGE OF EUROPEAN THEORY WITH THE FREE-SPENDING AND LIMITLESS SOUTHERN CALIFORNIA SUBURBAN LANDSCAPE. THEY HAD ARISTOCRATIC VEINS AND FACTORY WORKERS' HANDS, TONS OF COOL MATHEMATICAL RIGOR AND NO FANCY STUFF. THEY KNEW THEIR KIND WOULD SOON BE EVERYWHERE, THE WAY BIG CARS AND SCOTCH HIGHBALLS WERE EVERYWHERE. THEN THE EARTH REVOLVED A FEW TIMES. ECONOMIC CYCLES PASSED, AND SO DID THEIR MOMENT. THEY GOT SAD AND MAYBE A BIT MEAN, TOOK TO HUNKERING DOWN IN THE DESERT LIKE DISAPPOINTED IDEALISTS WITH GUNS.

LUC SANTE 04.99

COMPLEXITY AND COMPOSITION

What good is a computer to an architect? Palladio found pen and paper perfectly ade-
quate, after all. And it is hard to imagine Frank Lloyd Wright at a keyboard. (It just
doesn't go with a cape and cane.) The most sophisticated piece of technology on most
architects' desks even today is an electric pencil sharpener.

     The salesmen for Computer Aided Design (CAD) systems will tell you
that you can increase professional productivity by replacing drawing boards with graphics
work stations, and they will probably quote impressive productivity ratios. They may
be right. But it is notoriously difficult to measure productivity in any meaningful way in a
service profession; and it is certainly absurd to apply the industrial notion of productivity
to artistic activity (and I take it that architecture should be at least partly that). In any
case, we have an oversupply of architects in most developed Western countries, and every
year there are more people trying to get into the profession than there are places. It could
be argued, as a matter of social policy, that it would be better to create employment opportunities by decreasing individual professional productivity.

     You might take the view that achieving higher architectural quality,
rather than doing projects more quickly and cheaply, is the proper end of computer use.
That is an attractive ideal. But there is no extensive body of distinguished computer-aided
architectural design work to point to—at least not yet. At best you can find a few isolated
tours-de-force to offset the leaden banalities that many firms are proudly popping out of
their shiny new CAD systems.

     We will not, in fact, find the answer by looking for ways in which com-
puters can perform traditional design functions more quickly, or cheaply, or thoroughly,
or accurately than a human architect. There are some ways, but that is largely beside the
point. The real importance of computer graphics for architecture is that it provides new
ways of representing buildings, of manipulating those representations, and of interpreting
them in various useful ways. A design process supported by a computer graphics system is
qualitatively different from one carried out with pencil and paper: it has an altered pace
and sequence; brings information to bear on decisions in new patterns; renders the visual
effects of geometric, color, and lighting decisions with unprecedented speed and precision;
and so allows architectural ideas and effects to be explored in ways that were unimaginable
before now. Computer graphics promise architects an aesthetic adventure—one that is
just beginning.

     What are these new ways of representing buildings? We can best begin
to understand them by considering some canonical definitions of architecture.

     One traditional way to represent a building design, for example, is by
means of lines—usually drawn on paper. When we use this method of representation,
architectural design becomes (at one level of consideration) a matter of manipulating lines.
In his TEN BOOKS OF ARCHITECTURE, the great Italian Renaissance architect L. B.
Alberti defined architecture, in these terms, as follows: "We shall first lay down, that the
whole art of building consists in the design, and in the structure. The whole force and

182

rule of the design consists in a right and exact adapting and joining together the lines and angles which compose and form the face of the building." By "lines" Alberti meant straight segments (vectors) and circular arcs. Operations of "adapting and joining together" lines to produce compositions were performed by executing Euclidean constructive procedures (for parallels, perpendiculars, bisectors, tangents, and so on) with straightedges and compasses. Lines could be projected from three-dimensional space onto a two-dimensional surface by the newly invented (or rather, reinvented) method of perspective.

Another way to think of a building is as a collection of surfaces bounded and divided by lines, and made visible by light. This focuses attention on surface qualities of color, reflectivity, and texture, and the creation of relationships between these. In his polemic VERS UNE ARCHITECTURE, the young Le Corbusier set forth a stirring definition of architecture in these terms: "Mass and surface are the elements by which architecture manifests itself....Architecture is the masterly, correct, and magnificent play of masses brought together in light."

183

This is not merely an esoteric matter of aesthetic theory; it has direct technical implications for computer graphics. If we conceive of an architectural composition as a collection of surfaces, a "wire-frame" vector representation of a building will not serve us adequately; we will need to work with some kind of surface model. The simplest way to do this is to take closed planar polygons as data types. The shape of each polygon then becomes a low-level design variable. To define a composition, polygons must be located in space and assigned surface qualities, such as color.

Not all surfaces found in buildings are planar, of course. Cylindrical curvature is found on vaults and moldings, and spherical curvature is found on domes. Much more rarely, warped and spline surfaces of various kinds are found as well. So the surface modeling techniques that have been given so much attention in computer graphics have some role to play in architecture, though not so central a one as they play in automobile and aircraft body design.

Le Corbusier emphasized that the elements of a composition are "brought together in light." An architect is vitally interested in the lighting conditions, both natural and artificial, that will exist in and around a building, and how light will paint surfaces to create a visual experience. So a necessary adjunct of a surface model is a lighting model, which allows the characteristics of light sources to be specified and effects of light on surface to be displayed.

The simplest useful lighting model is based upon the cosine law for diffuse light incident upon an opaque matte surface. The light source is modeled either as a point in space or as a direction, together with an intensity value. The reflected light from a surface then is a function of the reflectivity of the surface and of the cosine of the angle that the incident light makes with the surface. This elementary lighting model, together with hidden surface perspective software and a raster display device, provides an architect with a very useful way to study building massing.

Architects are interested in sunlight; the ways the sun casts shadows on and around buildings at different times of the year, the patterns of sunlight penetration (insulation) through openings, and the thermal effects of sunlight incident upon the exposed surfaces of buildings are all vital architectural issues from both technical and aesthetic viewpoints. Two basic kinds of calculations are required to determine sun-lighting effects: calculation of sun position as a function of latitude, longitude, date, and time of day; and calculation of the pattern of east shadows as a function of sun position and building geometry. Calculation of sun position requires evaluation of some complicated trigonometric functions, whereas calculation of east shadows is isomorphic to the problem of generating a hidden-surface perspective of the building from the viewpoint of the sun. Both these calculations can be carried out by hand (indeed, there is a traditional architectural subject, sciagraphy, that is concerned with them), but they are extremely tedious and time-consuming. Use of a computer saves a great deal of time and effort, and allows more thorough explorations of sunlight and shadow effects to be carried out.

184

Much monumental architecture of the past (from the pyramids onward) was essentially a matter of opaque volumes, and the shading and shadowing effects of natural light. But Gothic cathedrals and baroque churches also made important compositional use of natural light transmitted through translucent and transparent planes of glass. Then the Industrial Revolution of the nineteenth century made possible spectacularly transparent steel-and-glass structures like the Crystal Palace and the intense artificial illumination of interiors. Since then the revelation of form through layers of glass and the nighttime effects of internally illuminated transparent buildings have been major concerns in architectural composition. It is fairly straightforward to extend a lighting model to deal with transparent as well as opaque surfaces so that an architect can use computer simulation to explore transparency effects. Essentially the illumination at any surface point is calculated by considering both reflection and transmission effects.

Not all surfaces used in buildings are smooth and matte. Some are shiny, so that highlights become part of the visual experience. Some have a metallic luster. Some act as mirrors, so that reflections appear. Many have texture. Furthermore, a building, or a space within a building, may be illuminated by multiple light sources, and the effects of interreflection within a scene may be visually important. Where accurate rendering of complex lighting effects is required, the technique of ray-tracing may be employed. This is computationally expensive, but it can produce extraordinarily realistic results.

It is sometimes suggested that use of computer graphics forces an architect to deal in barren computational abstractions, places the emphasis in a design process upon technology rather than upon the subtleties and complexities of visual experience that enrich and enliven architecture, and give it the capacity to touch our hearts. But the techniques for simulating light on surface and effects of color and texture actually bring architects closer to the qualities of visual experience by rendering these quickly and accurately. These techniques have the same potential for liberating the architectural imagination that the technique of perspective construction had for the architects of the Renaissance and the technique of graduated watercolor wash had for the architects of the Beaux-Arts.
WILLIAM MITCHELL 09.85

ALL SHOW AND NO TELE

Donald Trump has finally come up with a plan for realizing his dream of building the
world's tallest building, thereby redeeming the honor of New York City, which has
suffered untold humiliation since Chicago built its Sears Tower to 110 stories and 1,454
feet—104 feet taller than our beloved World Trade Center. The plan is Television City,
an extravagant spread to be built on the Upper West Side's old Pennsylvania Railroad
yards and designed by Chicago architect Helmut Jahn (pronounced: YAWN). Not only
will Trump's project bring back the world's tallest building (150 stories and 1,670 feet
tall), it will also (according to Trump) single-handedly keep the television industry
from fleeing to New Jersey. To make sure his sales pitch sticks, he has been busy wrapping it up with an even more generalized appeal to the provincial loyalties of New
Yorkers. "New York is getting beaten on all fronts," he says, as if deeply wounded by
the city's loss of the world's tallest building.

185

     Behind this show of civic pride, though, one quickly gets the idea that
what Trump really wants is the collection of high-yield goodies that he has stuffed into
this package. Of course, the tower is only the lead-in to the main event. Trump proposes
to frame this behemoth with two sets of three 76-story apartment buildings (each about
the size of the Chrysler Building) lined up on either side, as well as another 65-story office
building at the south end of the site, and to surround them all with a 40-acre park open
to the public. All of which will sit atop a gargantuan underground complex that will
house garages, shopping malls, and, above all, a series of huge television production bays.
By contrast, the 150-story tower is merely the tip of the iceberg. If Trump's plan triumphs,
more than 40,000 people a day will flood into the neighborhood, most arriving on an
already enfeebled subway line.

     But simply because a project of this sort is both outsize and inappropri-
ate (not to mention unattractive) doesn't mean it won't get built. The city has a difficult
time saying no to men like Donald Trump, because they both seem to equate overbuilding
with civic achievement. PETER LEMOS 01/02.86

GUGGENHEIM, WRIGHT OR WRONG

Sometime this October the Bureau of Standards and Appeals (BSA) is expected to announce its decision on the variance application of New York's Guggenheim Museum. There are a lot of bets on that the bureau will turn the museum down. If the BSA says no, it should end, for the foreseeable future anyway, the question of whether the Guggenheim will be able to build its proposed, and highly controversial, seven-story addition by the architects Charles Gwathmey and Robert Siegel. The museum addition's opponents will have won their fight to save one of the city's most recognizable icons from what they see as its certain desecration. And the museum and its supporters will be forced to find other ways of exhibiting the Guggenheim's collection, none of which are likely to satisfy its needs as fully as the addition would have. Whatever the decision, the many partisans who have taken one hard line or the other in this case are bound to be either gleefully vindicated or sorely disappointed.

For most of the rest of us, however, there is nothing at all so clear-cut about this controversy as to inspire either great glee or disappointment. The complexities of the situation do not seem to warrant the kind of partisan heat and animosity that has been generated.

Should the BSA approve the museum's application and allow it to proceed with the addition, the original 1959 Frank Lloyd Wright building and the city will survive quite nicely, and the world will not come to a stop. Given the weekly parade of other far more brutal assaults on our urban and architectural well-being, the proposed Guggenheim addition is hardly a major threat. Contrary to what opponents to the project have said, the design by Gwathmey-Siegel—although it does intrude on the space over the small rotunda—is neither "crushing" nor "grotesque." Compared with other proposed museum additions currently on the scene, the Guggenheim's is extremely well conceived, sensitive, and even diffident in its relationship to the original Wright masterpiece.

Likewise the presumed "toilet-bowl effect," which many of the museum's opponents are fond of mentioning, seems to be a specious argument. It is true that due to the unfortunate juxtaposition of the rectilinear addition atop the bowl-shaped rotunda, the project, when viewed in photographs from just the right angle, does indeed have the appearance of a toilet bowl and tank. But if built, few people, if any, would find themselves viewing the structure from just that perspective. Although the museum somehow managed to release photos of the model taken from exactly that angle, the "toilet bowl" should be dismissed as merely a two-dimensional effect.

On the other hand, there is certainly merit to the opponents' argument that the proposed gains that would accrue to the Guggenheim from the new construction don't justify the many aesthetic risks that seem inherent in the project. As the museum has repeatedly made clear, the additional exhibition spaces would allow it to show double (from three to six percent) its now "hidden" collection. As foes of the plan have pointed out, this minimal accretion of exhibition space may not warrant even the slightest intrusion on Wright's original building.

It may be that some alternatives suggested by the addition's opponents eventually would become necessary. Although the museum has repeatedly asserted that it cannot abide having its usable space spread out over several blocks, some such compromise may be its only solution. Apparently it already has passed on one excellent opportunity. According to Elizabeth Ashby, of the Carnegie Hill Neighbors, which has opposed the Guggenheim expansion from the very start, a rather large, vacant apartment building fronting Fifth Avenue between 95th and 96th Streets was on the market last spring for $4.5 million. This building would have afforded the Guggenheim a convenient and politic way of acquiring an additional 18,000 square feet of space four short blocks away. When Ashby pointed this out in a letter to Peter Lawson-Johnson, president of the Guggenheim board, she received a curt reply: the museum could not expect its staff to "sprint" from one location to the other. But if the BSA turns the museum down, the Guggenheim may be hard-pressed to find an equally attractive alternative now that, presumably, the apartment building is off the market.

The most compelling argument in the opponents' arsenal, though, has been the question of the eventual landmark status of the Guggenheim. Until 1989, when the Guggenheim becomes eligible for landmark status, the variance application now before BSA is all that stands between the museum and its proposed tower. If any institution other than an art museum of the Guggenheim's stature had attempted to alter significantly such a major architectural monument just three short years before it was to be reviewed for landmark status, the entire city would be crying foul. If architectural preservation in this city is to have any meaning at all, then it seems fair that the Guggenheim should be willing to wait three years and submit to the normal landmark process. Space needs or not, such a major institution should not stoop to slip by on the inadequacies of the Landmarks Preservation Law. PETER LEMOS 10.86

I LOVE THIS HOUSE. MY CHILDREN WERE BORN HERE. THE ONLY THING THAT BOTHERS ME IS THE FIRES AND THE EMPTY LOTS.

ROLAND LOPEZ 07/08.89

WHEN YOU'RE DOING A HOUSE, YOU'RE NOT REALLY AN ARCHITECT. THAT TITLE IS TOO FORMAL. YOU'RE A DREAM MAKER.

WILLIAM TURNBULL 04.84

Living room of the Little House, designed by Frank Lloyd
Wright. Courtesy **Metropolitan Museum of Art**

DESIGN IS **BUILDINGS**

TO TELL THE TRUTH

It is a measure of the utter shambles to which the postmodernist revisionists have reduced the field of architectural theory that the paladin of the movement, the Anglo-American architect Charles Jencks, could have published an article recently in which he dubbed Frank Lloyd Wright a premature postmodern eclectic. And it is a matter of delicious irony that he chose to claim Wright as one of his own in the very moment when two other events were occurring, either one of which would make hash of his argument. The first was the opening of the reassembled living room of the Frank Little house of 1912, one of Wright's great Prairie-style houses, in the American Wing of the Metropolitan Museum of Art. The other was the publication in the October 1982 issue of the Journal of the Society of Architectural Historians of a previously unknown letter from Wright to prominent architectural critic Russell Sturgis defending the functionalist origins of his designs for the Larkin Building of 1904.

No one but a blind man, confronting the lovely room of 70 years ago, could fail to realize that he stands face to face with an authentically original and dazzlingly new example of Modern architecture. Never before—not even in the Larkin Building and Unity Temple of a few years earlier—had Wright demonstrated more clearly how completely he had purged his designs of all historicizing anecdote and inherited iconographic devices. And no one understanding the English language could find a more reasoned or explicit description of the way in which Wright had accomplished this remarkable artistic and ideological achievement. One needs only to compare the Little living room with any other upper-class American home—say, the Hyde Park mansion that McKim, Mead, and White had done for the Vanderbilts a couple of years before—to see that Wright's design represented a quantum leap from eclecticism. Just as one needs only to compare Sturgis's confused and turgid defense of fin-de-siècle Beaux-Art-ism with Wright's straightforward explanation of his attempt to express the functional requirements of a modern office building for a big industrial operation.

How then does Jencks arrive at the proposition that Wright is, like Jencks and his cronies, a shameless eclectic plagiarist? It probably stems from his ambiguous use of the term eclecticism. The orthodox dictionary definition—"choosing what appears to be the best from diverse sources, systems or styles...free selection and borrowing"—can in a very real sense be described as the process through which all human beings pass in the course of becoming adults: the very act of learning is itself eclectic. The child studies the modes of behavior of his parents and peers as a first step in evolving his own modus vivendi. All the sensuous stimuli of his environment play upon him, and he responds by "trying them on for fit." But the mark of maturity—above all in the artist—comes when all these alternative modes of expression have been sorted out, discarded, or adopted, and then assimilated, abstracted, and distilled. The discrete components of the cultural milieu are thereby integrated into the personal mode of the adult. In the great artist this culminates in the authentically new, the unmistakably original, mode of thought and action. This is the orthodox role of eclecticism in the process of maturation.

THE CHAIR MUSEUM

In photographs the Vitra Design Museum is incomprehensible. It looks weird—as if some jokester kidnapped the Guggenheim, unwrapped its spiral, and teased it into dreadlocks. In a way, someone has. But in person, at close range, the cluster of forms begins to have logic, and what appears awkward in photographs turns out in real life to be quite graceful. The small, strange museum is rationally made and beautiful.

Architect Frank Gehry's first European commission is a milky white building that sits on an expansive lawn in front of a factory near the town of Weil am Rhein, Germany. Basel, Switzerland, is just across the river, a short taxi ride away. And the nearby hills, visible from the museum's front door, are on French soil.

192

In the clear light of a late summer afternoon in the hours before dusk, as I walk around Gehry's building, its irregular forms—forms that the precise terms offered by architectural dictionaries can't describe—unfold like the plot of a movie.

Gehry's building demonstrates that there are many ways to express function, that a skylight or a stairwell can assume new dramatic shapes without compromising practicality. More than any work by Henry Moore or Alexander Liberman, this polymorphous mass expresses the possibilities of form, the different ways that surfaces can interact with light, and the ways that shadows can exaggerate and alter shapes. More than the Claes Oldenburg piece—a group of giant, elongated hand tools situated on the grass near the museum—this building is effective sculpture. In short, the Vitra Museum is architecture that works as art.

The Vitra Museum is known informally as the Chair Museum. It sits in front of the Vitra factory—a showcase of industrial architecture with buildings designed by Gehry and Nicholas Grimshaw, a walkway by Antonio Citterio, and an entryway by Eva Jirinca—where chairs and shop fixtures are manufactured. The museum is the outgrowth of Vitra director Rolf Fehlbaum's penchant for collecting famous chairs. And given the circumstances, one would expect that this museum—in a building that is a work of art—would be a place where the chair is treated as art. But instead of transforming designed objects—chairs—into little aesthetic monuments, Fehlbaum and curator Alexander von Vegesack have tried to make this a museum where a chair is a chair.

Like other showcases of design, the Vitra Museum has elevated the status of chairs, placing the work of Eames, Thonet, Rietveld, and Breuer on pedestals. At the same time it is experimenting with ways to make the chair—aspects of its design and manufacture, its place in our culture—accessible both intellectually and physically. In the same way that Gehry has made a highly aesthetic building that is also user-friendly, Fehlbaum and von Vegesack have made a museum about highly aesthetic objects that undercuts their status as art and reminds us that a chair is also a humble industrial product.

"The fact that this place is not in some city but in front of a factory has a meaning," Fehlbaum says. "It's right that it's in front of a factory."

"Design is not art," von Vegesack declares. KARRIE JACOBS 12.90

Islamic Cultural Center, designed by Skidmore,
Owings & Merrill, on 96th Street in New York.
Photograph by **Wolfgang Hoyt/ESTO**

A DISLOCATED MOSQUE

Religious institutions have historically signified neighborhood identity and stability, but the mosque that opened for worship on 96th Street and Third Avenue tells a different story. Wedged in the gulf between condo towers advancing from the south and the rows of public housing to the north, it is an anomaly, reinforcing the sense of dislocation that now defines the area.

Like the two high-rise condos that share the same intersection, the mosque was built on 96th Street because the proximity of poverty and housing projects meant that a sizeable and accessible chunk of Manhattan real estate could be had at reasonable cost. Designed by Skidmore, Owings & Merrill (with a separate minaret by Swanke Hayden Connell), it is the first purpose-built mosque for the 800,000 Muslims in New York; but scant few of them live anywhere near it. Before Friday services, the Congregation—an average of 2,000 strong—descends on the area, ringing the mosque in triple-parked cars. Just as quickly they're gone, returning to jobs and lives elsewhere. Their impact on the neighborhood is as narrow as the single and upwardly mobile condo-dwellers, who use their apartments as mere stepping-stones while pursuing jobs that will soon (hopefully) allow them to afford better.

Both high-rises contain only rental units—and both have fancy names to conceal their not-so-fancy addresses. One corner is occupied by the colossal Normandie Court, the Chrysler of condos, which is too big to fail. Developer Ira Milstein defaulted on his federally secured tax-exempt bonds but managed to keep his hands on the property anyway. Tenants of Milstein's monster don't have to bother with 96th Street: the main entrance to the block-wide building is on 95th Street, and shuttle vans are provided to whisk them safely to jobs downtown.

On another corner is the soon-to-be-completed Monterey, a convex mono-lith that promises future tenants "California Dreaming in the New York 90s." The handiwork of Costas Kondylis Architects, this theme-park condo will include—no kidding—facilities for downhill and cross-country ski training, golfing, and alpine rock climbing: bribes for braving the uncertainties of 96th Street. An advertisement on New York City buses touts that with the money you save on living in the Monterey, you'll have plenty left over for a place to get away to in the Hamptons or Fire Island (and thus have to spend less time in your apartment).

Even amidst this company, the new mosque is no doubt a symbol of pride for New York's Muslim community. But 96th Street is in desperate need of a defining and stabilizing influence, and the mosque seems unlikely to provide it. Instead it adds to the area's transient quality; everyone is focused on being or getting somewhere else. Say a prayer for 96th Street. HUGO LINDGREN 07.92

195

SECURITY AT THE MEGA MALL

Set to open to the public on August 11, Mall of America will be the largest shopping cen-ter in the United States, covering 4.2 million square feet of retail space on three levels. The gargantuan complex is spread over the 78-acre former site of the Metropolitan Stadium for adjacent Minneapolis; includes four anchor stores, more than 350 other shops, and two seven-level parking decks for more than 11,500 cars; and surrounds a seven-acre enclosed amusement park, Knott's Camp Snoopy.

The mall is so large, in fact, that its customers—developers expect 40 million visits a year—will be offered services that include greeters, foreign-language inter-preters, courtesy help phones like those in airports, package checking and delivery, special rooms for parents to care for small children, and even a tram system on the top level to carry weary shoppers from store to store.

But part of creating a welcoming, convenient environment that subtly and continually directs every visitor's focus toward opportunities to buy is making cus-tomers feel safe. Thus security measures play a large role at Mall of America, as they have at its smaller predecessors. However, such measures must function unobtrusively to main-tain the upbeat atmosphere for shoppers.

In designing the mall, developer Melvin Simon & Associates and archi-tect of record HGA/KKE of Minneapolis faced two major challenges in ensuring visitors a sense of security. These were the mall's daunting size and the design of its parking decks, according to project manager Dennis McLauchlin. The architects mitigated the effect of its huge size by laying out the mall in a series of small vistas whose scales are meant to seem intimate and nonthreatening. Visitors arrive through one of eight plazalike entrances mid-way along the east or west streets. From here the streets lead to large skylighted atrium "courts" at the four corners, where the anchor stores have their main entrances.

But there is a flip side to Mall of America's warm and bubbling public spaces. A sprawling basement level houses supply routes, offices (for managers, maintenance workers, and security staff) and loading docks in a plain concrete-block, fluorescent-lit maze that extends up through all levels with a network of service corridors. Unlike in urban shopping districts, the service alleys—and even the service workers—are totally out of sight. The 10,000 people who work at Mall of America know certain portions of this backstage space, but the 100,000 daily visitors to this Midwestern shopping factory won't see any of it—unless they misbehave.

Standard practice for security officers is to get suspects out of sight immediately. If a word from one of the mall's 20 strolling security guards won't suffice, an offending visitor may be directed to follow the officer into the service corridor—and then to the mall security headquarters in the basement. Noisy teens, couples having a spat, sus-pected pickpockets, or shoplifters can be pulled into the netherworld at will by a guard following the cardinal rule: don't disturb shoppers' peace of mind.

Parking decks, a prime site of violent crime in malls, induce the most anxiety, especially in women. At Mall of America they were designed from the start to be—

and to feel—as safe as possible. No parking space is more than 300 feet from a door into the mall; and solid walls, which might conceal attackers, have been eliminated within the decks. For the same reason, the walls of the garage's elevators, stair towers, and skyways are all glass. The height between the floors of the parking decks was also increased from the seven-foot minimum to an average of nine feet, to make the garages feel more open. With more than three times the quantity of light as the average parking structure, the Mall of America's decks are bright enough to read in, according to the developers.

Each garage will be patrolled by a security officer in a car, with a third patrol car outside covering the grounds. Each deck has 49 closed-circuit surveillance cameras, monitored 24 hours a day by two officers in the security dispatch center, and 65 emergency call boxes. Dispatchers will send an officer with a two-way radio in response to any alarm. Director of security Keith Davidson will not provide details about how his staff will handle any type of disturbances or emergencies.

Despite their policelike uniforms, meant to blur the distinction between unarmed security officers and police, mall guards are not officers of the law. At Mall of America, the Bloomington Police Department has an on-site police facility (which it has not yet decided whether to staff) built into the basement level.

But the need for police intervention is rare, because mall managers have a powerful legal weapon at their command: a Supreme Court decision several years ago gave them the unassailable right to remove and ban from their private property anyone they choose. Unlike their beleaguered counterparts on the streets of America's cities, security officers in shopping malls can legally remove disruptive visitors and even potential troublemakers—which is to say, people who aren't there solely to spend money.

Included in this category are reporters. Managers may be unlikely to remove working reporters from the premises, but they can easily prevent them from talking to mall customers, and insist that they work with the mall's public relations office, whose ultimate goal is controlling, or "spinning," any news that might appear unfavorable.

Before recent coverage of the popularity of "mall walking," for example, mall managers routinely tried to ban senior citizens who gathered for companionship and exercise to walk laps in safe, quiet malls. Teenage "mall rats," on the other hand, are a fixture at any mall because they spend enough money to make them worth tolerating.

As for the rest of the citizenry? Forget it. Those people who cannot afford to shop but are still a part of our modern society—from the homeless and indigent to political protesters and religious evangelists—have been removed and rendered invisible. The sense of security fostered by America's shopping malls depends on their ability to keep the unfamiliar and threatening out of sight and out of mind. And that's the way their customers like it. JOHN VOELCKER 07/08.1992

197

I DO MAKE A DISTINCTION WHICH I THINK WE HAVE LOST. THE DIFFER- ENCE IS THAT ART MUST MOVE YOU, DESIGN NEED NOT.

199

DAVID HOCKNEY 07/08.84

SIR NORMAN FOSTER'S UNEXPECTED GUESTS

The cool, gray patch of pricey real estate that sits beneath Sir Norman Foster's Hong Kong and Shanghai Bank is the most austere of architectural spaces. It is an ambiguous zone—part private and public, part interior and out-of-doors. Rendered in granite and steel, the garagelike space belongs both to the street and the structure that towers over it. Sitting in the heart of Hong Kong's prestigious Central district, this place is dramatically transformed every weekend. On Sundays the hushed chamber of Modernism is turned into a colorful bazaar, as hundreds of guest workers, mainly single young women from the Philippines and Thailand employed as domestic helpers, gather there with friends to socialize, eat, and buy and sell goods.

Such gatherings of foreign domestics in Central is nothing new: the area has been used for years as a meeting place for Hong Kong's maids, amahs (nannies), and other workers. **The original gathering point was Chater Garden and Statue Square,** just north of the Shanghai Bank building. It did not take long, however, for surrounding neighborhoods to be annexed, especially as the number of foreign domestics rose in the 1980s. Today there are approximately 130,000 such workers in Hong Kong, mostly Filipinas.

In spite of its Spartan appearance, the bank plaza is well suited for public gatherings in hot, wet Hong Kong. During the summer temperatures commonly reach 90 degrees, accompanied by extreme humidity and sudden downpours. The darkened space is cool and dry by comparison. Built on a gently sloping surface, the plaza also has the quality of an amphitheater, with just enough grade change to make sitting much more appealing than on a level floor.

Sunday congregations of guest workers there and at other nearby areas have become a contentious issue. You would think the domestics were an invading army rather than the housecleaners and nannies without whom Hong Kong would be in disarray. Shop owners in Central have complained vociferously about the throngs of "birdlike Filipinas" who leave the area littered with rubbish. Others have voiced concern over the implications for tourism: legislator Alfred Tso-Shiu-wai warned recently that the sight of the thousands of maids might "put off" visitors. "It's not scenic," he pointed out.

The lot of domestic helpers in Hong Kong is an unenviable one. Most earn less than $450 a month—in a city where a shoe-box apartment costs more than twice that—and must leave Hong Kong within two weeks of the termination of their contract. Fear of this rule has frightened many women into remaining silent about incidents of abuse and sexual harassment. Once a worker has complained, she is likely to become tagged a "troublemaker" and find it impossible to land another contract.

Recently there has been a movement to establish recreation centers for the maids throughout the city. But the plan has encountered strenuous opposition and drawn out legions of NIMBYs. Until a suitable alternative is at hand, the Sunday streetscape of Central will continue to host massive ritual gatherings of Hong Kong's domestic workers. And the formidable architecture of Foster's masterpiece will continue to be enlivened by strains of Tagalog and the scent of homemade food. THOMAS J. CAMPANELLA 03.95

REDESIGNING THE OVAL OFFICE

In 1993, METROPOLIS invited several architects and designers to informally redesign what may be the ultimate home workspace: **The Oval Office.** It seemed about time to rethink that room, then occupied by a President eager to usher America into a new age, shaped by high technology and a growing concern for the environment. Here, designers **John Kelly** and **Noah Carter** transform the Oval Office into a combination trading floor, conference room, and television broadcasting station.

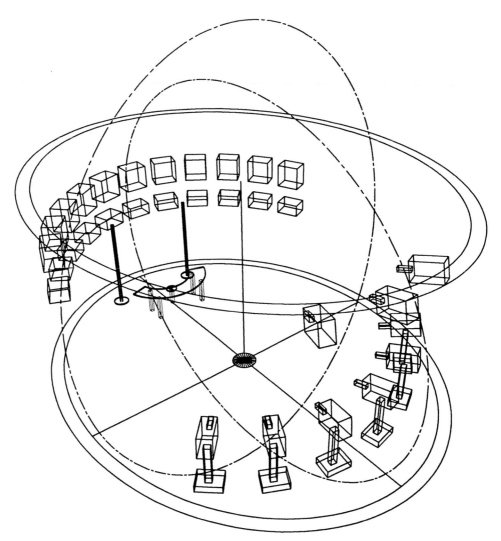

THE COMMITTEE FOR ARCHITECTURAL NEGLECT

BEN KATCHOR 06.99

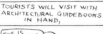

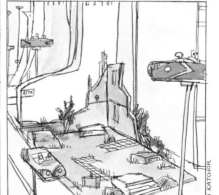

THE OFFICE BUILDING DEMYSTIFIED

BEN KATCHOR 08/09.99

WHAT ARCHITECTURE CAN DO

As he addressed an American Institute of Architects (AIA) symposium audience last year, Mississippi architect Samuel Mockbee relished the irony of the moment. What gave him such a kick was the program's lineup. Peter Bohlin, partner in the Pennsylvania firm Bohlin Cywinski Jackson, was asked to discuss his plans for the Seattle-area home of cyber-czar Bill Gates; then came Mockbee, to talk about the home designed and built by his Auburn University students for Shepard Bryant, a fisherman from Mason's Bend, in the backwoods of Alabama. "You have the home for the wealthiest man in America, followed by the home for the poorest man in America," Mockbee recalls.

206

This kind of incongruity is familiar to Mockbee. Such invitations to speak have been arriving steadily since his work began to draw notices nearly a decade ago. And as a professor with a storyteller's gift of gab, he is rarely reluctant to speak his mind. Known to family and friends as Sambo, he is a bear of a man with an avuncular nature, a laid-back Mississippi drawl, and a mischievous kind of Dennis the Menace spark in his eyes.

Having spent all of his 52 years here, Mockbee harbors a great affinity for the region's soulfulness, and yet he is sensitive to the contradictions inherent in its rich cultural heritage and in contemporary life. Plantations are restored as historic monuments to a time of peaceful gentility; visitors drive past miles of placeless strip malls to reach them. The civil rights movement may have made racial equality the legal standard, but prejudice and severe economic disparity persist. This awareness fuels his search for an architecture that serves society's have-nots with the dignity he believes they deserve.

"I would like to think that we can develop an architecture that is about American democracy, where we can create well-designed buildings and places for everyone and not just those who can afford architects," Mockbee says. "Perhaps it is Frank Lloyd Wright-ish to talk about an architecture that expresses the democracy of America, but as corny as it sounds, it's right. It's what we need to be aiming toward." This is not a popular approach these days, as the government continues to curb the construction of public low-income housing and developers cater to the affluent suburbs. But democratic architecture is Mockbee's mission.

In tandem with architectural partner Coleman Coker, Mockbee has achieved notoriety for designs that draw upon the regional vernacular. However, for the last two decades his professional life has cycled from practice to teaching and lecturing, and back again. (This semester he is a visiting professor at the Yale University School of Architecture.) His sporadic practice is run from what he calls his "young architect's house" in Canton, Mississippi: a gray clapboard structure that reflects his Modern aspirations before they were honed by regionalism. But most of his time is spent at Auburn University, his alma mater, in the town that shares the school's name, some 50 miles from Montgomery in the center of southern Alabama. From here, and from a small-town outpost on the other side of the state, Mockbee leads the Rural Studio, an intensive design-build program for architecture students that serves residents of one of the poorest counties in the state and the nation.

Unlike the efforts of Habitat for Humanity, whose volunteers build and repair homes—often in a single weekend, like an old-time barn raising—the approach of the Rural Studio is far more personalized. Students must first get to know the people for whom they are building, so the design corresponds to their needs. Thus the main difference between Habitat and Rural Studio, according to Mockbee, is spirit. Although the stripped-down Habitat designs may provide shelter, he feels they are ultimately dehumanizing. And this, he insists, is a mistake—and downright un-American. A house for a poor person, "may be small, but the quality of that house has to be as good as one for Bill Gates," Mockbee says. "The standard is, 'If I found myself in certain circumstances, would I want to live in that house?'"

Mockbee has been building for the poor since the early 1980s, when he offered to help a nun in Canton secure housing for a family whose home had been reclaimed by the city. A crew of volunteers built the new house, following Mockbee's inventive specifications of salvaged materials to keep expenses to a minimum. Such experiences fueled his search for a new form of practice, which became part of the inspiration for the Rural Studio.

Launched in 1993 by Mockbee and an Auburn architecture school colleague, D. K. Ruth, the program was also sparked by their desire to expose students to all that will be required of them in actual practice. Although Mockbee respects his more theoretical colleagues in the academy, he believes that architectural education also requires more hands-on training than most students experience, so they'll have a better idea of what it actually takes to build something once they leave school.

During a three-term school year, three teams of a dozen undergraduates design and construct a new homestead for a low-income family, which often includes one or more outbuildings in addition to a house. Each year several seniors design and build their final projects out here as well; this spring seven seniors are hard at work in Mason's Bend on a gazebo, an artist's studio, and a playground for the local family resource center. Not only do students explore a more "democratic" form of architecture, they get a crash course in the fundamentals of professional practice.

Thus, in addition to designing and conferring with their clients, Rural Studio students pound nails, dig footings, and frame structures—all on an extremely limited budget, which is usually provided by a handful of corporate sponsors, such as the Alabama Power Company. This immersion is "designed to get the students to cross a threshold of understanding," Mockbee says. "They begin to see that they are the ones stepping into the client's world, and not those folks stepping into their world." JIM ZOOK 04.97

Interior and exterior views of Butterfly House, designed
and built by Auburn University Rural Studio sophomores.
Photographs by **Timothy Hursley**, The Arkansas Office

I WOULD LIKE TO THINK THAT WE CAN DEVELOP AN ARCHITECTURE THAT IS ABOUT AMERICAN DEMOCRACY,

WHERE WE CAN CREATE WELL-
DESIGNED BUILDINGS AND
PLACES FOR EVERYONE AND
NOT JUST THOSE WHO CAN
AFFORD ARCHITECTS.

SAMUEL MOCKBEE 04.97

COME AND GETTY

The fantasy was this: against the uniformly dreary assessments of the Getty Center I'd rise in defense of a project that couldn't possibly be that bad. **After all, it has been branded in the press as the product of everything from cultural imperialism to elitism, autoplagiarism, and gigantism. Burdened by a huge budget, an extended gestation, and its brush with the millennium, the Getty has also been saddled, it seems, with a duty to account not just for its place in Los Angeles but in the culture itself.**

Some of these criticisms would have been made about any project representing such a huge concentration of resources. The relevance of the Getty's old-fashioned style of bigness and its Olympian character in a city of sprawl, where needs and neighborhoods are so evidently dispersed, has been legitimately questioned. I, however, have never had any problem with the idea of a big complex on that Brentwood hill. The site is superb and commanding, clearly no place for false modesty. And I'm down with the Acropolitan solution: pristine temples artfully deployed and glinting in the sun.

Nor does the institutional magnitude of the Getty trouble me. Much of the criticism of the project, understandably, has equated the museum component with the institution itself. Although the collection isn't fabulous (despite quite a few wonderful items), its strengths are those of an academic collection rather than a concentration of masterpieces. The ancillaries, though, are what make this an amazing place: the superior research labs, the luxurious scholars' center with its excellent library, the public education programs, grants, and conservation subsidies. There aren't many institutions like this anymore, and the creation of the center is more akin to the founding of a university than to the opening of a museum. One of the strongest arguments for the consolidation is that the Getty's various components work synergistically, in peripatetic, cross-fertilizing interchanges.

Of course, the museum is the focus for most visitors, and it is easily the weakest architectural piece of the complex. Indeed, it seems willfully so. The logic is to concentrate painting on the upper level and to create a sense of intimacy by breaking down the scale with a set of semiconnected pavilions. The result is a cumbersome and confusing circulation pattern, which—given the proportions of the buildings—accords de facto privilege to the vertical. I found myself in a circulation yo-yo, taking too many long hikes up and down stairs, and confronting too many elevators.

Another problem is the size of the galleries themselves. The lofty skylights and high pyramidal ceilings in the upper rooms are based on John Soane's beloved little Dulwich museum—Richard Meier himself allowing the historicist camel to poke its nose through the flap of the tent—but here they mainly seem too small, wrested from a building of a different scale. This strategy for intimacy is both out of sync with the grandeur of the Getty's enterprise and cramped in practical terms. On a Sunday, with thousands of visitors, it's a jungle (never mind the acute shortage of bathrooms). To be sure, the natural lighting is appropriately elegant and pellucid, but the cost in scale and proportion inside and outside is simply too high.

The vertical attenuation and scale breakdown are exacerbated by the quality of the gallery spaces themselves. Much has been made by a variety of writers (including Meier, who issued an unprecedented book-length apologia) over the imposition of a decorator—Thierry Despont—who was responsible for doing up the period rooms in period style. I'm strictly with Meier on this one. I've got no problem with museums installing period rooms from the period, but the ersatz is just tacky. Even the relatively undecorated rooms are done in lugubrious colors and unimpressive detail. It all feels somehow wrong.

Hardly an original insight, but the Getty is in Brentwood, land of O. J. and Monica Lewinsky. In this enclave of parvenu posh, the reigning sensibility is the decorator's, and the Getty certainly begs the alpha question of Angelene decor: Consistency? Brentwood answers with a kind of radical eclecticism in which anything goes with anything as long as someone's sanctioning taste is involved. This is more or less the strategy at the Getty (and at most old-line museums of encyclopedic grasp), which collects all over the map, from Louis XIV bric-a-brac to Old Master paintings to the jugs and shards of Classical antiquity.

Ironically, the decorator rooms resurrect the specter of kitsch that the institution sought to escape in its move from its previous quarters. The mainline Modernism of the complex stands in deliberate contrast to the legendary kitsch of its predecessor, the reconstructed Roman villa (complete with underground parking) overlooking the beach at Malibu. (That museum is itself being renovated by architects of Classical proclivities, who are treating the phony villa as if it were in fact an archaeological site, a truly poisonous conceit.)

There's another much spoken of intrusion on the Meier project that also raises the kitsch quotient. At some point in the development of the buildings, the museum—worried, it seems, about the project's remorseless stiffness—decided to invite the artist Robert Irwin to create a large formal garden in the cleft between the museum and the scholars' center. Meier had already designed this space, and he was reportedly furious to have yet another collaborator foisted on him. The two were apparently so overcome with mutual loathing that they were unable to integrate or even connect their two projects. Indeed, the most symbolically fraught moment in the whole complex is the dirt DMZ (as everyone refers to it up on Parnassus) that stretches between Meier's plaza and Irwin's garden. As a result, on a rainy day one walks in the mud.

Irwin does his bit to advance the kitsch by producing an unusually vulgar piece of work. Tiny mounds of earth are retained behind enough inch-thick Cor-Ten steel walls to build a battleship. Hundreds of plant species have been assembled and laid on like a smorgasbord, echoing the grab-bag diversity of the institution itself. The geometric layout might seem to tithe Meier, the master geometer, but the scheme is klutzy and overwrought, filled with circles and switchbacks and a surfeit of undercooked detail, the antithesis of Meier's cool grids and curves.

Most striking, though, is that Meier himself has produced a kind of kitsch. Modernism—in its austerity and rationality—is the historic enemy of kitsch, but as

211

Meier's particular brand of Modernism becomes increasingly self-referential, it enters a territory where relevance is adduced through excess and sentimentality, the nurseries of kitsch. The Getty is nothing if not excessive. Meier's kitsch involves both the number of built elements and the extreme deployment of his regular kit of parts—the orthogonal grid, the piano curve, the pipe railing. This sheer repetition of detail—however artful—dulls the sense of the particular that is central to artistic achievement. What seemed precise in Atlanta's High Museum or the New Harmony Center becomes a blur when multiplied to enormous proportions. Travertine is a beautiful, sensuous material, but the acres of it at the Getty—used simply as surface—are just gross.

The neighbors also contributed to this failure. Meier—whose whole career has been devoted to making white buildings—was obliged to promise that he wouldn't do so here lest the locals be blinded by reflected light. Bad move. White is the most volumetric color, emphasizing shape over detail, and it is Meier's signature. The royal road to disaster in this project undoubtedly began with the demand that the buildings be beige, the first decorator compromise. Most of the metal cladding panels are an ambivalent tan, suggesting shade where there is none, dulling the crispness of the buildings' edges and adding complication to an architecture that has always sought to pare.

The buildings display their sentimentality by self-consciously evoking the icons of the past—the Acropolis, to be sure; the whiff of Tuscany in the plaza and framed views; Hadrian's Villa; Soane's museum—but most especially in the almost parodistic use of Corbusian forms. One has the sense that the referent long ago ceased to be Corb and has now become Meier's riff on Corb. This impression is heightened by the many Meier buildings on the hillside, facing each other in various juxtapositions. Completely lacking in irony, Meier's compulsive repetition produces Meierland.

Searching for a reading of multiple buildings, we rely on certain paradigms—the acropolis, the campus, the office park, the theme park. The Getty elides them all. Certainly it's the shining temple complex at the brow of the hill, collegiate in both form and purpose, but it also recalls corporate headquarters designed in the seventies and eighties. And with its mechanically controlled sequences—from car to garage, to robot train, to plaza, to cafe, to attraction—it offers more than a suggestion of the theme park, a reading reinforced by the touchy-feely ad banners suspended from thousands of L.A. lampposts, picturing a young African-American boy and offering the invitation to visit "your Getty."

In 1967 I spent some months living and working on a kibbutz. Shortly after the Six Day War, I went to the newly united Jerusalem to check things out and offer my services. The task I was assigned was helping to clean up the old Hebrew University campus on Mount Scopus, which had been abandoned to the Jordanians in 1948. Like the Getty, the complex enjoyed a certain Acropolitan splendor, crowning the little mountain. The buildings were also the product of one hand, that of Erich Mendelsohn in his Holy Land phase. They were earth-toned as well, clad in the luminously golden local stone. Although I was unenthusiastic about the rough dressing of the stone at the time—I was into a more Meieresque, machined look in my impressionable youth—I came to appreciate the complex for the way it appeared to be not on the hill but of it.

The Getty does have its visual pleasures. The views over the city are marvelous and the landscaping luxuriant. The complex organizes many wonderful vistas: the view from the delightful cactus garden through the museum court to the drum of the rotunda is one of the best. The scholars' building is a very good piece of Meier—which means a very good building—and is clearly the privileged working environment in the complex. These pleasures, though, are obscured to nuance-dulling extent by the repetitive details—by the fact that the complex doesn't grow from the site but overwhelms it. In the end the Getty isn't the Acropolis, the summary artifact of long cultural development, but an act of recall. We'd been hoping for a vision. MICHAEL SORKIN 06.98

213

THE AT&T BUILDING BY JOHNSON/BURGEE WAS NOT THE BEST, BUT WAS EMBLEMATIC OF THE TIME. IT MADE CLEAR THAT ALL THE THINGS THAT I AND OTHERS HAD BEEN ARGUING FOR WERE INDEED POSSIBLE AND COULD BE DONE REASONABLY WELL. IT MADE EVERYBODY TAKE SERIOUSLY THE FACT THAT THE PAST AND PRESENT WERE PART OF A CONTINUUM AND NOT TWO SEPARATE ARMIES AT WAR WITH EACH OTHER.

ROBERT A.M. STERN 10.89

Two technicians check out a development unit of the
TransHab inflatable module inside Chamber A at the
Johnson Space Center's Space Environment Simulation
Laboratory. Courtesy **NASA**

SPACE INFLATOR

"It was about as exciting as watching grass grow," architect Constance Adams tells me.
Her nonchalance is less than convincing. Inflating the TransHab may have taken
12 hours, but until that day she and her colleagues had never had a good look at what
they'd been working on for almost two years—what they hope will become the first
manned inflatable structure in space.

Adams, an intense woman in her early thirties with sharp dark eyes, is
one of the few architects in a sea of engineers and scientists at NASA. At an agency where
architects often feel they have to justify their place on the payroll, she's been given a
daunting task: to make the TransHab—short for "transit habitat"—well, habitable. If she
succeeds, she may do more than change the way NASA thinks about architects, she may
change the way the rest of us think about architecture.

Her path to NASA was a circuitous one. After graduating from Yale
Architecture School in the early 1990s, she worked for Kenzo Tange in Tokyo and Josef
Paul Kleiheus in Berlin, where she focused on large projects, from office buildings to city
plans. But in 1996, when urban-renewal efforts in Berlin began to slow down, she returned
to the United States.

While visiting her father, a history professor, in Houston, she took a
tour of the Johnson Space Center, and quickly made up her mind to stay. "How could the
child of a historian resist?" she asks. "This is the big historical effort of our time. NASA
cares less about how things are traditionally done, because there are no real traditions yet
[associated with] putting people into space."

But as Adams soon discovered, an absence of tradition often has some
major drawbacks.

Just three years earlier NASA had set up a bioplex, a laboratory for testing technologies that might eventually be used in the Mars habitat—closed-loop, advanced
life-support systems that recycle air, water, and waste. The bioplex's eight airtight chambers simulate the conditions of life in space for crewmembers, and Adams's assignment
was to design their living quarters. With the project's short history, though, there was little
in the way of research for her to go on.

To determine the basic requirements for making a space habitat livable,
she interviewed the American astronauts and Russian cosmonauts who had served for
at least a year on the ill-fated Mir space station. Working with NASA psychologist Janis
Connolly and mathematician Francis Mount, she collected data about personal habits and
socialization patterns, and began to develop what she calls "socio-ergonomic analysis," a
way of understanding how in closed habitats members of a group behave almost as if they
were a single entity.

But a Mars mission lasts at least two years—a lot longer than a quick
trip to the Moon or a typical tour of duty on a space station—and Adams and her colleagues were still a long way from figuring out what goes into making the kind of place
where six people can coexist happily for extended periods.

215

Snapshots by David Carson

"Lincoln Center could just as well be in the Mojave Desert."

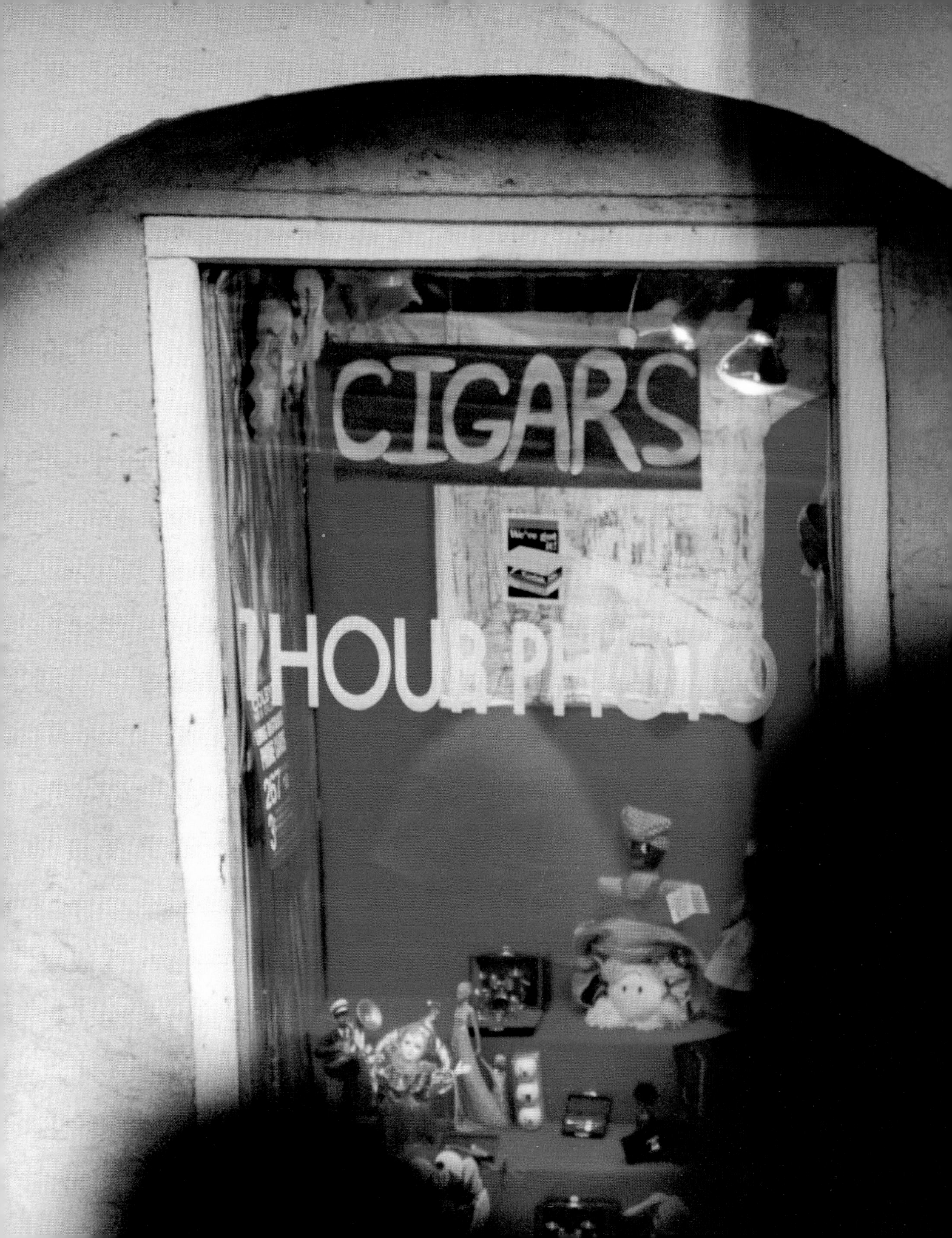
CIGARS
HOUR PHOTO

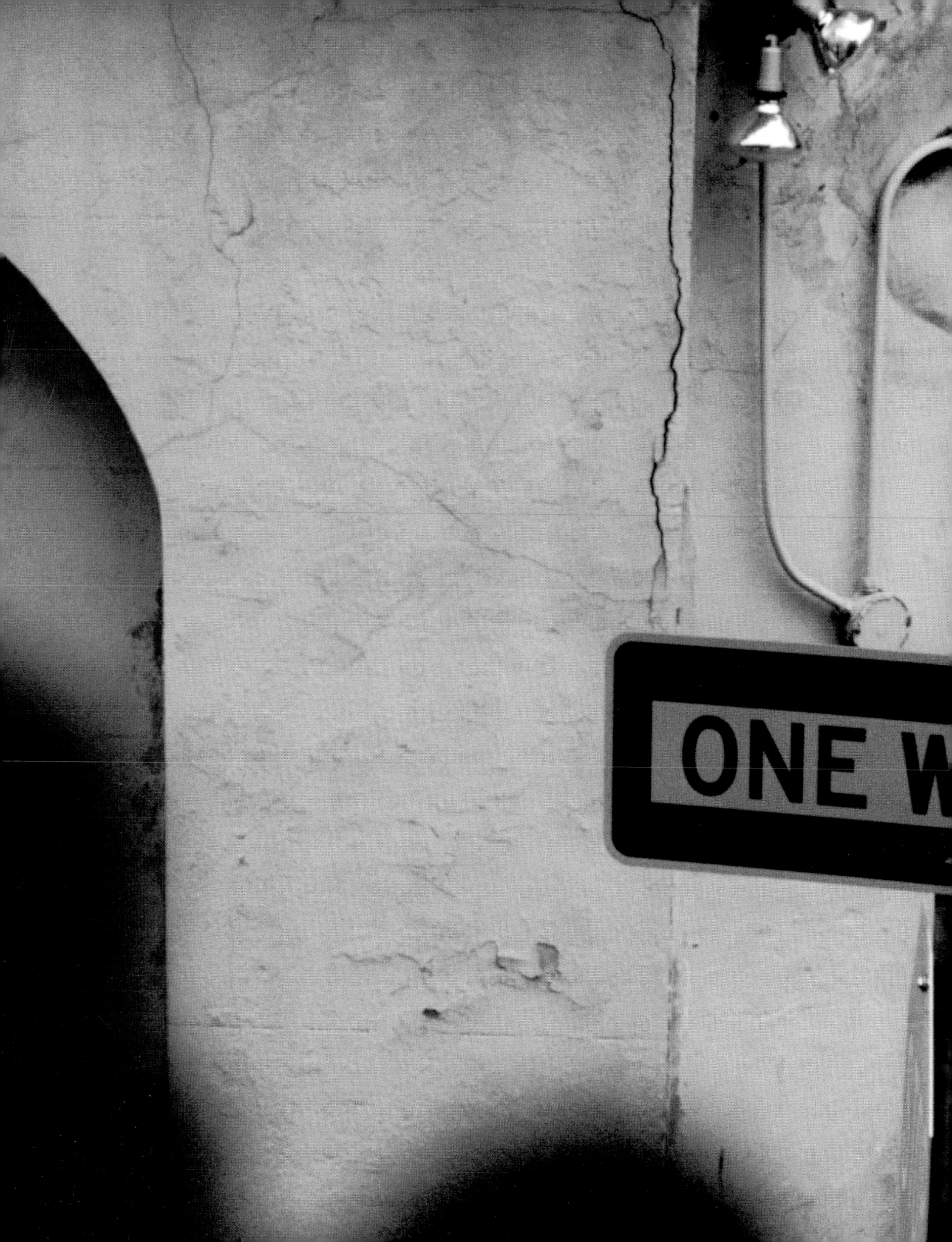
ONE W

"The present is what somton in the past would have called a ridiculous future."

CITYLIMITS

"The USSR is a typeface," Jeremy Wolff says. "Lincoln Center could just as well be in the Mojave Desert," Roberta Gratz said in 1982. "A shantytown of glowing polygons," is how Karrie Jacobs described virtual reality in 1990. And Marisa Bartolucci suggests that the storefront studio of NBC's TODAY SHOW at Rockefeller Center, where its fans gather each morning, has become an essential part of many viewers' everyday landscape. What all these statements make clear is that **our sense of place is derived from more than simple geography**, and the articles they have been drawn from try to determine the coordinates we use to locate and place ourselves in the landscape.

"We are suffering from a lack of space, but also from a lack of understanding," writes Veronique Vienne in a contemplation of the dressing room—but that thought applies elsewhere on the American landscape. Certainly it is true of single-room residences in New York City. The understanding that is begged for must address myriad complex questions: **Will neighbors complain? Are social workers needed? What city services are needed? What do people who have been living in shelters need?** In the new American urbanism, the questions have more to do with whether the social rituals that fostered the configuration of small towns across this country for generations can be recreated in any logical way in the congested suburbs.

If there is a message here, it might be that for a glimpse into the future it is more rewarding to listen to people's personal stories and hopes than to corporate imagineers and image-makers. Alyssa Katz refers to the "rapid shifts in perspective," in the computer game Riven, but it is how we acknowledge these shifts in the real world that help us to reshape and reform it. Barbara Flanagan dreams of a progressive habitat that is safe for young children. Riding his bike through the Ukraine, Jeremy Wolff finds poetry in the visual incongruity of American logos and heroic Russian socialist icons. But the most poignant projection of all may be that of Nicolasa Lopez. Speaking of the evolving fortunes of the **Longwood Historic District in the South Bronx**, she says simply: "It was beautiful. I hope I live to see what the Bronx can be again."
Akiko Busch

226

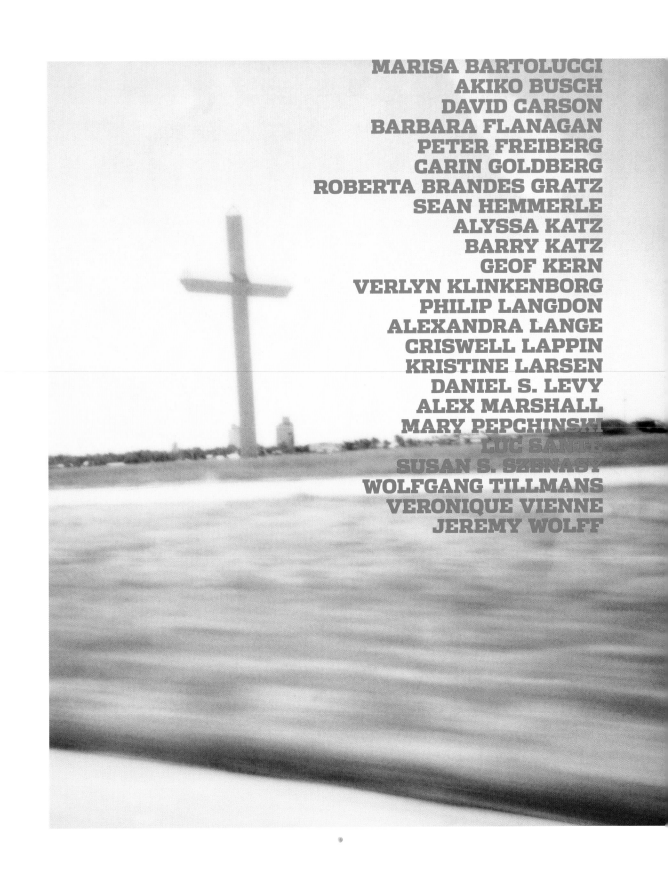

MARISA BARTOLUCCI
AKIKO BUSCH
DAVID CARSON
BARBARA FLANAGAN
PETER FREIBERG
CARIN GOLDBERG
ROBERTA BRANDES GRATZ
SEAN HEMMERLE
ALYSSA KATZ
BARRY KATZ
GEOF KERN
VERLYN KLINKENBORG
PHILIP LANGDON
ALEXANDRA LANGE
CRISWELL LAPPIN
KRISTINE LARSEN
DANIEL S. LEVY
ALEX MARSHALL
MARY PEPCHINSKI
LUC SANTE
SUSAN S. SZENASY
WOLFGANG TILLMANS
VERONIQUE VIENNE
JEREMY WOLFF

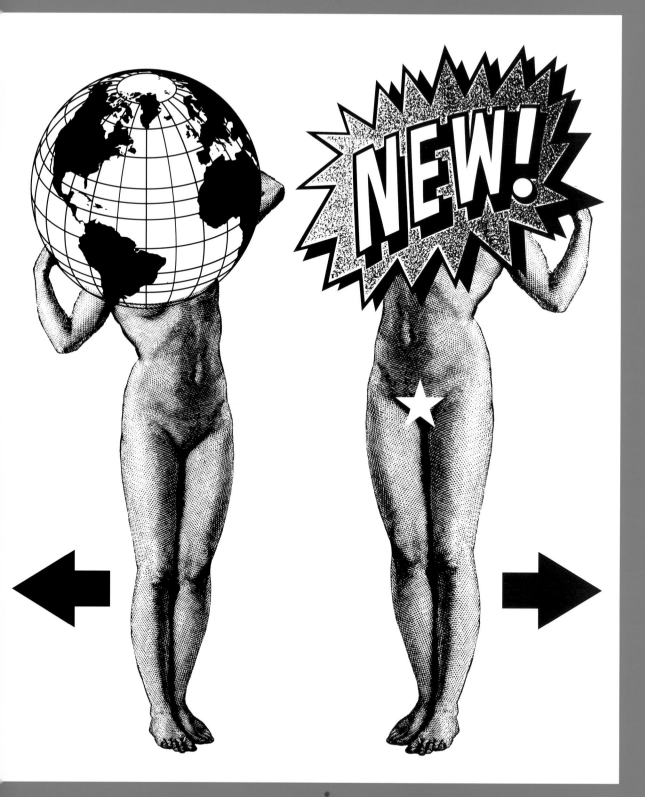

INNOVATION AND ITS DISCONTENTS

In THE FUTUROLOGICAL CONGRESS, a novel of slapstick futurism by Stanislaw Lem, a character named Ijon Tichy and his colleagues are surreptitiously doped with drugs called benignimizers—including substances like Euphoril, Empathan, and Ecstasine— and attacked with LTN (Love Thy Neighbor) bombs. In the chaos Tichy finds himself thrust forward cryogenically into a time that may or may not be real. This future also possesses a stunning pharmacopoeia. "A few grams of dantine," Tichy notes, "and a man goes around with the deep conviction that he has written THE DIVINE COMEDY." Experience is reshaped by mascons, which are not "those mechanical dogs they used to have at football games," but drugs that mask the appearance of reality. "Hardly anyone studies history now," Tichy also discovers, "history having been replaced in the schools by a new subject called hencity, which is the science of what will be." Hencity: not a city of hens, but a study of hence.

I feel, and you probably feel too, that hencity is already well established here and now, and has been for the past 50 years and more. If things had worked out the way they were meant to when I was in grade school, for example, I would be writing from a snug cabin somewhere near one of the Moon's grand promontories, with a view of distant Earth—a reborn planet where small, clean nuclear generators power vast hydroponic farms and where cities serenely thrum with airborne mass transit bearing citizens of unparalleled equality from one pleasure-dome to the next. Oh well.

There were several episodes of epidemic hencity—waves of futurological daydreaming—in the twentieth century. The post-Hiroshima and post-Sputnik episodes overlapped and intertwined their energies in now familiar, if largely unfulfilled ways, in the West, impelled by the grim hencity of Soviet communism. At the moment we're living through hencity of unusual intensity. What lies ahead, pundits say, is a kind of nano-Pangaea: all of Earth's continents fused, metaphorically and electronically, into one, thanks to new genetic, computer, and communications technologies, as well as a much anticipated burst of microscopic manufacturing.

What's always surprising about such predictions is the way they fail to reckon with the obduracy, the friction, of this very old, very real Earth—a planet of stone, mud, fire, water, and flesh. It's not that "what is" inevitably falsifies "what will be," but that all this innovation yields unexpected side effects once it encounters the weight and the visceral complexity of reality. The actual proportions of the collective world-room we find ourselves about to enter are slyly warped, so that everything looks different than expected, more archaic somehow and strangely gritty. The growth of the Web, for example, has been the occasion for almost apostolic zeal about the future. Yet what has driven so much of its innovation—in video-streaming, 3-D simulation, privacy concerns, and the handling of financial transactions—is pornography. The Web may look like a whole new souk, but the air there is full of familiar, ancient, earthy scents.

For Tichy, all it takes is a whiff of dehallucinimide and the unyielding truth peers out from beneath the psychochemical veneer of his world. "I looked out over the windowsill," he writes. "Seen from the forty-first floor, the street was a ravine, and at the bottom of it ran a glittering river of automobiles, windshields, and polished tops flashing in the sun." But when the drug kicks in, so does reality. Instead of midtown traffic, he sees "a most unusual sight. Holding their hands out chest-high and gripping the air like children pretending to be drivers, businessmen were trotting single file down the middle of the street."

That's the kind of vision that allows Tichy to see the vanity of the present and the absurdity of the future, the emptiness of hencity. It leads to an axiom of sorts: that the present is what someone in the past would have called a ridiculous future. "The criterion of common sense," Tichy decides, "was never applicable to the history of the human race. Averroes, Kant, Socrates, Newton, Voltaire—could any of them have believed it possible that in the twentieth century the scourge of cities, the poisoner of lungs, the mass murderer and idol of millions would be a metal receptacle on wheels?"

In the end we're all a little like Ijon Tichy, thrust day after day into a future that seems both illusory and altogether too real, where beneath the fresh paint, vacuum-formed plastics, silicon chips, and DNA dreams, you can see the arousing and dissipating of passions that are all too human. We live in an epoch of unparalleled innovation, with a wealth of new ideas, products, and designs showering down upon us moment after moment. But it may also turn out to be an epoch of disenchantment. There's something almost postcoital about the way Americans react to innovation—a flush of excitement followed by an all-too-familiar tristesse. It comes about because what we want isn't new tools, new foods, new cars, new houses, new networks, or new electronics. What we want is a new us—the very thing the American marketplace always promises but can never deliver. Newness in an age of newness wears off at the speed with which humans adapt to novelty, which is in the blink of an eye. It leaves us always hungry for the next new thing, always certain to find ourselves disappointed all over again. The dernier cri lapses into a horse whisper. VERLYN KLINKENBORG 2001

230

IT IS IMPROBABLE THAT A CITY OF THE EIGHTIES WOULD EVER BE LOVINGLY RESTORED.

ANDREE PUTMAN 10.89

HOW TO OPEN A DOOR

When I was a small girl in rural Hungary, I used to read about doors that opened as if by magic. Later I found out what the magic was about. It was someone's imagination that opened those fairy-tale doors. Still later I began to notice that some things around me had the same wondrous qualities, which keep those magic doors returning to my memory.

Intrigued by the infinite possibilities for combining imagination with memory, I was delighted to find people who shared my enthusiasm. Almost every one of them were designers and architects. They talked about the things we all do—things like eating, reading, and walking—but they approached our everyday movements in a special way: as design problems. This was like stumbling into a secret society whose aim was to remake the world. And I could take an advance peek at the plans. I was, frankly, awed.

231

But time and living have taught me a thing or two. Now my fascination with the process that creates spoons or houses or communities is tempered with an awareness of human frailty and folly. As a result I can identify some of the sources of my frustrations that come with living in this wonderful and wearing city. Much of our current discomfort comes from the designed environment. It need not be this way.

Observe one morning your fellow passengers on any of the newer local buses. More than half will ignore the MTA's instructions about how to make a graceful exit. People of all sizes and ages push through the back doors, with great exertions to spine and arm. Not a good way to start a day that is likely to bring other, small design failures, like glare on the computer console.

Why then aren't bus riders making use of considerate technology, devised to eliminate unnecessary physical exertion? The door, after all, opens like Sesame when it's gently pressed on the right spot. The MTA identifies it as a Safety Exit Door. Further down, at foot level, on this machine for leaving are two small acetate labels, each printed with bright yellow letters that read: "Air assist door." Then again, "Door opens automatically when: 1. Green light is on; 2. Tape is touched."

And so we've been told, three times no less, the obvious. We're standing in front of a door. But where is the "tape"? For most of us, that's the sticky film that holds the wrappings on gifts.

On some buses alert riders have located two thin, yellow, plastic bands centered at the top of the door. This must be the "tape." So someone with a black laundry marker has printed on it "press to open." Surely this could have been part of the original design of the buses. Instead, there were too many instructions.

It's all in the details, as a very famous architect warned. And when the details are neglected, design gets a bad name and so does the creative spirit. The same persons who were clever enough to devise the magic door should also know something about the way the rest of us are likely to use it.

I cannot give up on the magic door. SUSAN S. SZENASY 04.86

BRINGING DOWN THE HOUSE

Lincoln Center did not "revitalize" Manhattan's West Side.
That it is credited with such impact is a myth gaining increasing popularity for the simple reason that the more often it is repeated, the more often it is repeated again. And it is time this myth was seriously challenged.

Lincoln Center is just what its name implies—a self-contained center without streets, without any connection to its surrounding urban fabric, without anything to relate it to its neighbors. It sits alone in isolated glory and could just as well be in the Mojave Desert.

Centers like this—whether civic, cultural, or shopping—are alien schemes imposed on the texture of a singular place. They don't mend torn pieces of urban fabric. They destroy what exists. They replace. They are imbued with revitalization attributes they don't deserve. Their promoters use them to promise what can't be delivered. When the promise does not follow construction, few care enough to look back to recognize the mistaken assessment.

Lincoln Center was a trendsetter for marbleized entertainment centers that look more like giant mausoleums than seats of culture. Taste in contemporary public architecture seems to diminish in proportion to increase in size, but that is beside the point.

Since my return to New York in 1960, I have lived in three locations on Manhattan's Upper West Side, the polyglot area from 59th Street, where Midtown ends, up to 125th Street, where Harlem begins, and bordered on the west by the Hudson River and on the east by Central Park. All the West Side areas in which I have lived are among the improved areas whose rebirth has been popularly attributed to the construction of Lincoln Center. While it has been responsible for starting many things—especially some imitations in other cities that look worse than the original, if that is possible—Lincoln Center is not the cause of the West Side's renaissance. This assumption is wrong and harmful. It would be bad enough if this myth were confined to New York. But it has been used around the country to gain acceptance for similar cultural centers.

The Lincoln Center idea was born in the early 1950s. The site was selected when urban renewal was still at its height. Ground was broken in 1959. The first building (Philharmonic Hall) was completed in 1962 and the last in 1966. These dates are significant: they predate by many years what is currently identified as the rebirth of the Upper West Side. That renaissance did not truly take root until the mid-1970s. (Renaissance is a term I use here reluctantly, because by now the West Side is so "renaissanced" that it is almost homogenized—and that has never been my criterion to measure urban rebirth. But since there are so many ways in which the West Side rebirth is truly genuine, I use the term anyway.)

The West Side's renaissance began as it did in many urban neighborhoods across the country. "The city" was a rediscovered choice for many people deciding where to live. Lifestyles were shifting away from suburbia, where economics and auto dependency forced the value hunter to look to urban neighborhoods for the inexpensive, down-at-the-heels housing bargains that the energetic young could "do over." With this housing opportunity came some suburban amenities—the barbecue, the swing and sandbox, the garden—all in the backyard or at the park around the corner.

All over New York—not only in the vicinity of Lincoln Center—"brownstone revival" neighborhoods emerged slowly in the 1960s and reached unspeakable heights by the 1980s when real estate values shot through the ceiling. Chelsea, the West Village, Murray Hill, and Clinton in Manhattan; Brooklyn Heights, Cobble Hill, Park Slope, and Fort Greene, in Brooklyn—none of those neighborhoods had Lincoln Center as a stimulus. Yet renewal was happening just the same, at less inflationary rates. It was the natural, regenerative urban process taking hold. It was not produced by Lincoln Center.

What all those neighborhoods had was more basic than anything Lincoln Center ever offered: good-value housing stock; diverse populations that appealed to those seeking alternatives to static, one-class living; a sense of neighborhood where people easily get to know one another; the assortment of locally run stores that provide a welcome alternative shopping experience; accessible mass transit; diminished need for the increasingly expensive car. Those were the things that made all of those neighborhoods—including Lincoln Center's West Side—so appealing. They still do.
ROBERTA BRANDES GRATZ 10.82

233

I CAME FROM A JEWISH, LIBERAL FAMILY OF MODEST MEANS, AND MY POLITICAL VALUES MAKE IT HARD FOR ME TO THINK OF WASTE AND OSTENTATION. THIS TRANSLATES INTO MY WHOLE THING ABOUT CHEAP MATERIALS; IT CLICKS WITH MY BELIEF THAT YOU CAN MAKE BEAUTIFUL SPACES OUT OF NOTHING.

FRANK GEHRY 04.84

BUILDING FOR BUSINESS

Most people do not expect or demand a private office for themselves, but 90 percent of office workers do complain that they are forced to share their workspace with too many people. Privacy, in its various forms, is lacking.

Nearly everybody finds it impossible to have a confidential conversation. Even managers find their job performance impaired because of a lack of acoustic privacy, in some instances because the walls stop short of the structural ceiling and because there are unwritten rules against closing the door ("Team players keep the door open").

The "open-landscape" office was originally promoted on the grounds that it freed up communication (although the major reason for its widespread adoption in recent years has been its ability to economize on space).

However, a design research group called BOSTI (Buffalo Organization for Social and Technological Innovation) has done research that indicates that "as the degree of enclosure increases, the sense that the environment supports communication goes up." This does not mean that totally enclosed private offices are needed. Rather, it indicates that the partitions in an open-plan office should be tall enough and numerous enough for workers to feel they have more control over who sees them and how often. Partitions should be fitted with sound-absorbent materials and complemented by "white noise" systems to prevent conversations from wafting into the wrong ears.

Aesthetics turns out to be a troublesome issue for designers, particularly designers attached to the International Style. "Attractiveness, or aesthetics, counts for almost everybody" in enhancing environmental satisfaction and thus influencing job satisfaction, according to Michael Brill, the group's director. But white, gray, beige, marble, chrome, steel, baked enamel on metal are roundly rejected, Brill reports. Saturated colors—bright oranges and reds, for example—are not liked either. The survey shows that only wood and fabrics are acceptable for walls and that wood and wood-grain laminate are preferred for work surfaces and desks. No matter what any architect may have been taught about honesty in materials, fake wood is better accepted than forthright metal.

Office workers' preferences run to "pastels, soft colors like peach and sky blue." Brill sums up the survey's exploration of taste preferences by observing that "they're really the colors of traditional homes and old-line offices." The message seems to be that "the designer should go to his or her grandmother's house and look around."

There was a time not long ago when Modernist architects might have been able to counterattack by saying that what they're being urged to do is pander to popular taste and overrule their own aesthetic education. But the rise of postmodernists with a radically different palate (and palette) makes it clear that no single style can be designated as educated taste. If there is an ethical question in matters of taste, Brill argues, it is not whether architects should be free to act on their own sensibility but whether it is right "to impose the tastes of one person, who will never live there, on ten years of performance." The appropriate questions for the designer to ask, he says, are: "Who are these people? Where do they come from? What do they like? What do they need?" PHILIP LANGDON 03.83

THE MEGALOMANIA OF ARCHITECTURE

For centuries convention held that the higher emotions were evoked solely by nature, and that worldly items, the constructions of mankind, were fleeting at best, corrupt at worst, capable only of arousing brute reflex. The Romantics opened the gate wide enough to admit ruins, which is to say human productions on their way to being reabsorbed by nature—these could inspire awe by way of humility. It took the birth of photography to fully enfranchise the thing, to convey the grandeur and pathos of the man-made object, to allow for the emotions invested in stuff. The exponential mushrooming of manufacture over the past century and a half caused the object to dominate photography, displacing nature: the inclusive lens can lie and ignore but in the long run cannot deny the news that leaks into its field. From there the thing moved to claim its place in the sublime prospect, if not without some resistance, felt even today.

235

The photographer's task in drawing out the thing is hardly passive. On the one hand, objects are generally compliant and most collaborate agreeably with the photographer, only too happy to be cast as extras, as fill in some general scheme, as "telling detail." Rarely are objects seen to bristle or smolder with controlled resentment. Their ambition is to proliferate; photography assists them in this pursuit by broadcasting their qualities, making even their decay appear glamorous, so that they have no problem attracting suitors. Architecture, by contrast, is notoriously controlling and demanding of the photographer. When facing a lens, architecture becomes jealous of the sky, the trees, the ground, and transient humans, all of which it contrives to shrink, push to the margins, trivialize. What architecture requires from photography is acquiescence to its megalomania. Each building wants to be represented as a universe: Its proportions will be the norm, and a cowed deference the permitted reaction. So buildings have worked to reduce their depiction to a handful of standard tropes: the noncommittal middle-distance rendition, like the headshots of officers in a corporate report; the remote heroic view, in which the subject is silhouetted against a complicit sky; and the close-up, which permits the sitter to assume the entire frame, and suffer whatever passing trivia—people, dogs, vehicles—to occupy center stage for what is understood to be a stray and insignificant moment.

LUC SANTE 04.99

Babbacombe Model Village, Torquay, England.
Photograph by **Geof Kern**

236

Left: Sabbathday Lake, Maine; right: Cologne.
Photographs by **Wolfgang Tillmans**

THE ZEN OF SHOPPING

To semiologist Roland Barthes, the function of the Japanese package was "not to protect in space but to postpone in time." That hardly appears an apt description for clothing stores commonly associated with instant gratification. Yet the analogy of the package and the shop is a safe one. Postponing a purchase is a comfortable possibility in a low-pressure shop that seems designed to encourage contemplation. Such a serene space, set in a nervous city, can linger in the memory like an ancestral shrine, a place to be revisited religiously.

242   Not surprisingly the Japanese have become the most successful purveyors of emptiness, which may be seen in the remarkably restrained retailing spaces that are American outposts for Japanese fashion empires with French names. These shops offer total integration, not only of materials but also of the sexes. Here both women and men feel at ease and often look good in similar clothing. Other shops, those designed by Americans for American merchants, still separate the sexes. But often the interior design succeeds in integrating the old with the new, the lasting with the ephemeral, in spacious settings that have reminded one writer of "Shogun concrete."

           The Japanese ability to integrate conservative social patterns with sophisticated technology is a compelling model for American architects and designers looking for ways out of a maze of historical styles. This time they're learning from Japan. As Martin Friedman, director of Minneapolis's Walker Art Center, wrote, "Despite trappings of modernity, the past is not only alive there, it is a shaping force in the Japanese contemporary culture." Some highly visible and memorable shops around town remind New Yorkers of that attractive possibility. In these shops altarlike slabs of granite, stone, marble, wood, steel, and concrete isolate a special piece of clothing in an artful display. Clearly an attempt has been made to show an everyday object as a highly valued, rare item, in the same way that art is shown in a gallery or museum. With the elimination of multiples— there is one, one-of-a-kind shirt instead of 30 in many colors and sizes—the customer is assured of the possibility for unique self-expression through dressing. This artful expression of the self is attached to a large price tag.

           Ideas of how to combine the expensive pieces into something fresh and new are provided at the occasional interruptions to the space, often on large slabs. Here an attractive ensemble is stretched out as an offering in a temple. But the offering is merely a prelude to the larger ceremony. The clothes come alive, they move and drape on the attractive bodies of youthful salespeople who come and go in outfits they've gleaned from the racks, where only one of each style hangs.

           The glamour of celebrity adds to the excitement of shopping when the omnipresent television screen, always located at some site crucial to the shopper's decision-making, catches the customer's attention. This might be at the mysterious entrance where the timid are separated from the adventurous who dare to push through the doors. Or the screen might be near the "cash wrap desk," as the merchandising trade calls the old cash register that has metamorphosed into a small silent computer. At such points of potential hesitation, the artful video reinforces each decision. It presents a perfection of fantasy as a joyous procession of reedlike models with magazine-cover faces.

Coincidentally the video images of clothes in action also help the space planners' intentions for keeping props to a minimum. There's no need here for bulky mannequins—that space can be left empty, to create distances between products and people. The shop's resulting openness calls attention to permanent templelike surfaces that surround everything.

Giving a sacred aura to a container of worldly activity is not foreign to American memory. This integration of seemingly contradictory aspects of life was already brewing here in the seventeenth century. In the Midwest and New England the Shakers built ascetic, luminous rooms to house their daily lives. Their harmonious artifacts are products of a simple all-embracing belief in "hands to work and hearts to God," as was foretold by the sect's founder, "mother" Ann Lee.

In less than a hundred years, in the midst of nineteenth-century material excesses, the East Coast transcendentalists wrote and lectured extensively on spirituality, detachment, and self-control. Although more verbose than the Far Eastern philosophers who inspired them (a Zen master can express a thought in a brief haiku, a Japanese poem that is always 17 syllables), Americans once more gave their voices to eternal yearnings for something beyond the material.

The hundred-year cycle of American spirituality renewed itself in 1960s counterculture. A whole generation searched for ways to connect the many scattered concerns of modern life. Although specialization and standardization produced a life of material abundance, that life of many parts was increasingly difficult to comprehend. Once more the East, with its philosophy of integration, was a source of inspiration. Popular teachers like Alan Watts assured their audiences of an eternal life that is an "on/off pulsation." Like the transcendentalists a century before him, Watts put the individual in charge of understanding the world. It is up to men, he wrote in 1966, to transform "this immense electrical pulsation into light and color, shape and sound, large and small, hard and heavy, long and short. In knowing the world we humanize it."

During that same turbulent decade, Barthes—whose work subsequently induced a generation of American architects and designers to consider the products of their work as "instruments of meaning"—was also drawn to the East. After a trip to Japan he began to decipher some of the signs of that culture. He observed in EMPIRE OF SIGNS that "all of Zen" is concerned with ways to "halt language, to jam that kind of internal radiophony continually sending in us, even in our sleep." The way of Zen, he discovered, was "to empty out, to stupefy, to dry up the soul's incoercible babble"—the unstated aim, in fact, of these shops. Twenty years after those words were written, people living in computer cultures stressed with information overload are beginning to understand the importance of emptying out. SUSAN S. SZENASY 10.86

243

IBA Social Housing, by Peter Eisenman, Berlin.
Photograph by **Reingard Gorner**

DESIGN IS **PLACES**

3 NEW YORK ARCHITECTS IN BERLIN

For almost a generation, John Hejduk at Cooper Union, Peter Eisenman through the now defunct Institute for Architecture and Urban Studies, and Raimund Abraham at both Pratt Institute and Cooper Union have influenced architectural thinking in New York. Highly regarded in this country for their provocative and poetic ideas about architecture, all three are currently involved in building new projects in Kreuzberg, an old and still ravaged neighborhood of West Berlin.

The cause for their activity is West Berlin's International Building Exposition, the government-sponsored Internationale Bauausstellung Berlin (IBA). Culminating in 1987, the 750th anniversary of Berlin's founding (being celebrated separately by both East and West cities), IBA's primary focus has been to provide examples of well-designed subsidized housing. Although the building projects have included renovation of existing structures and planning, it is the building of new architecture by designers of international repute that has currently transformed parts of West Berlin into a textbook of contemporary building art.

In Kreuzberg, Hejduk, Eisenman, and Abraham are all building on a short street called Friedrichstrasse. Because of the street's proximity to the center of old united Berlin, Friedrichstrasse was largely destroyed during the Allied bombardment of World War II. Even as late as 1987 the street and its surrounding neighborhood, Kreuzberg, still contain a rough patchwork of buildings. Stone commercial structures, dating from the late nineteenth and early twentieth centuries, contrast with quickly made fifties-style housing projects. Bombed-out building lots interrupt the continuous flow of urban structures and streets. Finally, this array of dissimilar buildings and raw spaces ends in the gray, concrete Berlin Wall. Once Friedrichstrasse was the heart of Berlin's thriving prewar film industry. Today the street's lone monument occurs where Friedrichstrasse intersects the Berlin Wall. At this point a makeshift guardhouse, an auto stop, and a break in the wall comprise the fragile architecture of the infamous Checkpoint Charlie.

One unique aspect of the IBA in Kreuzberg was the absence of a master plan for the new housing projects. Seeing the still devastated area as an existing "fragmentary site," Abraham explains that the new IBA buildings were "developed as new fragments. Within this concept, each architecture has a new presence."

For the architects from New York, the leitmotif of the new presence among the history and ruins of Berlin was significant. The focal point of Hejduk's main housing complex is a 14-story tower that will rise gently above the surrounding 5- and 6-story buildings. Around the corner from this complex a smaller apartment house is also under construction. Standing on piers, it is part gatehouse and part clock, an animated fragment that will describe time vertically by the motion of two sliding metal side panels. (On either side of the structure are two integrated columns with numbers inscribed from 1 to 12, starting at the building's base and rising to the top.)

Eisenman's housing and museum at Checkpoint Charlie is the most striking of any of the completed IBA projects. Partially sheathed in a metal and glass skin,

245

DESIGN IS **PLACES**

this project appears as a fragment of the future cast against the background of the pre-World War II structures of Friedrichstrasse. Intentionally lacking the terraces and winter gardens of the traditional Berlin apartment house, the facade is composed of two intersecting oblique planes. The piquant geraniums and lace curtains placed within units reveal a yearning for symbols of home and hearth.

Whereas Eisenman's housing has a futuristic patina, Abraham's mid-block building suggests the mystery and enigma of a ruin. The front and rear facades are composed of attenuated precast concrete members, sculptured elevations that Abraham calls "topological facades." He is also concerned with incorporating vernacular elements, such as generous terraces and a well-articulated rear courtyard, into this new fragment for Berlin.

Why is there such an appreciation for new architecture in present-day Berlin? Hejduk passionately feels that Berliners are typical of a different climate in Europe. "Europeans put the mind to work," he noted. "They are interested in the 'cerebral' and the 'head.' "Eisenman feels that in Berlin "people are not interested in commercial architects. They are more interested in an avant-garde tradition. For example, IBA didn't ask Meier, Gwathmey, or Graves to participate." The Austrian-born Abraham sees the polarity between the European intellectual and the American pragmatist mindsets as being "a consequence of capitalism; in America, professionalism supersedes ideas."

With Josef Paul Kleihues, the Berlin architect who is the director of IBA, currently teaching at Cooper Union, one wonders if a similar architectural exposition could occur in New York. Certainly the need for innovative housing solutions is imperative. Abraham feels this might be possible, because of the force of Kleihues' presence in New York. However, he adds, "Europe is provincial. It is easier to establish a focus. America is more complex and has more problems."

To the casual observer it seems almost ironic that all three American architects should be building in such immediate proximity to Checkpoint Charlie. This is perhaps the most American area of West Berlin. Even its name is a reflection of Berlin's occupied status ("Charlie" is a letter in the American military alphabet: A = Alpha, B = Bravo, C = Charlie, etc.).

As one observes these new building sites, one cannot escape the tour buses passing by the place where Soviet and American tanks confronted one another 26 years ago. Uniformed American soldiers photograph each other by the checkpoint. The adjacent Berlin wall is decorated by New York graffiti artist Keith Haring. Were the Americans Eisenman, Hejduk, and Abraham placed near the infamous Checkpoint Charlie for any particular reason? "No, Checkpoint Charlie belongs to the world," Eisenman says. "Jack Kennedy said 'Ich bin ein Berliner!' " MARY PEPCHINSKI 09.87

246

BRINGING UP BABY

Nathaniel Weiner marches around the room with the stern authority of a Bauhaus professor. He paces, stops abruptly to lift a ruler against the plaster, and proclaims in accented English: "Dis wall goes here." He paces again: "Dis window goes here." And again: "Dis bed goes here."

I'm delighted. What a brilliant, commanding performance for someone barely two years old. Certainly he combines the best traits of both parents as he begins to sculpt space like his mother (a former architect), and to satirize grown-ups like his father (a working humorist). But I'm worried, too. Nat's new opinionated interest in his environs tells me it won't be long until he realizes the truth: at best, his domain is haphazard. His own mother has failed to provide the bright, accessible, creative, sanitary, efficient, memorable place he deserves.

What Nat's world needs is more design. Not more possessions (nice relatives have furnished those) or "good design," but a safe and stimulating environment. Once Nat's father and I found a design scheme that assigned everything its proper size, shape, location, and schedule, we would all save time, money, and stress. By liberating our reserves of patience and resourcefulness, a redesigned habitat could make us better parents and more gracious hosts. Inevitably one well-designed solution would inspire another, until we had created the momentum of a progressive household.

So why haven't we—two concerned parents with the privilege of working at home—got our act together?

Time, of course. Although we had plenty of it in our reckless twenties, we must have spent all of it somewhere else since. Now, time-impoverished in our thirties, we keep one step behind all our household duties. Planning ahead is a costly luxury. Because design requires advance planning, we put it off—rejecting all design measures in the process.

Just because we don't practice design, however, doesn't mean we restrain ourselves from preaching it. Nat's father and I are always eager to teach new parents our old discoveries, and these begin with reveling in contradictions.

LIVING WHERE YOU NEVER WANTED TO LIVE BEFORE
IS PRETTY NICE AFTER ALL

Ten years ago, on an architectural field trip to Hartford, Connecticut, we visit the house of home-efficiency advocate Catherine Beecher (author of AMERICAN WOMEN'S HOME, 1869). I think: How tedious to live so reclusively in a Victorian hulk of a suburban house while writing books and obsessing about kitchen flow plans. None of this domestic stuff for me; I'm off to the big city to build high-rises and postpone kids.

Last year we left New York City to move into a hulking Eastlake Victorian house (circa 1870) in nonhip but affordable Bethlehem, Pennsylvania, where we write books and debate issues of household engineering. We still love the big city but laugh at its cost of living.

This setting suits our extremely domestic life. The three floors of the house provide great public/private/office zoning. The secret stairs of the former maid's suite allows an au pair girl her privacy. And the nooks, banisters, and dormers inside—and the grass outside—delight Nat nonstop.

Although this house was originally designed for a resident brood (families of six preceded us), our need for workspace cuts the place down to size. The original six bedrooms have become two bedrooms, two offices, one studio, and one acoustic drum room. The traditional living room, dining room, den, sunroom, and kitchen hold great quantities of books, toys, and derelict furniture while we figure out how to build swings and a sandbox.

248

ONE HOUSE IS NEVER ENOUGH

Disguised in his trucker hat and wraparound sunglasses, Nat jabs his plastic bat, yelling, "OK, play baseball, now! Nat hit!" He knocks the Nerf ball across the room and circles the house for a home run. After a hard morning of base hits, he trades his bat for a security blanket (a raggedy tie), settles down into his crib, and looks up to say, "Mommy, Nat cozy."

Because they're as fragile as they are tough, kids really need two houses to contain their changing moods and shifting stages of life: one vast, rugged, and indestructible; the other soft, petite, and warm. Raising a baby to toddlerhood, parents need both houses within the span of two years—and within the course of the day. The successful designer will combine the two ideal houses into a single elastic home.

PRIVACY GOES PUBLIC

Nat's grandmother calls Friday night: "Hi. I'd like to drive up tomorrow." We say, "Gee, next weekend would be better. Some friends...." She says, "I'm coming to see Nat, not you." "See you tomorrow," we say.

There's still another reason that the houses of new parents need to be simultaneously bigger and smaller than those of their previous lives: they become at once more public and more private. The private-public proportion begins shifting as soon as the new baby comes home from the hospital. Because everyone feels fragile and vulnerable—including, presumably, the baby—the atmosphere is charged with a special kind of nervous intimacy. Mother seeks out quiet, pillowed corners for her breast-feeding sessions; rubbery baby things proliferate; parents nap heavily under the eerie blue glow of VCR-projected movies. The whole house gets privatized.

At the same time the house needs to go public. Suddenly even the smallest domain needs to function expansively, as friends and family increase the frequency of spontaneous visits, and holiday celebrations become more baroque. Also, lots of strangers are on the way: babysitters, the babysitters' friends and relatives, birthday-party guests, neighboring mothers and kids, the guys who deliver pizza and Chinese food.

TEMPORARY IS HERE TO STAY

"Nat, do you remember when you were a baby?" He answers, "Yes, [but] I not baby now."

The complex question in designing for kids is: How long does childhood take, anyway? In Nat's mind, his is over already. From his parents' point of view, this is only the beginning.

Misled by books, TV, and my own mother's recollections, I once believed childhood was a speeding phase. After making some recent calculations, however, I was surprised to find how long it takes to raise one or more children. For example, assuming that at the age of five a child reaches the age of reason—a time for restoring adultlike normality to the house, for better or worse—then parents who have two children spaced by the recommended three-year sibling gap will experience eight years of pre-five upheaval. Three kids, three years apart in age, total more than a decade of rambunctiousness.

How many childhoods does the average house survive? If just three of the above-mentioned well-spaced three-kid families spent those early-childhood years in the same dwelling, at different times, that would put 30 kid-years on the house.

What's so surprising is that the largest family houses are designed and scaled to ignore the presence of kids: common commercial floor plans remain inflexible, materials are unsympathetic, fixtures are unadaptable. Americans are willing to solve their domestic design problems by changing houses when their families expand or contract, falter or prosper. As they switch addresses, they pack in or pack out all the boxes of temporary equipment used to adapt the houses to kids.

If everyone stopped treating childhood as a fleeting phase, consumers might agree to pay more for adaptable, long-lived solutions as designers and manufacturers saw fit to research and deliver them.

SAVVY PARENTS BECOME SUPERSTITIOUS DESIGNERS

I ask my younger sister, a corporate bank lawyer, for advice about baby decor. She has no kids yet but prepares far in advance, reads voraciously, and knows about everything. "Try yellow. I read that it stimulates the brain and makes babies smarter," she says. Even though I hate that color, I dutifully hang a wall of translucent chrome-yellow curtains in the baby's room. Several months later, I notice that they've worked on Nat!

Modern mothers may start out scientific, but they soon become superstitious. Did Frank Lloyd Wright really blossom because of his mother's pushy interior design—engravings of Chartres Cathedral papering the nursery walls and Froebel blocks strewn on the floor? Better to get the blocks now and save the skepticism for later, many mothers believe.

But if evocative design can form a great person, perhaps it can break one, too. Mothers with no previous record of sexism ban pink in the boy's room and shop for virile shades of blue. Parents who once put no stock in environmental influences suddenly attribute great power to inanimate objects. They engage in voodoo design, hoping against hope that the nursery's artifacts—fine art, handmade quilts, plush animals—will work subliminal wonders. BARBARA FLANAGAN 07/08.88

249

Wedding chapels in Las Vegas.
Photographs by **Sean Hemmerle**

IT'S A GOOD THING WE DIDN'T CALL MEMPHIS 'ALASKA.'

MARCO ZANINI 07/08.85

SURVIVING URBAN BLIGHT

The Longwood Historic District is an architectural oasis in the heart of the South Bronx. This is Fort Apache, named after a local police station that was seen as a lone and embattled outpost in the untamed urban wilds of northern New York City. But as neighborhoods like Longwood show, lawlessness and hopelessness are not universal here. True, the bulk of the South Bronx went into an economic and social tailspin in the early 1960s and currently possesses gaping building shells and fields of tall grass littered with car parts and garbage. Yet Longwood's seven blocks of two-and-a-half-story houses contain some of the Bronx's finest intact turn-of-the-century residential buildings. Fortunately the neighborhood was only singed by the arson that consumed much of its surroundings. The 137 buildings in the Longwood section are generally well tended, and the neighborhood became a New York City Historic District in 1980 and was placed on the National Register of Historic Places in 1983.

252

Life abounds on streets made stable by the presence of longtime residents, private home-owners, and the work of the Longwood Historic District Community Association (LHDCA), which was formed 12 years ago. Salsa music swings from small grocery stores and children play on jungle gyms and slides in the middle of the block. On Sunday afternoons large extended families dressed in their Sunday best stroll from church. Men tinker with their highly polished, jacked-up cars; young couples lug laundry bags; girls skip rope. An old woman sets a plate of food on her stoop for stray cats.

Longwood was originally part of the township of Morrisania, an amalgam of villages, farms, country homes, and the Morris family manor in what used to be southern Westchester County. Annexed by the Bronx in 1874, this union of municipalities was incorporated into greater New York City in 1898, and was connected with Manhattan in 1904 by the IRT subway line. The mass-transit link accompanied a building boom that lasted until the Depression.

The small district lies to the west of Longwood Avenue and comprises Hewitt Place, Leggett Avenue, and Dawson, Kelly, Beck, and East 156th Streets. It was almost completely developed by the realtor George B. Johnson, who purchased the Samuel B. White estate about 1898 and operated his business out of White's mansion. Most of the buildings were built between 1897 and 1900 by the Long Island architect Warren C. Dickerson.

Almost all of Dickerson's buildings are two-and-a-half-story semi-attached structures, neo-Renaissance and mildly Romanesque Revival in style. They were planned together and built in mirror image, which along with their uniform scale and style makes a cohesive, pleasing cityscape. To avoid monotony and enliven the ensemble, Dickerson variously arranged similar materials throughout. He designed each double house for two to three families, coupled the iron-railed stoops between round and angular masonry bay windows, and separated the units with a driveway and an iron gate. Many homes were built with Roman brick, carved limestone, and brownstone ornamentations with Ionic, Corinthian, and composite-style pilasters and columns framing doorways and windows.

All the buildings' bays have imbricated shingled roofs with false mansard fronts and polygonal and cone-shaped tops that jut into the sky, creating little rooftop exclamation points. Some of the Romanesque Revival structures have raised rusticated basements.

Things are not perfect in Longwood. There is a drug problem on Beck Street, and dealers openly hawk their wares on Longwood Avenue. A number of homes and apartments are abandoned, sporting appliqué windows, with red and blue flowerpots and white shutters, which the city hopes will hide the obvious abandonment. One or two buildings have been faced with tacky artificial orange, yellow, and pink fieldstone. Even so, there is a sense of permanence. The seven-story Prospect Hospital towers over Kelly Street. Although this early 1960s white-brick building is in visual opposition to its neighbors, it has helped stabilize the area. A pharmacy is located in one of the Kelly Street basements, and there are doctors' offices in some of the other houses.

Pine telephone poles still line the sidewalk along Dawson Street, the district's widest road. Except for the lots on Longwood Avenue and a few abandoned buildings at its edges, Dawson Street's houses are well tended. Lace curtains hang behind wrought-iron door-gates, window boxes rest on sills, and polished brass shoe guards glint in the afternoon sun. Most of the beige-and-brown Roman bricks are clean and repainted, while splayed lintels and running bands enliven exterior surfaces. Some double oak doors have been restored and crowned by clear and stained-glass transoms and fanlights. Slender Ionic columns and composite-order pilasters border doors and rough-cut Romanesque arches frame upper windows. There is the occasional discordant note, such as new brick railings and chain-link fences, but the overall effect is harmonious.

Roland Lopez, a solid mustached man who walks with the assured swagger of the homicide detective he once was, acts as director of the LHDCA. The house where he grew up is still occupied by his mother, Nicolasa. Her front parlor has high plastered ceilings and the original light brown parquet floor with a dark wood trim. The house has a heavily carved oak staircase to one side, a parlor up front, a dining room and kitchen to the rear, and bedrooms upstairs. Brass hardware and a tiled entrance floor greet visitors, and there is a garden in the back.

"These houses are made to last forever," Nicolasa Lopez says. "Many years back people said, 'sell and move.' But selling is not the answer. I love this house. My children were born here. The only thing that bothers me are the fires and empty lots." When she moved to the neighborhood in the 1940s, she remembers, "It was beautiful. I hope I live to see what the Bronx can be again." Her son concurs. He agrees with the motto, "Don't move, improve." Leaving is not the answer. Home ownership is what maintains a community. DANIEL S. LEVY 07/08.89

A TRICKSTER IN TOMORROW'S OFFICE

For Japanese architect Isao Hosoe, the modern office is obsolete. In the seminar entitled "Work Encounters/Domesticity" that he taught last year at the Domus Academy, the postgraduate design school in Assago, Italy, Hosoe suggested that students assume the role of the mythical trickster. If a designer is going to break through the rigidity of the corporate office structure, Hosoe believes, he must employ "discontinuity, anomaly, and madness." Students were advised to consider such key elements of human life as delight and drama, play and status, even sexuality.

Crucial to the students' projects was the determination of just what "domesticity" should mean in an office context. Hosoe pointed out that the familiar workplace with its executive offices and paneled conference rooms resembles the plan of the ancient Roman house, the archetype for the Western concept of domesticity. Founded on the ideas of permanence, order, and privacy, both plans depend on symbolic and hierarchical divisions of private and public space.

Because the electronic office is about communication, flexibility, and shared activity, Hosoe urged students to eschew these traditional notions. Instead he encouraged them to turn for inspiration to non-Western concepts of domesticity: the multifunctional Japanese house, in which the divisions between private and public spaces are mutable; or the lightweight transportable nomads' tents, which when configured with others in a circle, create an intimate social space where home and public life intermingle.

Eakachat Joneuraiatana found a model for an office system in the Chat, the holy umbrella of his native Thailand. A transparent umbrella veils an office island where a management team might work. The petal-like curved panels that compose the dome lift up or down to articulate social openness or privacy. The station's unexpected shape also brings an element of playful exoticism to the ordinarily nondescript office interior.

Exploring corporate notions of status and hierarchy, Yasuhiro Asano designed three chairs that give new meaning to the phrase "clawing one's way to the top." The simple secretary's chair perches on a single avian leg, while the middle manager's chair can scale corporate heights with its winglike armrests and eaglelike legs and claws. Gabriela Raible's office-dividing panels are based on the Kiva, the sacred meeting places of the Southwestern Pueblo Indians. The open area of the Kiva, simply demarcated by stones, was used by the Indians for informal gatherings; below ground there was another secret chamber for religious ceremonies and political meetings. Because office culture requires places for casual as well as more serious convocations, Raible designed adaptable dividers. Constructed from transparent metal netting stretched across articulated frames, her panels can bend into concave pod shapes. When arranged in their erect form, the panels create an open, inviting meeting place, but when bent inward, they form a more intimate formal space.

One of the most striking models was by Yoshei Ota. A simple, narrow column when not in use, his workstation opens out like a fan to reveal a desk, computer, and video screen, as well as two fan-shaped partitions for privacy. No doubt Hosoe would approve. MARISA BARTOLUCCI 10.90

SOVIET SIGNS

I was staring at a sign somewhere in the Moscow subway when I had this realization: the USSR is a typeface. The World's Largest Country, the Russian Empire, the Second World, the Communist Threat: all were conveyed in those solid block letters. The Union of Soviet Socialist Republics is hard to picture beyond the archetypal image of Moscow's Red Square: the impregnable fortress, the secular cathedral, and the vast pedestrian space. This image came with me to the Soviet Union, and it had as much bearing on what I saw of life there as a type style does on the meaning of a sentence.

In the fall of 1990 my friend Tom Freisem and I bicycled 1,200 miles through three republics of the Soviet Union: south from Moscow in the Republic of Russia, to Kiev and Odessa in the eastern Ukraine, through Moldavia, to Lvov in the western Ukraine, continuing across Poland and on to Berlin. For five weeks, unescorted and at ground level, we moved through industrial cities, primitive villages, and empty farmlands. Across this wide-reaching landscape were the ubiquitous signs, slogans, images, and icons of the Communist Party, a weird mix of propaganda, public art, and practical signage.

In Moscow and other big cities along our route, vestiges of a richer history remain. Beautiful old buildings echo other European capitals and house museums, opera, and theater. Famous names evoke a wealth of literary tradition. In these cities, the socialist icons blend in scale and weight with the monumental architecture of the fortresses and cathedrals: the 100-foot Lenin posters on the Kremlin walls, like the fifteenth-century Kremlin itself, were tourist attractions.

Outside the old city centers little remains of the traditional aesthetics that connect this vast federation with its religious heritage and with European and other ethnic cultures. Here the socialist slogans and logos are more serious, if more incongruous. Where the churches have been demolished, the great houses sacked, and the farms collectivized, these public images are eye-catching but disconcerting.

Every collective farm, administrative district, and neighborhood has some large sign or structure marking it. Most incorporate the hammer-and-sickle icon with images of what the region produces: agriculture, textiles, and machinery. The graphic pieces themselves are aggressive and self-important: modern-looking sculptures attempting to inspire modernity in chicken farms (bird factory is the Russian term), airports, and towns.

Every main street is called Ulitsa Lenina (Lenin Street), and there is a statue of Lenin, in one of three familiar positions, in every town square. This is where Tom and I would stand around, if the town had no hotel, until our high-tech bikes and Clowns from Mars outfits drew a crowd. In the village of Nenashevo, the local Communist boss showed up first, a squat balding man in a suit who told us to catch the train to the next city. But peasant women passing by took our side, shaking bunches of carrots at the People's Deputy: "What's the problem? Help these boys!" A man with a thick mustache listened in, and then gestured for us to follow. In his two-room flat, he made us rice soup and left to stay with friends so we'd have space.

255

DRESSING-ROOM POLITICS

The American dream is a myth. We are not born equal. But we get an equal opportunity to feel great—every morning—under the shower. American plumbing is the great social equalizer. The shower, in the land of the free, is not a convenience, it's a privilege: it turns ordinary citizens into crowned heads. We, the people, start the day naked but regal, our heads truly crowned in water.

I had to come to the USA to experience the baptismal power of this particular ritual. In Paris, where I grew up, there are no decent showers; what you get is a meager handheld contraption that spurts like a watering can.

Unfortunately in America, as soon as you step out of the shower stall, you lose your prerogative. Turn off the water, and the bathroom becomes a grim and slippery cell. The decor is spartan and bleak; the tiles are usually ugly, the furnishings minimal. French bathrooms, on the contrary, are real rooms—often with a window and enough space for a small table and a couple of side chairs. They encourage people to linger and dally in the nude, take their time and, if they feel like it, read for a while.

There is no such thing in America. As you tiptoe out of the steamed-up bathroom wrapped in a towel, you will not find a friendly spot to rest your bare bottom. You have to keep moving, like someone on the run. There is a furtive quality to the dressing process, too. Putting your clothes on is carried out like a clandestine operation: you ransack your drawers, looking for underwear; you pilfer your closet, hoping to find the right thing to wear; you leap on one foot while putting on your hose or your socks. The place soon looks a mess. Dressing in America is the most uncivilized act of the day.

Amazingly enough, working people manage to get it together. By the time they hit the streets, they appear to be winners, dressed for success and in control.

In most American homes that focal point is missing. There is no dressing room, boudoir, "lingerie" —just a crowded dressing table, a walk-in closet, or a side chair to throw your clothes on, if you're lucky. People instinctively elect various spots in their homes as a rallying point. For some it's the mirror. For others it's a basket holding gloves and keys. Two lovers take turns watching TV and commenting on the news. A young man fusses over his tie collection. My husband refills my coffee cup a couple of times to bring me back to the breakfast table, where he sits patiently while I run around. Dressing up in the morning can be a three-ring circus. And you dream of a carpeted alcove where you could quietly and methodically put on your clothes.

We are suffering from lack of space, but also from lack of understanding. Intimate details are kept so private no one knows anymore how to live. We learn from the movies how to take our clothes off, but not how to put them on. I can't think of a single scene in a film showing characters dressing to go to work. Is it so unmentionable and unsightly? Painters like Ingres, Bonnard, Seurat, and Degas have given us wonderful images of women at their toilette. So why can't filmmakers do the same?

Photographers have replaced painters. The naked body, now recorded on emulsion, not canvas, is seen as explicit and erotic rather than intimate and personal.

258

We look at everything through a sharp lens; life is just a photo opportunity. Architects and their clients now design houses and apartments with the camera angle in mind—a living room being first and foremost a potential spread in a magazine. No one wants to publish dead space, empty hallways, and bare corners. As a result there is no mystery, no hiding place, no spare room in modern apartments. Every square inch is accounted for, shrink-wrapped and exploited. There is very little "in-between" space.

With the exception of the Shakers, few American designers have been inspired to create memorable objects relating to storage. In other countries wonderful dressing-room and closet artifacts are readily available on the market. I found a witty freestanding mirror with holes for eyes, designed by Carlo Cumini for Horn in Italy; a well-crafted Modernistic coat rack, from North Studio in Toronto; a totemic storage unit in cold-rolled steel and wrought iron, by Russell Bagley for Box Products in London; a two-panel screen that looks like a Venetian mask, by Massimo Iosa Ghini for Lisar in Milan. All it takes is one extraordinary object to transform nonspace into a zone of possibilities.

259

Today dressing for work has become a form of meditation. When asked to describe their grooming and dressing routine, most people talk about minute details with great seriousness, as if it were a ceremony—or a celebration. For many there is an irresistible quality of hope in the sunrise, and even on rainy days there is a feeling of expectation: am I really alive? You get up, stumble into the bathroom to check the mirror. The first look is the occasion for an intimate spiritual inquiry.

No matter what you see, the sight is always reassuring—I look like hell, therefore I am. For the next 30 to 60 minutes, you will accomplish a double task—preserve your private self and assert your public identity; become more human but less vulnerable; remember that it's the first day of the rest of your life—and shine your shoes.

Louis XIV built a majestic chapel next to his royal bedroom. All we want is a little dressing room.   VERONIQUE VIENNE 04.92

I COLLECT GLOBES WITH NO POLITICAL BOUNDARIES. THEY MAKE ME THINK ABOUT HOW WE MAY LIVE ON THE PLANET.

KEVIN WALZ 05.92

MULTICULTURAL TWISTS

Several months ago I found myself sitting in Frank Gehry's "Festival Disney" arcade, brooding over a cheeseburger and a glass of French Burgundy on how the most popular tourist destination in Europe managed to lose $1.5 billion in its first year. I was literally holding the answer in my hand.

Euro Disney is a massive exercise in applied multiculturalism, and the prognosis is not good. Like all colonial adventurers, Disney set sail intending to impose its rule over native subjects. A few concessions might be made to indigenous institutions—the simulated Matterhorn of Anaheim would be replaced by Big Thunder Mountain, since the real thing is nearby; Adventureland became Discoveryland, in deference to the restless European spirit. For the most part, however, the supra-cultural iconography of Disney was preserved intact, as was its antiseptic cleanliness, the ruthless efficiency of its technical infrastructure, the preternatural friendliness of its staff, and (it need hardly be added) its unequivocal ban on the sale of alcohol.

As the debt load grew and wing after wing of its sprawling designer hotels was closed off, the culture of Disney was forced into a more tolerant accommodation with the culture of Old Europe. The famous prohibition of alcohol was the first taboo to be lifted. Hence, the Burgundy with my burger. Other amendments to the constitution of the parent company will doubtless follow—if it is not too late. Next year the cafe waiters may be allowed to revert to their native surliness. And the year after?

The lesson of all this is simply that design at all levels—from a teaspoon to a theme park, as the saying almost goes—requires the fusion of two cultural realms if it is to be successful: the realm in which the designer operates, with all of its inherited memories, tastes, values, obsessions, and prejudices; and the realm within which the designed artifact will take up residence and establish an independent existence. The delicacy of this balance is what was underestimated by Disney. When there is a perfect cultural fit, the designed object melts into its background as invisibly as a Henry Dreyfuss telephone, or a Venetian gondola; it just seems to belong where it is, as it is, and we rarely pause to reflect upon just what it is that makes the relationship "work." But confronted by an American theme park in Paris, a London telephone box outside a bar in Palo Alto, the Queen Mary permanently docked in Long Beach, or the bizarre image of an electric yam pounder in the house of Amma Ogan's Igbo tribesman, we cannot help recoiling.

Jarring juxtapositions of this sort, we are told, are the mark of the postmodern, of an age that has either lost its confidence in the rightness of a single imperial style or has outgrown its need for it. During the heroic decades of Modernism, it will be recalled, an aggressive campaign was waged to neutralize the accidents of history and culture, of time and place. Technology would somehow define a uniformly objective aesthetic, and the impersonal norms of "modernization" would stitch together the peoples of the world. Although this fantasy is by no means dead, even at its most aggressive there was something fainthearted about it. This is because the object—with apologies to the philosophers—is never a wholly self-contained ding an sich (thing-in-itself), but gives and takes its meaning within a particular human, that is to say cultural, context.

Moreover, these contexts are never stable. Long before multiculturalism became the swan song of the freshman Western Civilization course, the Earth had been crisscrossed by the tracks of traders, warriors, explorers, missionaries, diplomats, pilgrims, students, tourists, and Federal Express. Then, as now, the products they carried with them shifted in meaning as they journeyed in different directions. The pivotal technologies of gunpowder, magnetism, and printing, for example, tended to support the conservative bureaucracy of China where they most likely originated; they proved revolutionary, however, when conveyed across the ancient Asiatic silk routes and dropped into the fluid social structure of Europe.

The same can be said of the "black stones" that, according to Marco Polo, were dug in Cathay and burnt for fuel (coal), of the vein found under the mountains of Chingintalas "that when crushed into a fiber is resistant to fire" (asbestos), and of the notes bearing the seal of the Great Khan with which Polo transacted his business "just as if they were coins of pure gold" (paper money). It took the genius of Western civilization to transform these discoveries into acid rain, cancer, and inflation.

It is clear that many of our most cherished (and not-so-cherished) icons are the result of centuries of interculturation. The English language is littered with evidence of the European debt to Islamic medicine, astronomy, and mathematics. In a profound sense, it may be said that the Arabs contributed nothing to Western civilization, but anyone who doubts the significance of "nothing" (zero comes from the Arabic sitr by way of the Medieval Latin zephirum) might try balancing a checkbook with Roman numerals. The word check, by the way, is derived from the Arabic sakk.

That the membranes separating the cultures of today's world have grown increasingly permeable—rendering the tasks of the designer increasingly complex—seems undeniable. Several artifacts have helped shape the virtual culture of postmodernity and are as representative of it as the Santeria altar is of Cuba or the mah-jongg tables are of Hong Kong.

First among them must surely be the various technologies of timekeeping, always in the vanguard of technological change. When the contents of Lemuel Gulliver's pockets were inventoried, his Lilliputian captors quite reasonably concluded that his watch must be the god he worshiped, or perhaps an oracle, because he never did anything without consulting it.

The clock having stealthily imposed upon us a common experience of time, it fell to the automobile to establish a common experience of space. The American landscape in particular—urban, suburban, or exurban—is shaped by our means of getting to it; no longer are we shaped by it. This historic inversion, the essence of what theorist Jean Baudrillard has aptly called the American "motopia" and writer J. G. Ballard, more ominously, the coming "Autogeddon," seems to be unprecedented.

Finally, there is the phenomenon of television, which has by now irrevocably restructured the innermost mental landscape of two generations. In retrospect it will

261

prove to have been the first tentative vehicle to travel down what more perceptive observers are already calling the Entertainment Superhighway. Its next incarnation, which will combine the functions now separately allocated to the television, the telephone, and the personal computer, will be ubiquitous within another decade.

The inevitably homogenizing effect of these technologies of time and space does not dispose of the problem of multiculturalism. To the contrary, designers should take multiculturalism seriously—but not too seriously. On the side of restraint lies the fact that although the reality of multiculturalism is very old, the discourse of multiculturalism is relatively new. Like all current intellectual fashions, it is full of untested generalities, unrestrained hyperbole, and unintelligible jargon—and must be treated as such.

In time, however, we are bound to see a shakedown in the multiculturalism industry, and some robust truths will emerge. First among these will doubtless be the moral truth that designers—no less than any other professionals—are bound to respect the diversity of tastes, values, fears, needs, desires, histories, and all else that make up the cultures and subcultures of the world.

As if that weren't enough (and alas, frequently it is not), it is also likely that a simple anthropological truth will emerge, and that is that ideas and artifacts that are culturally presumptuous may not travel well. At times this may result in mere embarrassment, such as John F. Kennedy standing with his back to the captive nations of Eastern Europe and solemnly declaring "Ich bin ein Berliner!" which is literally translated, "I am a jelly donut," or General Motors attempting to market the Chevy Nova in Puerto Rico: nova means "doesn't go." At times, the embarrassment may hit the bottom line with a deep and resounding thud. Whoever doubts this basic economic truth should seek out the managers of Euro Disney for a lesson in design and multiculturalism. BARRY KATZ 10.94

I LIKE THIS MALL. IT WOULD BE NICE TO REDO THIS MALL.

MARK LONDON 05.99

Following spread: web of steel, Seattle, Washington.
Photograph by **Kristine Larsen**

DESIGN IS **PLACES**

ACCESS

If we consider access simply in terms of legislation, we limit the dialogue to adaptive devices like ramps and Braille elevator buttons. But if we look at the question of access as one of greater social exchange and integration, we can address the bigger questions.

TV commercials, perhaps the most up-to-the-minute barometers of who we think we are, feature middle-aged and older people. Cotton Inc. shows Americans as a diverse group of races, ages, and sexual orientations living, loving, and dying in the "fabric of our lives." New York Telephone's "We're All Connected" campaign puts the elderly in touch with friends and family. Breakfast cereals, coffee, and weight-loss systems are only some of the products now sold by older people. Indeed statisticians tell us that by the year 2010 one in four of us will be over the age of 55. And by 2020 the baby boom will have attained senior status and four million of us will be visually impaired.

As our population grays, as our bodies become less flexible and our minds more introspective, our image of ourselves will also change. The need to conquer impossible odds will become less urgent. Indeed barriers of all sorts may lose some of their symbolic importance. We may even find a different way to travel the open road, which is what my father did during the last year of his life. His is an American road story with a twist. When he took to the road, my father was 78 and suffering from pulmonary fibrosis, a disease that made it increasingly difficult for him to breathe. And so he could think of nothing better to do than to drive his car across the country. My family had lived in an old New England house, partially heated by a wood stove, and in previous years he had split logs for exercise. Now he could no longer do this, and the climate in the Northeast, along with a house that was too large, made him feel isolated and depressed.

And so he got behind the wheel of his car. For my father, Route 40 was a barrier-free environment. The Pontiac's bucket seats reclined at such an angle that his driving position helped his breathing. He headed south, where even in January he could keep his window open. For lunch every day he would pull up to the drive-in window of a McDonald's and order a milk shake. Afterwards, he'd pull over to the side of the road, put the seat into a deeper recline, and sleep. After that he would keep on driving until late afternoon, when he'd stop at a motel, where he was usually able to get a ground-floor room because it was difficult for him to climb stairs. He did this all through the Blue Ridge and Smoky mountains, through the plains of the Midwest, and on to the deserts of the Southwest. And then he did it all the way home. For those months, one thing and one place led beautifully to another. I would call this access. I would also call this beating the odds.

People might find things wrong with this story, like the nutritional value of food from McDonald's. But to me it makes two beautiful and important points. The first is that my father's last year conformed to his itinerary of pleasure. The second is that his breathing disability, for those several months, did not make his world smaller; rather it served to expand his landscape for thousands of miles. And this is what access is all about: how we keep our landscape wide open in spite of our disabilities and sometimes even on account of them. AKIKO BUSCH 11.92

263

IN SEARCH OF HOME PLACE

I have been thinking about place in a place unlike any other I have ever lived in. It is a compound of government-built housing, surrounded by a low chain-link fence, set on the Hopi Reservation in northeastern Arizona. Doctors and pharmacists and optometrists and physicians' assistants and nurses live here, the men and women who staff the Indian Health Service Hospital in Keams Canyon. No one lives in the compound or works at the hospital for much longer than three years. The floors of the houses are linoleum, the exterior walls are lightly stippled stucco, and the soil is too sandy, the climate too dry, for gardens. Yet the compound is full of children, born in the midst of a temporary assignment because their parents are sure of the trajectory their lives are taking. Blue propane tanks stand beside each house and trailer. There are three streets: High, Middle, and Low. Except for the portable outhouses posted two to a street after a recent water crisis, this could be an ordinary neighborhood—the houses a little too seedy, perhaps, the inhabitants too medical—in any town in America.

But at the end of Middle Street there is a stile over a livestock fence, six steps up, five steps down. On the far side the ground drops away swiftly, and after a few more strides you find yourself in a watercourse, a streambed where the footprints of women and children and dogs are swept away after even the slightest of rains. On dry days—and most days here are dry—the doctors come with their partners and children to the wash, which to the boys and girls is a narrow meandering sandbox bordered by yucca plants and chamisa and juniper. The dogs lie in the sun. The two-year-olds throw sand at each other. Infants cling to their mothers. Around them the land rises into small barren hills latticed with horse trails ending at the abrupt red walls of the mesa, which form a long narrow canyon in whose shadow the compound lies. At dusk you can hear an owl calling from a cavity in the smooth rock walls of the mesa and you can hear nighthawks beginning to chitter overhead. The wings of ravens creak as they fly by. But in the bare afternoon the only sound you are likely to hear is the wind or the noises of a Hopi man—an ironworker by trade—training his quarter horse in a corral just up from the wash.

I have walked along the hills above the wash and found shards of pottery lying on the surface of the earth after heavy rains. Some are ridged by strict geometries, some are sinuous, and some are painted with broad black lines. I pick them up, turn them over, and put them back. You can distinguish them from the flat bits of rock that fill the wash by their slight but even curvature and by their consistent thickness. After a while you don't even need to pick them up to know that they are pieces of pottery—a sign that this has been a home place for someone. So is the water heater that lies in the streambed a ways up the wash and the section of dirt bank that spills over with broken glass and rusted cans. In the late afternoon in early spring, when the light begins to level off and the wash fills with the glow from the rocks along the edge of the mesa, it can be hard to keep your eyes to the soil. I find myself looking for loftier ground, a place where I can see the peaks near Flagstaff, which have been the cardinal point of reference for as long as humans have lived along the edge of this mesa that snakes its way westward across the desert.

The doctors' compound at Keams Canyon lies, in one sense, just around the corner from the great Hopi mesa-top villages, which cluster at the edges of First, Second, and Third Mesas only a few miles eastward. But in another sense it could hardly lie further away from them. I am not alluding to any of the romanticized distinctions that visitors bring to this reservation—distinctions between modern and ancient, rich and poor, Indian and white. I am thinking of the act of situating oneself. Frail as these villages can look when you walk through them on foot or when, driving past them, they appear only as a series of slight crenellations along the top of the mesa, they have what is, in human terms, an almost geological endurance. And though I see in these villages only a maze of narrow passageways, opening now and again onto a plaza filled with the smell of burning cedar, though I lack a sense of the rich human associations that arch back over centuries here on the breaking edge of a wave of stone, I still know a home place when I see one, even when it belongs to a culture not my own.

Yet I have learned here that looking across cultural borders requires an act of conscious translation. What seems familiar may not be familiar at all. In a village like Walpi, on First Mesa, what speaks of home to me is the arrangement of houses, the continuum of stone and timber, the rhythm of confinement and space, light and shade. To me, the landscape is a frame, and within it, centered, lays the village, the house. But the inhabitants of Walpi, of Mishongnovi—and even of the more modern houses that cluster along the foot of the mesa—have less invested in the idea of domicile than I do. For them the home place is found less in the house, in the arrangement of buildings, than in the land itself—the circle the horizon makes. And for a bond like that, landscape is already too abstract a word.

Another thing I've learned here is that we use the word native loosely. There is, for example, the old habit of calling indigenous non-European peoples "natives," as if to suggest—ambivalently—the permanent historical exile of whites outside of Europe. The word expresses an intrinsic connection between place and personhood. We usually don't think too carefully about it, since everyone, we assume, is a native of somewhere. It seems to come with the territory. But what surprises me is that we think of nativeness as something entirely passive. You're born and you grow up and, without thinking, you take on the coloring of the immediate world, pick up its accents, become a native. We all notice the glibness of children this way—how eager they are to imitate what they see around them. But that eagerness, that imitative power, is fluid: given the chance in a diverse, mobile culture like ours, children slip the mold with ease. Here's what I conclude. It takes a long time to make a native. It takes the steady press of years to do the job, and it's pretty easy to end up feeling like a native of nowhere. For me this raises a larger question: To whom belongs the greater pathos—the existential rover, the Cain, the Wandering Jew— or the person who has always lived in one beloved place and in whose face is written the shape of the land where he was raised?

Just as we take it for granted that nativeness is something that comes upon us unawares, we also take it for granted that there is a natural link between human consciousness and the landscape. It must be so, because, like all other creatures on Earth,

267

we are as a species the unconcluded product of constant adaptation. To what have we adapted if not our environment? There is a strain in human nature that tends to sanctify the home landscape, to convert its landmarks into the icons of a primal story that binds the listener throughout his lifetime to the scene where that story is set. But we would hardly be human without the awareness of alternative places and settings, even if we know them only through myth, stories, and dreams. That awareness draws us away from the home place and yet reinforces what you might call the closure of the home place—the sense that it is defined differently from all other places.

      I have spent a lot of time among the doctors in this compound. Though they are here now, they carry with them an extraordinarily strong sense of where they have been and where they are going. This is partly because, like anyone who has a graduate degree or who has served in an institution as widely scattered as the Indian Health Service, they carry about with them a geographical resume. They were in Mescalero, now they're here, but in six months they'll be going to Yakima. Today they're in the emergency room, tomorrow they're at the clinic on Second Mesa, and this weekend they'll be on educational leave—at a medical conference—in Chicago. They know about each other's medical geography, what school they attended and where they did their residencies; but they don't know nearly as much about the towns in which their colleagues were born or the houses in which they were raised.

      The children who were born to the residents of this compound will not be natives of this beautiful, delicate place. They will leave too soon, and, I suspect, they could never be natives here anyway. The schools aren't good enough, and there is nothing in the landscape, for Anglos at least, to compensate for that deficiency. Of one or two of the doctors or their partners, you might say that they have never been here at all, though others have found themselves wedded to the light and the dry air and the stones in the wash in ways they would never have imagined. Many of the doctors try to keep their patients at something of a distance, the way they would in any practice, anywhere. Some have sought what are called "cultural friends"—that is, they have made an extensive acquaintance among the Hopis and Navajos. But none of the doctors, even those who choose to remain with the Indian Health Service, will carry away anything more than a memory of this place, with perhaps a few kachina dolls and a Navajo rug and a large selection of books about Native American history. These doctors, like me, are inherently natives of a different kind of place, a more abstract place, which is defined by one's awareness of the alternatives to it. It is not enough to say that I, like them, could live anywhere. I must choose somewhere to live, with the alternatives strong in my mind. And in that I am significantly different from the patients who come to the hospital here, who are bound to this place by bonds of a kind that nearly every episode in my family's history has set aside, though my family is made up of farmers who have farmed the same land for most of this century.

      My father calls the farm where he was raised, and which is still being worked by his brother and nephews, "the home place." To me, the home place has become an abstraction. It is not a place I come from, but a place I hope someday to find. I must imagine coming into it, feeling the sudden force of recognition, knowing that this is the place that will begin to put all other places out of my mind. I have always taken for granted the primacy of the link between landscape and human consciousness. I have asked myself again and again the question I asked earlier in this essay: "To what have we adapted if not our environment?" I thought about listing for you all the towns in which I have lived—not a long list, but one that reaches from a tiny mining town in northwestern Colorado (where I was born, but of which I am not a native) to London, England. But after listing them, I realized that all the places I had lived were essentially the same, because the environment that humans have adapted to is not mainly a landscape at all—it is the presence of other humans. To know the truth of this you have only to watch the synergy of humans as they transform even a place as barren as government housing—which actively resists the homemaking instincts of its occupants—into a true community, whose focus is each other.

269

That much becomes perfectly clear, here in this compound, on the first day of spring, a Sunday. It is 70 degrees. When the sun has just begun to abate, and it's getting late enough that everyone will be able to retreat to dinner, a ball game begins on Middle Street. Children line up to bat at home plate, which is painted backwards on the asphalt. A patient father pitches. The compound dogs are playing the outfield. When a two-year-old gets a base hit, another father helps him scamper to first base. Parents cheer. A pinch runner is sent in. The score is a billion to a million. No one is counting strikes.
VERLYN KLINKENBORG 07/08.92

WHAT'S THE GOOD OF TALKING ABOUT AESTHETICS, PROPORTIONS, HARMONY, AND WAYS OF LIFE IN THE FACE OF ECONOMIC PRESSURE AND POLITICAL FACTORS? THEY MAKE THE ARCHITECTURE OF CITIES A GAME PLAYED BY EVERYONE, WITHOUT ANYBODY KNOWING THE RULES OR VALUES OF THE CARDS.

JEAN NOUVEL 06.94

I LIVE AT 69 ALBANY
AVENUE IN TORONTO,
BUT I ALSO LIVE IN
THE UNIVERSE...

RED
RODEO

VER
RENA

...AND I'M AT HOME IN
BOTH OF THEM.

JANE JACOBS 04.98

NEW URBANISM

A grand fraud is being perpetrated in America. Across the country, developers and planners are selling repackaged subdivisions as "new urban" communities. Billed as the modern equivalent of Charleston, Georgetown, and "Our Town" all rolled into one, these are supposed to be places where people of all backgrounds will be magically freed from their chaotic, car-dependent lifestyles to reunite in corner cafes along civic squares and lead healthy public lives.

Also known as neotraditionalism, New Urbanism is the much-hyped theory that planners can create cohesive communities by building subdivisions—though that word is never used—that resemble traditional towns or big-city neighborhoods. To do that, streets are laid out in grids (some are modified) without cul-de-sacs, garages are tucked into alleys behind homes positioned close to the street and to each other, housing types and prices are varied, and street-level retail turns up in or near residential neighborhoods. At Kentlands, a planned community in the Maryland suburbs of Washington, D.C., this strategy is meant to create what the sales brochure calls "the old-town charm of Georgetown and Annapolis ... in western Gaithersburg."

It sounds good. But although the virtues of the traditional city or town may be desirable, they cannot be replicated on empty land at the edge of town, where most of these developments are being built. This is not a matter of New Urbanism being right or wrong, but of understanding what is possible and what is not. Cities, even when drawn by a single hand—like Washington or Paris—take shape in the context of larger economic and social forces. Reproducing traditional cities, or saving the ones we have, would require recreating the conditions and systems that produced them. This may or may not be desirable; but in any case it is a sociological question with real economic consequences, a question that New Urbanism avoids.

New Urbanism is fast becoming the new standard for suburban development. Zoning boards and city councils around the country are demanding that new subdivisions conform to this idea, or at least to some of its superficial aspects. An avalanche of magazine and newspaper articles, books, and television shows preach that New Urbanism will save us from our suburban sins. But these new subdivisions cannot cure the ills of sprawl. They are sprawl. ALEX MARSHALL 07/08.96

272

REINVENTING PLACE

Our sense of place keeps getting vaguer as the postindustrial economy moves relentlessly forward. Megastores, downsizing, faxes, laptops, cellular phones, working mothers, the information superhighway—we find ourselves uprooted, adrift in an uncharted alien terrain.

In her book on the nature of place and place-specific art, THE LURE OF THE LOCAL (Free Press, 1997), art critic Lucy R. Lippard tells how she asked 20 university students to name a place where they felt they belonged. "Most could not," she writes. "The exceptions were two (traditionally raised) Navajo women and a man whose family had been on a farm for generations." For the majority of us, the connection to place has become distant and tenuous: we're more likely to visit with far-flung friends on the Net than with next-door neighbors on the porch, more likely to eat grapes from Chile than tomatoes from a family farm. In fact, these days locally grown tomatoes are becoming anomalous: financially squeezed by agri-businesses, small farmers are selling their land to real estate developers, who in turn sow anonymous subdivisions, reaping huge profits while further erasing the landmarks of place.

Being geographically unfettered has its rewards, however. Most important, this placeless culture has opened vast territories for individual exploration and opportunity; provided an abundance of products, from Italian plastics to Chinese-produced films; and created a whole new universe of easily accessed information. But in the midst of all that possibility, that longing for a "sense of place" still gnaws at us. Preservationists and historians work to protect what's left of it; developers and planners try to conjure it anew. Nevertheless, it continues to elude. Conservation efforts typically transfigure the charming into the quaintly commercial. For fear of spoiling the tried-and-true, contemporary architectural interventions are shunned, as are innovative zoning plans that might encourage new businesses.

Although this resistance to change can turn towns into lifeless museums, it's not without logic As a culture we seem utterly inept at creating "real places"— perhaps because we are so removed psychologically from our surroundings. As Lippard observes: "Sometimes it seems easier to communicate (or identify) with people long dead who were once stewards of a particular landscape than with today's property owner, even when the land is 'our own.'" And so, clinging to formulas of yore, we produce sterile, kitschy communities.

We've failed to accept that the old definitions of place no longer apply: place is now as much virtual as it is physical. As contrived as it may be, the mall outside the storefront studio of NBC's TODAY SHOW at Rockefeller Center, where its fans gather each morning, has become just as much a part of some viewers' everyday geographies as their own neighborhoods—possibly the most vivid part. Our notion of place, then, must be reinvented. It needs to embrace the "metaplace," but it also has to be grounded in physical place, and our own role in that place.

"Land is an amalgam of history, culture, agriculture, community and religion, incorporating microcosm and macrocosm," Lippard writes. She's right, but maybe a little too lyrical. That history and culture includes strip malls, toxic-waste dumps, blighted neighborhoods, 14-lane highways, abandoned factories, and neglected peoples. If we are at last to create a contemporary sense of place, we might say of "rootless rootedness," we need to acknowledge the ugly as well as beautiful, the disturbing as well as the cozy, the virtual as well as the real. It is this totality that today constitutes the "here." As Lippard contends, "Place continues as an absence to define culture and identity. It also continues as a presence to change the way we live."

Although we may feel light years away from the kind of "place" that Thoreau found in the woods near Walden Pond, there's still much to be learned from him. "I have traveled a good deal in Concord," he wrote, an observation as profound as it is ironic. For in the close and familiar await the exotic and new. MARISA BARTOLUCCI 09.97

274

FOR ME, THE INTERNET IS AN ENABLER....IT'S LIKE WHEN YOU'RE IN COLLEGE AND DISCOVER BEER PARTIES. SOME PEOPLE GO TO THEM ONCE A WEEK AND HAVE A NICE TIME. SOME DISCOVER BEER PARTIES AND SAY, 'WOW, IT'S GREAT. I CAN SELL INSURANCE TO OTHER STUDENTS THERE.' SOME PEOPLE GO TO BEER PARTIES AND BECOME ALCOHOLICS; AND SOME DON'T GO AT ALL. IT'S MORE A REFLECTION OF HUMAN NATURE THAN SOMETHING THAT'S GOING TO CHANGE HUMAN NATURE.

ESTHER DYSON 10.00

MAGICAL MYSTERY TOUR

The small temple seems out of place in this rocky, wind-whipped landscape, but maybe it's exactly what you're looking for. Inside, there's a five-pointed gold star on the floor; above, a star-flecked dome. And mounted on footlit pillars arranged in a pentagon, five football-size scarabs rest at eye level. Pull a cord on one—its wings flip open, revealing a glowing peephole. Peer in, and an amber-toned image reveals itself: a panel from a creation myth, in which robed men appear to be building a domed structure from scrolled plans. There's another door out of here, a gate of bronze crosshatches with a star set in the center, but no apparent way to open it. Beyond that, a gilded dome beckons. You'll get there somehow.

This entire world, known as Riven, was generated by computer. Yet the fact that "there" exists only on CD-ROM doesn't make it feel any less imperative to reach that tantalizingly vivid dome, which glistens under a bright blue sky. This is what puts Riven in the games section of the computer store: a delicately crafted tension between the promise of space and a forceful denial of access. As a player, your goal—in the course of carrying out the goofy mission of imprisoning Riven's twisted creator and rescuing his hostage—is to conquer that terrain and bend it to your needs. Access to the dome (a power plant, it turns out, that runs machinery on five islands) comes only with an understanding of the spatial relationship between the chambers surrounding the temple, which rotates at the push of a button, exposing new passageways and perspectives. Indeed, success throughout the game depends on your ability to interpret and manipulate what its creators call its "immersive environment," a faintly Victorian system of walkways, doors, levers, pipes, tracks, valves, power plants, even an underwater subway straight from the pages of Jules Verne.

Riven's popularity—1.3 million copies sold as of March—is all the more remarkable considering that aside from the occasional film clip, it's basically a computer-generated slide show derived from a three-dimensional digital model. The "places" you walk through are stills selected from the whole, as if captured on film by a compulsive tourist. Through rapid shifts in perspective that the computer model made relatively easy to deliver, one can examine a petroglyph in a rocky tunnel, scope out the horizon through a nearby hole in the wall, and then follow the twisting paths of ladders through a village of spherical huts, always comfortable in the illusion of continuity between the views. The limited processing power of PCs has resulted in an economy of images that speaks to how we interpret any environment, concrete or imaginary; many sites in this game offer just four perspectives, and some only two, but by unconsciously adding the visual information together we're able to perceive a whole. ALYSSA KATZ 06.98

275

276

277

Material excerpted from METROPOLIS magazine
for DESIGN IS.

ACKNOWLEDGMENTS

Over the years contributors to METROPOLIS magazine have included architects, designers, writers, editors, illustrators, photographers, and a wide variety of other talented people whose professional expertise is more difficult to catalogue. To all of them we are immensely grateful. Listed below are the publisher, editors, artists, and designers who have worked on the magazine staff and to whom we are especially indebted. Their work has shaped and reshaped the magazine over the years, and their skill and talent are reflected in this book.

PRESIDENT & CEO
Horace Havemeyer III

EDITORS IN CHIEF
Sharon Lee Ryder 1981-1986
Susan S. Szenasy 1986-

EDITORIAL DEPARTMENT
1981 to 2001
Marisa Bartolucci
Barbara Bedway
Aaron Betsky
Laura Bourland
Linda Bradford
Eric Brand
David E. Brown
Patricia Leigh Brown
Akiko Busch
Kristi Cameron
Tom de Kay
Irene Demchyshyn
Julien Devereux
Cathryn Drake
William Elison
Steven Robert Frankel
Diana Friedman
Victoria Geibel
Avilah Getzler
Renate Glaser
Amy Goldwasser
Kira Gould
Alisa Grifo
Anne Guiney
Jared Hohlt
Karrie Jacobs
Ben Katchor
Adam Lehner
Peter Lemos
Hugo Lindgren
Paul Makovsky
Elizabeth Mashinic
Noel Millea

Philip Nobel
Kate Norment
Cliff Pearson
Martin C. Pedersen
Stan Pinkwas
Claude Lubroth Reilly
Laura Riley
Jonathan Ringen
Janet Rumble
Steven Saltzman
Adam Shatz
Christine Liotta Sheridan
Michael Sorkin
Karen Steen
Gini Sykes
John Voelcker
Sarah Williams
Susan Woldenburg
Kevin Wolfe

ART DEPARTMENT
1981 to 2001
Stephen Barlow-Lawson
Esther Bridavsky
David Carson
Damian Chadwick
Jeff Christensen
Nancy Cohen
Design Hdqtrs
Jeannie Friedman
Lonnie Heller
Rona Fischer Hunter
Criswell Lappin
Carl Lehmann-Haupt
Ivette Montes de Oca
Peggy Roalf
Paula Scher
Helene Silverman
Karen Shapiro
Derek Ungless
William van Roden
Cornelia Walworth

281

PECAN C

Snap